The illustrated history of the

WORKS MINIS

in international rallies and races

Other titles by the same author

Healeys and Austin-Healeys
The Works Big Healeys
The Jensen-Healey Stories

As part of our ongoing market research, we are always pleased to receive comments about our books, suggestions for new titles, or requests for catalogues. Please write to The Editorial Director, G. T. Foulis & Company, Sparkford, Nr Yeovil, Somerset BA22 7JJ

The illustrated history of the
WORKS MINIS
in international rallies and races

Peter Browning
Foreword by Paddy Hopkirk
Second Edition

First published in 1971
Reprinted in paperback 1979
Second edition published in hardback 1996
Reissued 2005

A catalogue record for this book is available from the British Library

ISBN 0 85429 967 X

Library of Congress catalog card no 95 79121

Published by Haynes Publishing, Sparkford, Yeovil, Somerset BA22 7JJ, UK
Tel: 01963 442030 Fax: 01963 440001
Int.tel: +44 1963 442030 Int.fax: +44 1963 440001
E-mail: sales@haynes.co.uk
Website: www.haynes.co.uk

Haynes North America Inc., 861 Lawrence Drive, Newbury Park,
California 91320, USA

Printed and bound in Britain by J.H. Haynes & Co. Ltd., Sparkford

Contents

Greek to Timo – Aaltonen's Championship trail – victory on the Geneva, Czech, Polish, and Three Cities – Alpine clean sweep – Makinen's home win – RAC Championship finale.

Foreword by Paddy Hopkirk

The Mini has been a part of my life for so many years that I am delighted to write the foreword to this updated and enlarged edition of Peter Browning's *The Works Minis*.

The book brings back so many happy memories of the fabulous events of the 1960s, and the good times that I enjoyed with my fellow team members – Rauno Aaltonen, Timo Makinen, and Tony Fall, my co-drivers Henry Liddon, Ron Crellin, and Tony Nash, and all of the BMC mechanics and staff from Abingdon who were, without question, the best in the world.

And, of course, memories of the fantastic little Mini itself, which continues its worldwide popularity, as I discovered when I returned for a 30th anniversary commemorative drive on the 1994 Monte Carlo Rally.

In years to come this book will be a happy reminder of the most enjoyable era of my motorsport life.

Paddy Hopkirk

Paddy Hopkirk on the 1963 Tour de France.

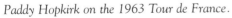

Acknowledgements

For this second edition of *The Works Minis* I must first repeat my thanks to those who helped with my researches for the original book 25 years ago. The late Doug Watts told me a great deal about the early days of the team; Cliff Humphries helped me put together the chapter on the technical development of the cars; Paddy Hopkirk, Rauno Aaltonen, and John Rhodes provided the basis of the chapter on competition Mini driving; Jeremy Ferguson and Iain Mills of Dunlop helped with background information on Mini tyre development; my former secretary, Sandy Lawson, researched a lot of the original Competitions Department records.

Drivers, co-drivers and team members who have been particulary helpful include Rauno Aaltonen, Tony Ambrose, Brian Culcheth, Paul Easter, Tony Fall, Stuart Turner, and Mike Wood.

The following have kindly made photographs available from their archives: Neill Bruce, Den Green, David Hodges, Bill Price, Maurice Rowe, Guy Smith, Chris Spennewyn, Mike Wood, Robert Young, and the British Motor Industry Heritage Trust/Rover Group.

The final chapter, which brings the story up to date with the post-Abingdon history of the cars, could not have been written without the enthusiastic co-operation of the Mini-Cooper Register, their ex-works Mini Registrar Basil Wales, and the many owners whose stories have been featured.

Finally my thanks to Paddy Hopkirk for contributing the Foreword.

Preface

When I wrote the first edition of *The Works Minis* I never expected that, some 25 years later, there would be the demand for an expanded and up-dated second edition.

In the original Preface I mentioned that there were so many good stories to tell about the works Mini's achievements, and about the fortunes of the famous BMC Competitions Department at Abingdon, that it was difficult to know when to stop researching and to start writing. I said then that you could write a book about every event in which the team took part.

During the preparation of this new edition I have had much the same experiences all over again, as so many more stories, fresh information and new photographs have come to light. Furthermore, such is the timeless appeal of the Mini today that there seems to be even more interest in the exploits of the famous little red and white rally cars and their crews.

That the Mini's sporting image lives on was reflected in the attendance of over 100,000 enthusiasts at Silverstone for the Mini's 35th Birthday Party in 1994 – exceeding the attendance figure for that year's British Grand Prix! A recent reunion dinner of former BMC Competitions Department drivers, co-drivers, and team mechanics was attended by almost 200 people, who had travelled across the world to be there amongst old friends. The camaraderie amongst those who were involved with the works Mini's international race and rally

Thirty years on and ex-works Minis and former works drivers regularly meet up again at classic car events – John Handley at the Annual Abingdon Works Show.

exploits over three decades ago is still as strong as ever. No other works rally team, past or present, could arouse such instant nostalgia.

The names of the leading works Mini drivers of the day have remained very much in the public eye. Paddy Hopkirk's return to drive a Mini on the 1994 Monte Carlo Rally, in celebration of his famous victory 30 years previously, was one of the talking points of the event. Paddy, and his former flying Finn team mates, Timo Makinen and Rauno Aaltonen, have all been re-united with Minis in recent classic car events.

The Mini has also remained one of the most popular competition cars for the amateur, continuing to introduce countless new enthusiasts to the sport, and it continues to provide one of the most popular, spectacular, and best-supported categories of club racing. This is without the hype and manufacturer's promotion currently afforded to most of today's one-make saloon car racing series.

It is significant that Rover's marketing of the recent production runs of limited edition Mini models – and, of course, the re-introduction of the Mini-Cooper itself – have reflected the heritage of past competition glories: Abingdon's traditional red and white body colours, Cooper racing car bonnet stripes, imitation competition wheels, rally spotlights, and Monte Carlo Rally stickers.

The more recent interest in classic car rallying, with many Minis taking part, has blossomed and, as can be seen from the final chapter of this book, it is good to record that so many of the original works rally cars of the 1960s have been traced and painstakingly restored.

This, therefore, is the story of how the achievements of the works-entered cars in international competition were to make the Mini the most successful competition car of its era.

Who knows, without the challenge and demands of international competition, the evolution of the Mini-Cooper and the Mini-Cooper 'S' may never have happened.

Peter Browning
Sandford-on-Thames, Oxford
December 1995

Chapter 1 _____

Abingdon Magic

Having the right cars, the right drivers, and the right support organization are the key ingredients for any team's recipe for motor sport success – whether you are running a club rally car or a Grand Prix team. The achievements of the works Minis, entered by the BMC Competitions Department at Abingdon, in international rallying, were unquestionably due to all of these magic ingredients coming together at the right time.

When in 1954 MG's Managing Director, the late John Thornley, persuaded the top brass of the newly-formed British Motor Corporation that its Competitions Department should be based at the home of MG at Abingdon, this certainly ensured that perhaps the most important ingredient of all for the team's future success was guaranteed – the right support and back-up organization. Steeped in pre- and post-war racing and record breaking achievements, with enthusiastic and experienced competition-minded people still in charge of many of the key departments, the MG Car Company was certainly an ideal base for the new team.

The Competitions Department was first established within the MG Development shop under the command of MG's designer, the late Syd Enever. There were three sections in the shop at that time: MG development, customer tuning, and competitions. With Syd's main responsibilities being racing and record breaking projects, plus the building of the MGA prototypes, it was soon clear that Competitions needed its own manager, and thus Marcus Chambers was appointed to lead the team.

Marcus was a big, jovial character, who very early on earned the nicknames 'Chub' and the 'Poor Man's Neubauer', the latter a reference to the famous pre-war Mercedes team manager. Marcus came to Abingdon with experience of production cars in competition, having served as the chief racing mechanic to HRG and having driven at Le Mans in pre-war years. He was pretty astute when it came to sorting out the rules and regulations of motor sport, a proficient linguist, a much travelled man and, to the delight of his colleagues, a lover of good food and wine!

Marcus would be the first to acknowledge the part that John Thornley played in those early days. John had come to Abingdon in the 1930s and worked his way up from the Service Department to be the long-serving and much respected Managing Director. When it came to decisions on competition matters, John was a man with experience and foresight, a born leader who had a unique way of transmitting his enthusiasm to those who worked under him. While he appreciated that the Competitions Manager likes to be left alone to get on with running the team as he thinks fit, John was always on hand to give advice and fight any political battles with the senior management. This he did for the Competitions Department with the same determination that he applied to his constant battle to see that MGs were designed and built the way that he and his team decided, and not necessarily as the management at Longbridge suggested. It was sad that early retirement through illness meant he was not in command at Abingdon to help us fight our last and most important political battle, against British Leyland's closure of the Department in 1970 – followed later by the even sadder demise of the MG factory itself.

European challenge

By the mid-1950s the British motor industry was flourishing, no part of it more so than the British Motor Corporation, the amalgamation of the giant Austin and Morris groups with their associated marques – Riley, Wolseley, MG, and Austin-Healey.

There was at the time a growing awareness of the value of motor sport successes in advertising. Chief rival to MG and Austin-Healey was Standard-Triumph, who had set up their competitions base at Coventry one year before BMC and were enjoying some success with the TR2. The European Rally Championship was seen as the best arena for competitions, as production car racing was only just about to start in the UK, and only on a national basis with little direct manufacturer support.

Until then the post-war European Rally Championship had been dominated by overseas teams and the best that British manufacturers could hope for were class wins, the occasional Team Prize, or a Ladies' Award. BMC had scored better than their rivals, claiming class awards with a wide variety of models and marques ranging from the MG Magnette, the more useful MG 'TF', the lumbering Austin Westminster, the graceful Riley Pathfinder, the more agile Riley 1.5, Austin A40, A50 and A105, the Morris Minor, and later the MGA. It was not, however, until the potential of the big Austin-Healey (first the 100-Six and later the 3000) was proven that the team could, for the first time, aim for outright rally victories.

The big Healey had been developed into a fast, powerful, rugged long-legged machine, ideally suited to the long-distance rough road events of the day, like the Liège and the Alpine. But it was by no means an all-round winner and there were events where it was starting to be out-paced by faster, light-weight, and more nimble opposition. The arrival of the little Mini-Minor was initially, of course, no threat to the big Healey's status but with the later evolution of the Mini-Cooper the team was for the first time able to field a potentially more versatile winner.

Team drivers

With two of the three ingredients for success in place – the right back-up and the prospects of more competitive cars – recruiting the right drivers was the last and perhaps the easiest to achieve.

In the early days of the team there were few full time professional drivers around, works drivers being mainly amateurs who were able to devote time to their chosen sport and receive a modest allowance into the bargain. Those who joined the BMC team were invariably drivers who had already achieved some success in their own cars, with or without some form of works support. Those who drove the first works 850 Minis included Pat 'Tish' Ozanne, Alec Pitts, Ken James, Tom Christie, the late John Milne, Mike Sutcliffe, Tommy Gold, and the late Derek Astle. Later there emerged the first of the 'professionals', like Nancy Mitchell, Peter Riley, Don Morley, John Sprinzel, David Seigle-Morris, and Pat Moss.

BMC attracted the best crews, mainly because the team was larger than its rivals and offered the opportunity of more drives in a wider variety of cars and models; in addition there was better back-up, on-event service, and generally growing professionalism. With the later arrival of the Mini-Cooper came the super-stars, like Paddy Hopkirk, the Finns Rauno Aaltonen and Timo Makinen, young Tony Fall, and, when the team turned to racing, the talents of John Rhodes and John Handley.

In the early days of rallying the role of the co-driver was principally to read the maps and, on certain long-distance events, do some driving. However, many of the earlier 850 crews

Left *The Alpine Rally was one of the toughest and most significant events of the 1960s, contested by most of the works teams. The early Mini-Minors were handicapped on the mainly up-hill stages by lack of power and the car's early Achilles heel, a slipping clutch. This is Alec Pitts on the 1960 event.*

Above Amongst the first to drive the works Minis was 'Tish' Ozanne, seen here (right) with co-driver Nicky Gilmour on the 1960 RAC Rally.

Left Peter 'The Bear' Riley (left) with Tony Ambrose. Peter crewed the early works Mini-Minors when he was not driving the works big Healeys, which were more suited to his size and driving style. Tony Ambrose was to become the most successful of the works Mini co-drivers.

When the first Mini-Minor arrived in the Abingdon Competitions Department it looked somewhat incongruous parked alongside the works big Healeys which, at the time, were spearheading the team's attack on the European Rally Championship. However, it was not too long before the rally-developed 1,275 Mini-Cooper 'S' was able to give the big Healey a run for its money. This is the team line-up for the 1964 Alpine Rally.

With the arrival of the Mini, the activities of the Competitions Department at Abingdon soon changed from the preparation of the wide selection of BMC cars to concentration on Mini development.

regularly swapped seats and were equally happy as drivers or co-drivers. Later there emerged a new generation of the dedicated professional co-drivers and 'car managers', of which the most successful Mini regulars were Ann Wisdom, Tony Ambrose, the late Henry Liddon, Paul Easter, Mike Wood, and Ron Crellin.

Thus, when the Mini-Minor first appeared on the scene, the BMC team was on the threshold of success, with the prospect of being in a position to put all of the key ingredients together – the right cars, the right crews, and the right back up. Nobody. however, could have forecast how the diminutive Mini-Minor was, in time, to play such an important role in the team's fortunes.

850 Days

When the first Mini-Minor appeared in the Abingdon Competitions Department soon after the official launch in August 1959, it was a somewhat incongruous sight parked alongside the brutal big Healeys, the spearhead of the team's European rallying assault at the time. Shop foreman the late Doug Watts recalled that he even refused to borrow the Mini to go down to the bank because he did not wish to be seen 'in such an insignificant little car'.

But just as it did not take long for the revolutionary features of the remarkable little car to appeal to the public the world over, so its inherent sporting potential was very soon to be appreciated by motor sport enthusiasts. This was perhaps not surprising when the alternatives to the Mini at the time were models such as the VW Beetle, Renault Dauphine, Fiat 600, Ford Anglia, Triumph Herald, and Standard 10. The Hillman Imp, the Mini's only serious sporting rival in terms of small car handling and performance, was still some three years away.

The late Laurence Pomeroy in his book *The Mini Story* admirably summed up the novel concept of the car:

Ideal conditions to demonstrate that the Mini-Minor was in a class of its own with its inherent advantages of front-wheel drive, small overall size, and superb handling. ('Tish' Ozanne on the 1961 Monte Carlo Rally.)

When conceived in 1957 no British car had been built in volume with either front drive or all-independent suspension; no car made anywhere in the world in serious quantities had used other than metal springs; no one had combined water cooling with a four-cylinder transverse-mounted engine; nobody had contemplated 70 mph with road wheels with a rim diameter of less than one foot; everyone had accepted that cars with an overall length of less than 11 feet must have rear seats suitable for bicrural amputees, or for children, or no room for luggage, or in some cases all of these disabilities put together. It was common-place that the very small car could scarcely exceed a mile a minute or climb, in top gear, a gradient steeper than one in fifteen. The Mini-Minor cut through these conventions with a design that has since technically dominated the small car world.

While the Mini's sporting potential may have impressed, its designer, the late Alec Issigonis, pointed out that it had never been conceived with competitions in mind:

> When the Mini was designed and in production I never gave competition motoring one single thought. We were pre-occupied in the design, in getting good road-holding and stability for safety reasons and to give the driver more pleasure, but it never occurred to me that this thing would turn out to be such a successful rally car.

Issigonis's right hand man on production and the senior project engineer of the Mini at Longbridge, Jack Daniels, was to play a significant roll not only in interpreting Issigonis's design brief but, in later years, in responding to the requests from Abingdon for more powerful and improved Minis for competition.

> Leonard Lord said that he wanted us to build a car that would knock all of the bubble cars off the road. Alec presented his thoughts on the Mini and right throughout our joint work together his was the inspiration, mine was the perspiration. He would go home at his normal time at six o'clock, we on the other hand were taking the cars out all night, coming back at around two o'clock in the morning.

Daniels and his team also had to bow patiently to the dogmatic ideals of the Mini's creator. For example, when Issigonis was once reminded that Swiss vehicle regulations required cars to be capable of being fitted with snow chains, Issigonis replied that you did not need snow chains with front-wheel drive and he refused to modify the wheel arch clearances. Probably his most famous quotation was when someone unwisely commented on the Mini's uncomfortable driving position with pretty basic seats and the 'lorry' styled angle of the steering

Despite his declared initial disinterest in competitions with the Mini, Alec Issigonis (right) was amongst the first to join the team's rally celebrations. Here he joins French journalist Jean Herbert (centre) and competitions manager Stuart Turner for a post-'64 Monte Carlo Rally dinner.

column. Issigonis replied that a driver should always be uncomfortable so that he was alert behind the wheel! The crews of the works Minis on long-distance events would disagree!

It was when the Longbridge test drivers were running the Mini prototypes that the phenomenal road holding and handling of the car was first realized, recalls Jack Daniels:

> Once we got the prototypes running they were sent out on a triangular test course around the Cotswolds. The boys soon began to realize that they could give things like Jaguars a run for their money, losing them on the straights but passing them on the corners. We were a bit scared, in fact, that we were giving the car too much performance.

The first Mini prototypes used a 948 cc engine mounted 'west-east' with the exhaust system at the front, and this had a top speed of around 90 mph. Carburettor icing was one of the reasons for the engine subsequently being turned around 'east-west', with the carburettors protected at the rear. To reduce power and improve smoothness, the engine was later reduced to 848 cc. The only disadvantage of the 'east-west' layout, as many owners were later to discover, was the problem of water getting onto the distributor.

Whether or not Longbridge approved of the Mini being used in competitions, private owners very soon demonstrated the potential of the car in all forms of club motor sport. It did not take long for it to be unbeatable in the 1,000 cc class, and not only because there was little 1-litre opposition.

Early trials

John Handley, later to become one of our top Mini racers, claims to be one of the first to buy a Mini for competition use when he took his local dealer's demonstrator, on the first day that the car was on sale, to a Hagley & District Light Car Club meeting and was laughed at when he said that he was going to use it for rallying!

I recall hiring an early Mini to take part in a driving test meeting at Denham airfield in west London, organized by the Harrow Car Club of which I was a member along with such luminaries as Pat Moss, John Sprinzel, Brian Culcheth, and saloon car ace Steve Soper. Some six of us drove the same Mini, which totally dominated the class once we discovered the art of handbrake turns and, for us, the revelation of front-wheel drive and a whole new experience in terms of handling. The poor Mini was totally trashed by the end of the day and finally expired with a broken drive shaft. I pushed it onto the main road, phoned the hire company and told them to come and collect it complaining that something had broken!

It was not long after this that rather more serious mechanical Mini failures in competition were to cause quite a stir. A team of 850s (one of which was driven by John Handley) had been entered for the annual Six Hour Relay Race organized by the 750 Motor Club at Silverstone. This was a wonderful event when teams of the most diverse cars, ranging from standard saloons to the wildest sports cars, raced in relay against each other on a handicap system. The Minis amazed everyone (including the handicappers) with their performance until the front wheels started to fall off. The strain of continuous high speed cornering (mainly right handers on the old club circuit) had found a weakness in the wheel construction.

Marcus Chambers at Abingdon was soon made aware of the problem and, with the support of John Thornley, quickly passed the bad news on to Longbridge, who were less than interested. This was despite Marcus pointing out that if the wheels fell off after an hour's fast motoring around a race track it might not be too long before the district nurse hurtling down a Welsh mountain road might find that her wheels fell off too! The matter was brought to a head when the RAC, as the governing body of the sport in the UK, actually banned Minis from racing until something was done! Marcus and his men then found themselves official suppliers of approved competition wheels (officially stamped), it being found that one of the two original suppliers had produced a faulty batch. That was the first of many instances when Abingdon was instrumental in proving that competitions could improve the breed.

Moving on to the international scene, the Mini's arrival coincided with the announcement of new International Appendix J regulations for production cars, which created two distinct categories for Touring cars (near standard) and Grand Touring cars (modified). Thus there were two options for Mini class wins while the GT category gave Abingdon the opportunity to try out a few modifications and provide a little more power than the standard 33 bhp and 70 mph top speed.

Viking debut

Marcus Chambers actually gave the Mini its international rally debut himself, by entering an 850 (YOP 663) on the Norwegian Viking Rally in September 1959 as support vehicle to Pat Moss, who was chasing points for the European Ladies' Rally Championship in an Austin A40. Despite having troubles with the deeply rutted roads, caused by the big wheels of the predominant local Saab entries, Marcus did well to finish, albeit 51st overall.

There are many different claims as to who was first to win an event with the Mini, but amongst the first to win a rally in one were Pat Moss and Stuart Turner, who entered a car (TJB 199) in the Knowldale Car Club's Mini Miglia National Rally. They won by some 10 minutes, despite Pat complaining that she found it desperately slow while Stuart reported that it was darned uncomfortable!

First works team

The first team of works Minis in an international event was less successful. Three cars, driven by Pat 'Tish' Ozanne (TMO 559), Ken James (TMO 561), and Alec Pitts (TMO 560), were entered for the 1959 RAC Rally. 'Tish' Ozanne was amongst the most active of the early works Mini crews and can claim to have been the first 'invited' works Mini driver when she ran a car in the German Rally one month prior to the team entry in the RAC Rally. Ken James, like many drivers of the day, was equally happy driving or co-driving and went on to partner the late Rupert Jones on several events. Alec Pitts was another of the regular pioneer Mini pilots, who was to be involved in more than his fair share of incidents.

The RAC Rally that year was moved from its traditional early season date to November in an effort to try and offer more testing weather conditions and attract more overseas entries as the final round of the European Championship. This was the first year when Jack Kemsley exerted his influence on the organizing committee with the result that the emphasis of the event started to move away from comic driving tests on the sea front to more serious and competitive road sections.

The works 850 Mini-Minors ran in two categories on international events, for standard Touring Cars and modified Grand Touring cars. In the latter class, modifications were allowed which gave the team the opportunity to try out a number of prototype items later to be fitted on the Mini-Cooper. The interior of the early works Minis, here being completed by Johnny Organ, was functional if not as professional as the later Mini-Coopers.

One of the most active of the early works Mini-Minor drivers was Alec Pitts, seen here with Tony Ambrose on the 1960 Alpine Rally.

Starting in Blackpool and running up to the Scottish highlands and down through Wales to the finish at the Crystal Palace race circuit in south London, the event was run in tough wintry conditions, which did not really suit the fledgeling Minis. All three cars failed to finish because of slipping clutches resulting from oil seal failure, an on-going 850 and early Mini-Cooper problem.

The event was memorable for the fact that the organizers got more wintry weather than they bargained for, heavy snow blocking roads in Scotland and causing organizational chaos. The regulations required crews to take the shortest route between controls but, with that route blocked by snow, the drivers were left to find their own way and thus try to achieve an impossible average speed. There were lengthy protests at the finish (led by one Stuart Turner, navigating for European Championship contender Wolfgang Levy in a DKW). By the time their protest was finally withdrawn, and Gerry Burgess (Ford Zephyr) was declared the winner, the Rally had almost been forgotten.

Portuguese problems

As a test run for the forthcoming Monte Carlo Rally, two Minis were entered for the Portuguese Rally in December, to be driven by Nancy Mitchell (TJB 199) and Peter Riley (618 AOG). Nancy Mitchell was the team's leading lady driver of the day and had done great things with MG Magnettes and MGAs to win the Ladies' European Rally Championship in 1956/7. 'Mitch' went on to drive Riley 1.5s and the big Healey with equal distinction. Peter Riley was a former Cambridge University student who had made a name for himself in club racing and rallying and who bravely tackled the 1959 Liège–Rome–Liège in a spartan Healey Silverstone. He had his first drive with the BMC team in the big Healey, which suited his large build and determined driving style. He was later to marry Pat Moss's regular co-driver Ann Wisdom.

Both Mini crews in Portugal finished the event, bravely supported by the intrepid Marcus Chambers, partnered by deputy shop foreman Den Green, entered in a lumbering Wolseley 6/99 carrying the team's luggage and spares. This was the notoriously unsporting event when most of the visiting entries were disqualified at the finish for having the wrong coloured competition numbers and local drivers were awarded most of the trophies! This actually cost Erik Carlsson the European Rally Championship title.

Monte sextet

By the 1960 Monte Carlo Rally, there was growing awareness of the Mini's sporting potential and confidence in the little car was reflected in the fact that, apart from Pat

Moss's venerable A40, Abingdon's team entry for the winter classic was made up entirely of six Minis (and there were a similar number of private Mini runners).

Peter Riley (618 AOG), Don and Erle Morley (TMO 561), and Alec Pitts (TMO 560) were entered in the improved Grand Touring car class, while Tom Wisdom (619 AOG), Nancy Mitchell (617 AOG), and 'Tish' Ozanne (TMO 559) drove in the standard Touring class. The results indicated improved reliability, for only the two ladies' crews failed to finish.

For Alec Pitts it was an eventful journey to Monte. Starting from Paris the dreaded clutch slip started on the first night and did not respond to the frequent injection of fire extinguisher fluid. Sand was then added to the mixture in an attempt to bind the whole transmission solid. Then, in thick fog, Alec ran into the back of another competitor, badly damaging the radiator and spinning across the road, knocking the rear wheel badly out of line. Pitts battled on until he hit a milk float just outside Monte, the impact wrecking the side of the car and punching the roof down, reducing visibility. The body was now so out of line that most of the windows had popped out and the doors had to be tied shut with string!

Pitts finally reached Monte with a car that was hardly driveable and then declared that he intended to complete the Mountain Circuit. This he achieved after many stops to attend to the ailing clutch and to retrieve parts of the Mini that fell off along the route. At the finish (placed 73rd) Alec offered Marcus £10 for the remains of the car, an offer which was readily accepted!

Pitts's intrepid co-driver was a young Oxford University student by the name of Tony Ambrose, soon to become the first of the true professional co-drivers in the team. Tony brought a lot of advanced thinking to Abingdon and was instrumental in pioneering more serious pre-event recces, pace notes, and practising. His long stay with the team was rewarded with the European Rally Championship title with Rauno Aaltonen in 1965 and, along with Henry Liddon, he was amongst the most successful co-drivers in the team.

First class win

The international class-winning potential of the Mini was demonstrated for the first time on the 1960 Geneva Rally by Don and Erle Morley (618 AOG) when they scored a class win, beating Erik Carlsson's Saab and a pair of DKW Juniors. 'Tish' Ozanne (617 AOG) was runner-up in the class while Alec Pitts (619 AOG), having further adventures, had to retire when he crashed into a mountain after coming round a blind corner to find another competing car blocking the road.

Don and Erle Morley gained their works Mini drive as a result of winning the 1959 Tulip Rally in their privately-entered Jaguar. The farming twins from Suffolk, who always went rallying in tweed suits, were one of the quietest and most polite crews in the business but also one of the canniest. They went on to an outstanding rallying career with sports cars – MGA, MGB, and the big Healey – winning consecutive Alpine Rallies in 1961/2.

On the Circuit of Ireland, privateer David Hiam was called in at the last moment to take over the entry of a strange yellow and blue Mini (TMO 559) prepared by the works in the Swedish national colours for Erik Carlsson, who was prevented from taking part at the last moment by a leg injury. Unfortunately the Mini was heavily penalized following a slight misunderstanding about the regulations concerning booking in early at controls. David Hiam was one of the most determined of early privateer Mini drivers in 16 BOJ and nearly got into the record books by being the first Mini to finish the Liège in 1963. Driving with Derek Astle, they were excluded by just two minutes after having dragged the ailing Mini for 90 gruelling hours of the Marathon. David was later to become the very efficient and popular Rally Manager for Dunlop.

Tulip trio

All three works Minis finished the Tulip Rally, John Sprinzel (TJB 199) coming second in the GT class, Tom Christie (TMO 560) third in the Touring class, and 'Tish' Ozanne (TMO 561) a worthy finisher.

John Sprinzel was a versatile and colourful race and rally driver, famed for his giant-killing exploits in A35s and his own Sebring Sprites. John went on to drive a variety of works and privately-entered cars. In his excellent book *Spritely Years* (Patrick Stephens 1994) John was, as usual, pretty outspoken about his first Mini drive:

> In 850 trim they were fun but gutless. They understeered like crazy and needed a lot of hand-brake-tugging to get around hairpins. Wheels broke, water seeped into the boot and footwells, and they were forever oiling up their clutches.
>
> For the Tulip Rally, Marcus asked me to drive TJB 199 which was a sort of prototype Mini-Cooper fitted with twin carburettors. This was a good deal quicker and co-driver Mike Hughes and I enjoyed ourselves immensely. Because of the modifications we were running in the 1,000 cc Grand Touring class and had a rally-long fight with Tommy Gold's Sprite and a Renault-Gordini.

Tough Acropolis

The rough terrain and the heat of the 1960 Acropolis Rally, with its tight time schedules and little time for service, was to be a tough challenge for the 850 with its low ground clearance, somewhat fragile front suspension, and tendency to overheat.

'Tish' Ozanne (617 AOG) got lost on the first night after the start from Trieste and later went out with broken front shock absorbers and smashed ball-joints. Scottish motor sport enthusiast the late Johnny Milne (619 AOG) went well right up to the final test, when he was forced to slow with leaking brake hydraulics. Mike Sutcliffe (618 AOG) lost time after a crash but soldiered on to the finish and got a standing ovation for his antics in the final circuit test, when the little Mini put up a stirring performance to overtake Ford Zephyrs and 3.4 Jaguars.

There were also cheers from the spectators at the British Grand Prix at Silverstone in July, when the Grand Prix drivers took part in an hilarious three-lap demonstration race driving a fleet of standard Minis. Chaos reigned on the grid when some of the drivers parked their cars facing the wrong way. Jack Brabham tried to lift the bonnet of the late Graham Hill's car to pull a spark plug lead off. Others tried to hide ignition keys and deflate front tyres! The result was an almost dead heat, with Hill just beating the late Bruce McLaren and Roy Salvadori. Hill reported afterwards that he had driven flat out in top gear the whole way at the Mini's terminal speed of 70 mph!

Alpine class

Back on the international rally scene, in the 1960 Alpine Rally the Abingdon team's development of the big Healey was rewarded with a fine second place overall by the remarkable Pat Moss in a 3000, Austin-Healey also winning the Manufacturers' Team Prize. Mini reliability was slowly improving and Tommy Gold (TMO 561) went well to win his class.

The Reverend Rupert Jones, one of the most enthusiastic of the pioneer works Mini pilots, did the Alpine in a modified car with Ken James (TMO 559) and recalled in *Sporting Cars* how the event was enlivened by the humour of Erik Carlsson who nicknamed Rupert 'The Bishop' and never failed to raise a laugh at the rallying Reverend's expense.

> Our position meant that on many tight sections Erik took us somewhere near the top of the pass. I held him for a few miles and then he hurtled on ahead. Having booked in himself with time to spare, he prepared for our arrival, it was typical Erik.
>
> 'Look out, Bishop comes. Stand back please, here is the Bishop.'
>
> We were leading our class. We had an experimental gearbox, destined to become the Cooper box, it was a joy to use, but pathetic disc brakes at the front, also experimental for use on later Coopers.
>
> Sometime late in the night, perhaps in that last hour before dawn, when one's guard is down, we booked into a control early. It was a measure of how well we were going but it was expensive as the penalty was as great as for being late and it lost us first place in the class for a short time.

Up-hill all the way for Ken James and the Reverend Rupert Jones on the 1960 Alpine Rally, an event which Rupert recalls caused them more than their fair share of adventures.

Later there was the long slog across country to Monza for a thrash around the circuit. At this time I was doing some circuit racing and two summers previously we had been at Monza to take some records on the banked circuit. I had walked the road circuit and thought that I could remember it well.

Anticipating the starter I had the wheels spinning fractionally before the flag dropped and surged (as well as one can with 33 bhp) forward, well ahead of my class mates. This meant that for the first lap, the quick boys who had not been quite so quick off the line, kept coming by and coming to the last tight right hander on the first lap, my mirror was full of cars, I was too busy looking at them, braked late and fade set in. The grass was very long and I had to indulge in some private and almost unobserved rallycross to regain the circuit and spend the rest of the race working hard to recover the class position.

We started the trek back to the finish with still some great motoring ahead of us and we did it again – booked in early. I was furious with myself and attacked the Col d'Allos going much too well. Two thirds up I met some banking that leapt out from behind a bridge. I thought we would

Tommy Gold – best remembered for early works TR3 drives with Standard-Triumph and, later, racing and rallying successes with a Sebring Sprite – gained a class win for the works Mini-Minor on the 1960 Alpine Rally.

David Seigle-Morris in his element on the comic skid-pan test on the 1960 RAC Rally where his team mate, Mike Sutcliffe, made the fastest time of the day.

ride up on it, but the front left hand corner embedded itself in this little piece of France and became slightly deranged. It soon became obvious that we were out, leading the class and with less than 200 miles from the finish.

By the time we reached Nice the final control was closed and everyone was out on the town, or out for the count. We joined the latter group, tired and defeated but wiser and enriched with memories.

Saab chasing

The 1960 season finished with the RAC Rally, where Jack Kemsley continued his endeavours to improve the event and, for the first time, competitors were supplied with a 'Tulip' type road book and did not have to map-read their way around the route. More significantly, there was a real special stage, a two-mile race across a craggy mountain track in Scotland. The event was to decide the European Championship between Rene Trautmann (Citroën) and Walter Schock (Mercedes) but this fizzled out when the Frenchman crashed in the fog 100 miles from the start leaving Schock as the Championship winner. The German somewhat unsportingly immediately retired and returned home.

The Minis were not outclassed. Tom Christie (TMO 560) put up a brave challenge against Carlsson's Saab until he was forced out when the flywheel came adrift. Front-wheel drive reigned supreme on the comic Wolvey skid pan test, where Mike Sutcliffe (TMO 561) set fastest time of the day to beat the entire field. David Seigle-Morris (TMO 559), despite clutch

Final test on the 1960 RAC Rally at Brands Hatch, where David Seigle-Morris (TMO 559) won the 1-litre class race, beating Erik Carlsson's Saab from pole position. Clearly the RAC Rally did not attract as many spectators in those days!

The ill-fated works Mini-Minor team leave Abingdon for the 1961 Monte Carlo Rally: (left to right) Peter Garnier/Rupert Jones, Tom Christie/Nick Paterson, and Derek Astle/Steve Woolley. Garnier crashed and Christie went down with food poisoning, while Astle's car was hit by a landslide.

slip, was consistently quick and even won the final class race at Brands Hatch to finish runner-up in the class and a worthy sixth overall.

The Minis won four of the speed tests against Rally winner Carlsson's three, the big Swede and his navigator Stuart Turner nevertheless being the undisputed winners and the only crew to finish unpenalized. There was much talk that Carlsson and Turner had practised the infamous Scottish stage many times but Stuart later confirmed that he had recced it only once, in a Mini which stopped halfway with drowned electrics!

Monte mishaps

The 1961 season started badly when a series of incidents eliminated all three works Minis on the Monte Carlo Rally – one of those events which are a team manager's nightmare when

Rupert Jones and Peter Garnier set out on the 1961 Monte Carlo Rally on their studded Dunlop Durabands. The crew were to be eliminated by a crash in France.

The 1961 Monte Carlo Rally Mini-Minors sported a rear-wheel driven distance recorder in an endeavour to gain more accurate readings than those given by the spinning driving wheels. Gerald Wiffen makes final adjustments.

circumstances outside one's control take over. Peter Garnier (TMO 559) wrecked his car when it was in collision with a farmer's Peugeot near Rheims, Peter breaking a rib; Tom Christie (TMO 560) went down with food poisoning; and Derek Astle's car (TMO 561) was hit by a landslide.

The 1961 Monte Minis sported a novel speedo/distance recorder drive developed by inventive shop foreman Tommy Wellman in conjunction with Smiths. This took the drive off the rear wheels to obviate the error through wheelspin from the conventional drive off the gearbox.

Moss's Mini debut

First works drive with a Mini for Pat Moss came on the Lyon–Charbonnières Rally (TMO 560) but this was not a happy debut, the transmission breaking when she was lying well placed.

First works Mini-Minor drive for Pat Moss and Ann Wisdom was on the 1961 Lyon–Charbonnières Rally – not a happy debut when their transmission broke.

The inventive driving style of David Seigle-Morris (left) and Vic Elford on the 1961 Tulip Rally – trying to emulate the sideways style of their Scandinavian rivals – (David steered and Vic tweaked the handbrake on the corners), was not too effective and did not endear them to the mechanics! Vic Elford was later sacked from the BMC team for his over-spirited antics but he got his own back when he later led the works Lotus Cortina and Porsche rally teams against the Minis!

Having driven just about every other car in the BMC Competitions fleet since she started rallying in the mid-1950s (MG 'TF', Magnette, MGA, Riley 1.5, Austin A40, and the big Healey) Pat demonstrated her remarkable natural skill by quickly adapting to the front-wheel drive Mini. Pat was one of the greatest lady rally drivers of all time – many who drove against her (particularly in big Healeys) would say that she was unquestionably the fastest. Like brother Stirling, she could adapt her style and apply her talents to any car and in all types of events. Pat's regular co-driver was Ann Wisdom, who appropriately shared her later Ladies' European Rally Championship honours.

There is a strange tale that Pat was actually responsible for the Mini getting its name.

The Tulip Rally was to become a happy hunting ground for the works Minis, and immensely popular with British private entrants. Peter Riley and Tony Ambrose gained a class win on the 1961 event.

Competing on the 1957 Liège with a Morris Minor, Pat had a phenomenal avoidance with a VW Minibus on a road section. She joked afterwards that she very nearly had a 'Morris Mini Minor Bus' and thereafter all of her rallying Morris Minors were called Mini-Minors. This was two years before the arrival of the real Mini!

Driving the underpowered Mini competitively in those days demanded considerable courage and, on tarmac events, some crews applied unorthodox techniques trying to emulate the sideways driving style of their Scandinavian colleagues. It was on the 1961 Tulip Rally that David Seigle-Morris and Vic Elford (TMO 559) decided that they might go a bit faster if they both drove at the same time – David steering and working the pedals while Vic set the car up in the corners by yanking on the handbrake! The pair developed this pioneer version of left-foot braking to some effect but failed to beat fellow Mini team mate on the Tulip, Peter Riley (TMO 561), who won the class.

David Seigle-Morris made a name for himself club rallying in a Mini (with Vic Elford) and went on to become one of the most consistently successful big Healey pilots.

Final sorties

The final 1961 outing for the works 850s on the Acropolis Rally was disappointing, probably because the crews were now having to drive the little under-powered cars well beyond their capabilities to keep up with the opposition. All three cars failed to survive the rough punishment of the Greek stages. Mike Sutcliffe (619 AOG) had to drop out with broken shock absorbers, front suspension ball joint problems, and finally a blown head gasket. Don Morley, partnered by Ann Wisdom (363 DOC), rolled off the road and was airborne for so long that Ann said she had time to start removing the valuable stop watches from the dashboard before they landed! David Seigle-Morris with Vic Elford (TMO 560) retired when the ever-determined Elford crashed on a road section, an incident that saw him sacked from the team.

One of the final works entries for the 850 was the much-used 363 DOC with the rallying Reverends Rupert Jones and Philip Morgan on the 1962 Monte Carlo Rally, where they finished third in their class.

Their prayers for the Mini to have more power were soon to be answered for, although the 850 had not enjoyed an auspicious international competition debut, the sporting potential of the little car had been clearly demonstrated. The Abingdon Competitions Department were not alone in calling for a more powerful Mini.

Last international outing for the works Mini-Minors was on the 1962 Monte Carlo Rally. The prayers for more power by the rallying Reverends, Rupert Jones and Philip Morgan, were to be answered by the introduction of the Mini-Cooper.

The Mini-Cooper and a New Era

Towards the end of the 1961 season two significant events were to affect the fortunes of the BMC Competitions Team at Abingdon: in September the Mini-Cooper was announced, and one month later Stuart Turner was appointed Competitions Manager.

The arrival of the 997 cc Mini-Cooper, launched in September 1961, came about as a result of the combined enthusiasm of John Cooper (World Champion F1 racing car constructor 1959 and 1960) and the Mini's creator Alec Issigonis. The two were pioneers in their own fields, for while Issigonis's front-wheel drive concept was to be a landmark in production car design, so Cooper had changed the design thinking of single-seater racing cars by proving that the correct place for the engine was behind and not in front of the driver.

John Cooper recalls how he first met Issigonis:

> Back in 1946 we went to the Brighton Speed Trials with our 500 Cooper special, the first one that we built, and I was matched against Issigonis who was driving his Lightweight Austin Special

John Cooper (far right) was always an enthusiastic supporter of Abingdon's rallying activities. Here he welcomes home the victorious 1964 Monte Carlo Rally team (right to left) Paddy Hopkirk, Stuart Turner, Erle Morley, Raymond Baxter, Timo Makinen, Henry Liddon, Rauno Aaltonen, Patrick Vanson, Tony Ambrose, and Don Morley.

and I beat him, and we became friends from that date. I knew him through the days of the Morris Minor and, of course, following on into the Mini.

In the late 1950s Jack Brabham and I decided that the old 500 single-seater formula should be replaced. The continentals were racing the Stangellini 1,000s which was called Formula Junior where you had to use an engine from a production car and only certain modifications were allowed. The 'A' series engine was then in the Morris Minor and the Austin-Healey Sprite and we thought that this was the engine to use. I went to see Issigonis and Donald Healey was there at the time and we decided to use that engine in our Formula Junior car. They went very well, Formula Junior became Formula 3 and in 1964 Jackie Stewart won the European Championship in a 1,000 cc 'A' series-engined Cooper.

When the Mini first came out most of the racing drivers had one as a spare car, people like Jack Brabham and Bruce McLaren, and we started to put Formula Junior bits on them then. Later I went and saw Issigonis and said why don't we build a production version for the boys. He reluctantly agreed to discuss it, went and saw George Harriman (then Managing Director of BMC) who said take one away and do it.

We took a car away and put a Formula Junior engine in it. I knew Jack Emmott, the Chairman of Lockheeds, well and we managed to get some disc brakes put on it because they were researching disc brakes on a Mini wheel at the time and they reckoned that if disc brakes would go on a Mini they would go on anything. We also added a remote gearshift.

We took the car back and drove it round the grounds of Longbridge and Harriman said that it was fantastic. I said you've got to make 1,000 to get it homologated. He said, 'I don't think we are going to sell 1,000.' In the end they sold 150,000.

They were originally going to call it the Austin or Morris Mini-Cooper but later it just became the Mini-Cooper. We finalized on a royalty arrangement of £2 per car. We also made an agreement whereby we prepared and entered the race cars for UK events with Tyrrell racing the Minis in Europe and Abingdon running the rally team.

Basic engine modifications for the Mini-Cooper involved increasing the stroke and reducing the bore to give 997 cc, as close as possible to the 1,000 cc class limit for competitions. Twin SU carburettors were fitted with a three-branch exhaust system and the cylinder head was modified. Other alterations included larger valves fitted with double valve springs, increased valve overlap, and raised compression ratio, giving 55 bhp at 5,800 rpm. An improved gear shift was fitted, there were close-ratio gears, and braking was improved with disc brakes at the front and larger drums at the rear. The only weakness of the car was crankshaft failure at sustained high revs; later a modified version with different bore/stroke ratio giving 998 cc was introduced. Top speed of the Mini-Cooper was 85 mph.

Stuart Turner

Stuart Turner would be the first to admit that he could not have arrived on the Abingdon scene at a better moment. Marcus Chambers had built up a superb team of mechanics that was already acknowledged as the best in the business. There were some good drivers and co-drivers under contract and the opportunity was now ripe to try the talents of the young rising stars from Scandinavia. The big Healey was established in winning form and now the Mini-Cooper was expected to add further strength to the team's attack on the European opposition.

Stuart studied accountancy until he caught the rally bug. He did his national service with the RAF, where he says that he learnt little of use other than Russian. In club rallying he was a demon navigator, winning the *Autosport* Navigators' Trophy in 1957, 1958 and 1959. He had been a member of the Auto Union, Mercedes, Saab, Standard-Triumph, and BMC works teams, his most notable success being with Erik Carlsson when they won the RAC Rally in 1960. Before he came to Abingdon he did a spell as rally editor of *Motoring News*.

Left *With the announcement of the 997 Mini-Cooper, the team at last had a more competitive car with which to challenge the opposition. Pauline Mayman on the 1963 Alpine Rally.*

The arrival of Stuart Turner as competitions manager at the end of the 1961 season, along with the introduction of the Mini-Cooper, heralded a turning point in the team's fortunes. Stuart (right) with top co-driver Henry Liddon (centre) and Rauno Aaltonen.

Stuart's arrival at Abingdon heralded a new era of professionalism within the team. He was a tremendous leader, a quick-witted thinker, ruthless in the field, and always ready to exploit any weakness in rival teams or loopholes in event regulations or organization. He had superb vision as to how the various elements of the sport would develop internationally and was inevitably always one move ahead of the opposition. Some found his blunt outspokenness and dry wit disconcerting and he had no time for bumblers. Without question, his reign at Abingdon established him as one of the most successful competition managers of all time.

Stuart recalls his excitement at coming to Abingdon:

> I was writing the rally column for *Motoring News* and to go from that to running the BMC team was the most magical thing of my life. I was about 27 at the time and when I went to a board meeting there would be the accountant, who was about 44, and everyone else was over 55. But the board was made up of people like Syd Enever (the head of Development), Reg Jackson (the chief inspector), Alec Hounslow (who had been Nuvolari's riding mechanic). And, of course, there was Alec Issigonis. I mean I was sitting beside legends!

Stuart moved on to join Castrol as Publicity Manager in 1967 then became Competitions Manager at Ford and later Director of Motor Sport, Ford Europe. He retired in 1990 and has enjoyed a new career as a lecturer and most entertaining after-dinner speaker as well as working on grass roots motor sport projects through the RAC.

Monte Coupe des Dames

Appropriately, the first competition outing for Stuart Turner and the new Mini-Cooper was on the 1962 Monte Carlo Rally, an event which was to become synonymous with Mini successes.

Pat Moss (737 ABL) won the Coupe des Dames despite one or two problems like a broken throttle cable due to hasty car preparation. Back-up support for the big Abingdon entry (an Austin A110, MG Midget, MGA, big Healey, Riley 1.5, and the Minis), was the works-supported Mini (11 NYB) of Geoff Mabbs with his then little-known 'co-driver', Rauno Aaltonen. Lying second overall to Erik Carlsson's winning Saab, Rauno (who, of course, did most of the driving) crashed on the Turini and the inverted car caught fire. Trapped by partly melted seat belts, Rauno resigned himself to death and described the experience as 'very peaceful but warm.' His reverie was rudely interrupted by Geoff's rough Bristolian accent saying, 'Get out you silly bugger!' Mabbs, himself burnt, rescued an unconscious Rauno from the blaze and in this dramatic fashion began the Finn's long and distinguished period with the team.

A fine Coupe des Dames award went to Pat Moss and Ann Wisdom on the 1962 Monte Carlo Rally, starting a year in which Pat was to claim the Ladies European Rally Championship title.

Rauno Aaltonen

Rauno was good at any sport which involved speed, skill, and courage. At the age of 12 he started racing speedboats in Finland and was seven times National Champion and, one year, Champion of Scandinavia. He took to motor cycle racing at the age of 16 and was soon a member of the Finnish Speedway Team. He also won his class in the Swedish Motor Cycle Grand Prix. He started racing and rallying when 18, with encouragement from his motor sporting father, and soon earned a works drive with Mercedes, partnering Eugen Bohringer, before joining the BMC team on the Monte in 1962.

Rauno was a great 'thinker' and theorist who never missed an opportunity to expound upon his ideas to everyone, which made him particularly popular with the press. He was quite a talented engineer and I remember him being seated at a dinner party next to Alec Issigonis when the pair used up every menu in sight and then the table cloth, upon which they redesigned the Mini's front suspension.

The 'Little Finn' as he was nicknamed (Timo Makinen was the 'Big Finn') was fanatically conscientious about having his cars just right – almost to the point of being irritatingly fussy. Co-driver Tony Ambrose recalls the occasion when they very nearly lost time on an Alpine Rally road section because Rauno insisted on checking his tyre pressures with his own gauge, just in case there was a discrepancy with the gauge of the Dunlop fitters who had just checked them. In contrast he got some pretty rude comments when he turned up to collect his rally car at Abingdon and asked the mechanics to modify the spares packing arrangements to make space for his heavy camera case when they had been slaving away to remove all unnecessary weight from his car!

Rauno, however, was a man of indomitable pride, very firm in his views and principles. He was one of the most gentlemanly characters in the sport and without question one of the ultimate professionals. He was the most successful of the works Mini drivers, winning the 1965 European Championship after a truly dominating season.

With the closure of the Competitions Department, Rauno completed a successful career with Lancia, BMW, Datsun, and Ford. He later worked with BMW again, offering advanced driving tuition courses to customers, and more recently has raced a BMW in historic events.

Rauno's partner on his first drive with the team, Geoff Mabbs, graduated from club motor sport to drive for a number of works teams including Standard-Triumph, winning the 1961 Tulip Rally in a Herald. Geoff was a motor trader by profession, a good engineer, and a use-

Rauno Aaltonen's debut with the team on the 1962 Monte Carlo Rally ended with a fiery experience but the 'Little Finn' was to become the most successful of the works Mini drivers. Rauno is seen here with co-driver Val Domleo (centre) and Pauline Mayman.

ful test driver. Always cheerful and with a great sense of humour, he later worked closely with Abingdon on the development of Triumph and Rover models for racing, rallying, and rally-cross. He drove the famous works Rover in a TV rallycross event at Lydden Hill with a furled umbrella, bowler hat, and a copy of the *Financial Times* on the rear parcel shelf, which directed some publicity away from the inevitably mediocre performance of the car!

Dutch treat

While the Monte proved the capabilities of the new Cooper it was on the 1962 Tulip Rally that Pat Moss and Ann Wisdom (737 ABL) scored the Mini's first outright international rally victory – dominating the event by setting the fastest time in their class on every stage to win by a comfortable margin on the class improvement system. Minis, in fact, took the first eight places in the 1,000 cc class.

The class improvement system (used primarily on the Tulip Rally) awarded the top prize to the car that won its class by the greatest margin. This was not always popular with drivers who had put up 'winning' scratch performances and the system could be manipulated by clever team managers who in the closing stages of the event could slow down supporting entries in the class to ensure a comfortable class-winning margin.

While the team's major effort for the 1962 Alpine Rally was to see the Morleys achieve their second victory in the Austin-Healey 3000, a Group II Mini-Cooper looked a good bet against the handicap system and a lone car (407 ARX) was entered for Rauno Aaltonen. Although the Mini retired with what were to become typical Alpine problems – gearbox troubles and over-heating – it was not before their performance had shaken the touring car opposition.

By now the Mini-Cooper was being campaigned to good effect by a growing number of BMC dealers around the world – none more successfully than BMC Sweden, who found no shortage of local drivers ready to try the new car in ideal Mini conditions. On the same week-end as the Alpine Rally, for example, Bengt Soderstrom won the Swedish Midnight Sun Rally in a BMC Sweden Mini-Cooper, and with Tom Trana and Hans Lannsjo they collected the Manufacturers' Team Prize.

Pat Moss scored another outright win on the German Baden-Baden Rally (737 ABL), again

First outright win for the works Minis was claimed by the redoubtable Pat Moss on the 1962 Tulip Rally, when her Mini-Cooper set the fastest time on every stage.

run on the class improvement system. Pat finished fifth on scratch behind two Porsche Carreras and a pair of works Mercedes. It was expected that the Mercedes team would win because they had the class improvement system carefully worked out so that team leader, Eugen Bohringer, won his class by the necessary margin from the other team cars. But even the great Mercedes organization makes mistakes and they got their sums wrong this time, giving the Rally away to the British ladies.

Moss and Mayman

Pat was now partnered by the late Pauline Mayman, Ann Wisdom having retired to marry Peter Riley. Pauline possessed the rare talents of both a top line driver and co-driver. She began as a navigator to husband Lionel in club rallies, then they both turned to speed events. Pauline drove a Cooper-Climax, a Morgan and a Lotus-Climax in races, sprints, and hillclimbs, holding the ladies' record at Prescott in 1958. After two seasons of international co-driving, she teamed up with Pat Moss for half a season in 1962 before returning to the driving seat the following year to become BMC's leading lady when Pat moved on to Ford.

It was typical Turner strategy that when Ford out-bid BMC for the services of Pat Moss, Stuart very quickly signed Val Domleo – Ford's only lady co-driver! It was perhaps more appropriate that Val should drive for BMC for she was, at the time, a research physicist with Morris Motors Engine Branch at Coventry. Val was to team up with Pauline Mayman for 1963 and later to marry Don Morley. The Moss/Mayman partnership went well on the 1962 Geneva Rally (737 ABL), finishing third overall and being class winners behind Carlsson and winner Hans Walter (Porsche Carrera) – a success which brought Pat the European Ladies' Rally Championship title.

The 1962 season closed with a monster BMC entry of four big Healeys, three Mini-Coopers, and an MG 1100 for the RAC Rally. Starting in Blackpool and finishing in Bournemouth, the event was extended to some 300 miles of forest stages. Main feature of the rally was the battle between the top Scandinavians, eventual winner Erik Carlsson (Saab) and the BMC Sweden supported Mini-Coopers of Tom Trana and Bengt Soderstrom, Trana beating Carlsson over several stages in a well-used Group II car. Rauno Aaltonen (977 ARX) won Group III, and with Logan Morrison (477 BBL) the Minis won the Manufacturers' Team Prize.

The new pairing of Rauno Aaltonen and Tony Ambrose started well with a win in the Group III class on the 1962 RAC Rally.

Timo Makinen

Another class winner on the RAC Rally was a little-known Finn, who won the Group II class in a 997 car (407 ARX) – Timo Makinen (or, as one national newspaper once called him, the well-known Scottish driver Tim MacKinnen!). Whilst I suspect that with Rauno Aaltonen and Paddy Hopkirk already in the team Stuart Turner did not really need any more talent, he was one of the first to realize that it is better to have Timo drive for you than against you!

During his time with the team through the 1960s, Timo was unquestionably the fastest rally driver around – if not the most successful. He had that incredible ability to get into any car on any rally and drive it faster than anyone else. On just about every event that Timo drove with BMC, if he did not win he retired with mechanical trouble when in the lead. But it should not be inferred from this that he was a car wrecker, although he was a lot harder on his cars than his team mates. Timo always had that driving edge over his rivals and thus demanded that little bit extra from the machinery. He really was the trail-blazer for the team when, on so many occasions, the opposition in pursuit of the flying Makinen retired too, leaving one of the other Abingdon cars to move up and win.

Co-driver Paul Easter recalls some facets of his long-term partnership with Timo:

> Once a rally started Timo was there to win – but on the recce it was something different. You would be driving through a town and if he saw a couple of nice young girls he would flip the Mini sideways to wave at them through the windscreen then flip it straight again and carry on. Wherever he went he was a big character, full of fun, wanting to give rides to everyone up and down the mountains – the mayor, the village policeman, the chap who kept the bar – and they would all be shouting for Timo on the event.
>
> His capacity for drinking and surviving was incredible. We maintained that the only time Timo did a complete run over the Turini on the Monte was on the Rally itself. We practised one side, practised the other, but he always stopped at the Ranch Bar at the top. One recce we met two gendarmes with a Jeep and Timo gave them quite a demonstration on snow driving over the summit.

First outing for Timo Makinen in a works Mini was on the 1962 RAC Rally, where he won the Group II class. The legendary Finn was without question the fastest rally driver of his era.

Paul Easter (left) and Timo Makinen were to become one of the closest and longest-standing partnerships. Paul cannot recall any event in which, if they did not win, then they retired with mechanical problems when in the lead!

Then they all sat drinking and later there was Timo in the police Jeep doing handbrake turns spinning all over the Turini while the two gendarmes were stoned out of their minds after a session with him in the Ranch Bar.

We would often meet up with the other team drivers on recce and sometimes swap cars. One time I went out with Toivonen in his Porsche 904 and I marvelled at the speed of this lightweight racer. Then Timo shot past us in our Mini with Toivonen's co-driver beside him looking decidedly amazed.

Controlling Timo was quite impossible. He did not like head sets and intercoms and said that the noise made his vision go 'woggly' or something. So I just used to shout the pace notes to him over the noise. Whether he could hear them with his crash hat on I don't know. Sometimes he would ask me to put the notes away and just let him get on with the driving.

His driving style, and particularly his left-foot braking technique, was amazing. We had the brakes on fire many times. I did not think brake fluid burned but I recall using fire extinguishers on the rear brakes on the RAC Rally, wheel cylinders on fire, rubber seals and brake fluid all flaming away on a cold frosty night.

Timo was the master of any car that he drove. I remember driving with him up the main promenade in Marseilles on an Alpine Rally recce in one of the Princess 'R' service barges, laden with spares and heavy roof-rack. This was the fashionable place where all the local poseurs drove their Ferraris and Lamborghinis. Inevitably, Timo could not resist showing them how a Princess 'R' could blow them all off through the traffic. Amazing!

Tony Fall also recalls driving with Timo:

On the occasions when I sat with him it was terrifying. After the Monte one year we were having a few beers at the top of the Turini. Timo was giving his joy-rides to people down the mountain and I was fortified enough to go with him. He was barrelling in fourth towards a hairpin and I was starting to tense up because I knew the corner well. I looked round and he was not even looking at the road but trying to pick up a pen he had dropped on the floor. He looked up, swore and launched into some of the most amazing avoidance manoeuvres I have ever seen. He decided to go back to the bar after that!

Timo started ice racing and rallying in Finland in 1960 with Volvo and Saab and then with a Mini prepared by the local BMC distributor, with whom he formed a long-lasting association. When he first came to Abingdon he spoke very little English and he communicated with the team in a mixture of Finnish and English which soon became known as 'Finnglish'.

The winning potential of the works Minis on a major international event was clearly demonstrated for the first time on the 1963 Monte Carlo Rally, when Rauno Aaltonen finished third overall.

In those early days he was a pretty irresponsible character, a big fun-loving playboy, always the joker and not too keen on hard work. But later he became a more disciplined performer, as his results showed.

Timo's most famous drive was winning the 1965 Monte Carlo Rally in appalling conditions acknowledged by many to be the finest rally drive in history. British enthusiasts will also recall his spectacular and valiant attempts to conquer the RAC Rally in a big Healey.

Timo joined Ford following the closure of the BMC Competitions Department, to score a hat trick of RAC Rally wins in the Escort. Later he took up powerboating, to become Finnish Offshore Champion and winner of the 1969 Round Britain Race. He returned to Monte Carlo to drive a Japanese-sponsored Mini-Cooper in 1994, but unfortunately the car was stolen on the eve of the event and its hastily-prepared replacement retired early.

Wintry Monte

Moving on to the 1963 season, the Monte Carlo Rally provided real wintry conditions and only 100 out of the 299 starters reached the Principality. The Abingdon Minis fared well and for the first time really showed their winning potential. Rauno Aaltonen (977 ARX) finished third overall and won his class behind Pauli Toivonen (Citroën) and Erik Carlsson (Saab). Logan Morrison (477 BBL) collected the 1-litre GT class, while the rallying Reverend

Another useful drive by Logan Morrison saw the Scot win the 1-litre GT class on the 1963 Monte Carlo Rally.

Joining the BMC team to drive the works big Healeys, Paddy Hopkirk soon found the Mini more to his liking following his first drive on the 1963 Monte Carlo Rally. Paddy is seen here with Nobby Hall, one of the true craftsman-mechanics within the Abingdon team.

Rupert Jones won his class in an MG Midget and Mini racer Christabel Carlisle had the ride of her life partnering Timo Makinen in the big Healey to win the GT category.

Paddy Hopkirk

The name of Paddy Hopkirk appeared on the BMC Monte entry list for the first time in a Mini (407 ARX) although, as Paddy recalls, he had joined the team in 1961 initially to drive the big Healey: 'The big Healey was winning the Alpine Rally and just about everything else at the time and then Stuart Turner joined the team. I had great faith in Stuart and the Healey so I joined them too, but in fact hardly got my hands on the Healey. By then the Mini was up and coming and I preferred front-wheel drive – it was more forgiving.'

Paddy Hopkirk's first regular co-driver was Bristolian Henry Liddon who, along with Tony Ambrose, was to become one of the most experienced and successful of the works co-drivers.

Paddy started competition driving while at Trinity College, Dublin, in the 1950s, and joined BMC after successful careers with Standard-Triumph and Rootes. Although he drove the big Healeys with his usual skill and determination, he found that he was immediately more competitive in the Mini and, although used to tarmac rallying, he was soon equally at home on the loose.

Paddy is one of the legendary British motor sporting personalities whose name has remained very much in the public eye. His good humour, quick wit, flashing smile, and lilting Irish accent, plus a name that rolls off the tongue, all helped. But Paddy worked hard at personal promotion and was always immensely popular with the press. The quality which endeared him to the team was that he was always a 'trier' from the drop of the flag – and it did not matter whether it was an unimportant test day at Silverstone, a televised rallycross, or the final decisive stage of a big rally. Paddy would always give of his best behind the wheel, whatever the rewards. Paddy's Monte Carlo Rally victory in 1964 was without doubt one of the most publicized and popular rally wins of all time.

After the closure of the BMC Competitions Department Paddy concentrated on his motor accessory business but came out of retirement to drive a Mini to win the 1990 Pirelli Classic Marathon and was entered in a Rover Mini-Cooper on the 1994 Monte Carlo Rally, the 30th anniversary of his famous Monte victory.

Paddy would be the first to pay tribute to the part played by his long-time co-driver, Henry Liddon. Determination is the quality that seems best to describe the tall, bespectacled Henry. Either on a recce or in an event, nothing would prevent him from gaining his driver and the team the best possible advantage. Henry probably did more rallies in more countries than anyone and this gave him particular expertise when it came to assessing the nature of events. He was renowned for the accuracy and detail of his road books – a laborious and unglamorous behind-the-scenes job that contributed so much to success. After the closure of the BMC Competitions Department, Henry joined Ford and later moved on to mastermind Toyota's domination of African rallying, sadly losing his life in a plane crash on the Ivory Coast Rally.

With the imminent arrival of the 1,071 Mini-Cooper 'S', the final outing for the works 997 cars was on the 1963 Alpine Rally, where Pauline Mayman and Val Domleo won a Coupe des Alpes, the class, and the Ladies award.

The ebullient John Sprinzel, who never really seemed at home with the Mini and always preferred his Sebring Sprites, made a rare appearance with the works team on the 1963 Alpine Rally and was less than impressed when the steering column came detached from the rack just a few miles from the finish and a certain class win.

Alpine honours

The 1963 Alpine Rally should have been an historic milestone for the Morleys, who were eligible for a gold Coupe for three consecutive wins, and for Paddy Hopkirk (Healey), eligible for a silver Coupe for three non-consecutive Coupes. However, Hopkirk crashed on the very first stage, having made fastest time, while the Morleys went out with a broken experimental differential on the big Healey. The final honours were left to the Minis.

The event saw the first outing for the 1,071 Cooper 'S' (see next Chapter), driven by Rauno Aaltonen to an outright category win. Of the 997 Coopers, Denise McCluggage, a larger than life US journalist, retired with a broken drive shaft coupling (17 CRX), while John Sprinzel (977 ARX), heading for a class win, crashed just a few miles from the Marseilles finish when the steering column came disconnected from the rack. Pauline Mayman (18 CRX) won a Coupe des Alpes and the Ladies' Award, while the Minis took the Manufacturers' Team prize with the support of Terry Hunter's private entry. Not since 1958 had so few cars arrived at the finish, but of the 24 that made it, eight were Mini-Coopers.

By now Stuart Turner was visualizing the further development of the Mini and gathering around him the strongest driving team for the future. The performances of the 997 Mini-Cooper showed promise but failed to capture the all-important outright victories that were now expected of such a strong and talented organization.

The new 1,071 cc Mini-Cooper 'S' was to bring that success.

The 'S' Type

Of the many engine tuners who had turned their hand to improving the performance of the 997 cc Mini-Cooper, none had been more successful than the late Daniel Richmond of Downton Engineering. His work was much respected by Alec Issigonis and many were the meetings with John Cooper, Stuart Turner, and Alex Moulton (of rubber suspension fame) at Downton's Wiltshire base – invariably over a gastronomic lunch, when the discussions about fine wines and good food were as important as those about developing more power for the Mini. It was the evolution of the Downton big-bore 1,071 cc engine that led to the announcement, in May 1963, of the first 'S' type Mini-Cooper.

The power unit of the old Cooper was raised from 55 bhp to 70 bhp, with a revised bore/stroke ratio, the bore being increased to 70.6 mm and the stroke reduced to 68.26 mm, which involved off-set bore centres. Most of the other significant engine modifications came from experience with the Formula Junior engines. Nimonic valves with hidural guides were fitted, there were modified valve springs, and forged rockers were now used. There was a new nitrided crankshaft with redesigned connecting rods which allowed the use of larger gudgeon pins. A modified oil pump was used and a double spring-activated clutch was fitted. The gearbox was improved, with needle-roller bearings for the idler and first motion shaft. With the wider ventilated steel 4½-inch J wheels it was also possible to improve the braking, with larger diameter discs at the front and the use of a vacuum servo unit. There was a higher ratio steering rack and an optional second fuel tank was offered.

As a 90 mph road-going car, the improved performance, handling, and braking of the 'S' type gained it immediate appeal as one of the most versatile and lively of all the Mini-Cooper variants. The new model was to add yet further strength to Abingdon's rally programme.

With the Mini-Cooper 'S' offering as significant a power increase over the Mini-Cooper as that model had done over the Mini-Minor, the new 1,071 brought hopes of yet further achievements for the team. Paddy Hopkirk on his memorable drive on the 1963 Tour de France.

One month after the arrival of the 1,071, Rauno Aaltonen astounded the touring car opposition on the 1963 Alpine Rally by winning the category outright.

Aaltonen's Alpine

Only one month after the announcement of the 1,071, a lone car (277 EBL) was entered for Rauno Aaltonen on the 1963 Alpine Rally, to support the team of 997 Coopers which were in the hands of John Sprinzel, Pauline Mayman, and the American lady journalist Denise McCluggage.

Rauno's performance in the new car was the talking point of the event, for he led the Touring category from start to finish and collected a coveted Coupe des Alpes. On many of the stages the Mini came close to, and even beat the times of the big Healeys. Rauno's only problem was overheating, which was cured by the mechanics running the car with the heater on full power and diverting the outlet pipes underneath the car – not strictly legal, but effective!

Hopkirk's Tour

The performance on the Alpine was immediately endorsed in the next event on the calendar, the 1963 Tour de France. Run for nine days over 3,600 miles, with nine circuit races (12 hours of racing) and seven hillclimbs, Paddy Hopkirk's 1,071 (33 EJB) not only got up amongst the big 7-litre Ford Galaxies and 3.8 Jaguars to come third in the touring category, but finished third overall on scratch and won the handicap category.

It is always hard to quantify the value of competition successes but Hopkirk's achievements on the Tour de France (which attracted 20 minutes of live TV coverage daily), sparked a remarkable sales impact for the Mini in France. The BMC dealer in Montpelier reported having taken orders for nine Mini-Coopers before the event was over, while the main Paris distributor placed orders for three times his annual Mini quota at the London Motor Show.

Paddy Hopkirk on the 1963 Tour de France, when he mixed it with the 3.8 Jaguars and the 7-litre Ford Galaxies to finish third overall on scratch and win the handicap category. Run for nine days over 3,600 miles and including nine races and seven hill climbs, the Tour attracted tremendous media coverage in France. Here Paddy Hopkirk (No 38) has some fun with Timo Makinen.

But not all of the excitement took place abroad. Paddy Hopkirk (8 EMO), now in brilliant form, came home for the 1963 RAC Rally where, placed fourth overall, he was the top British finisher, not very far behind the leading Scandinavians Tom Trana, Harry Kallstrom, and Erik Carlsson. Paddy, in fact, was fastest, or equal fastest, over 20 of the 30 special stages.

Paddy recalls the somewhat dubious practice of using pace notes for this event:

> We were the first to use pace notes and on the RAC Rally Stuart Turner had cars going ahead over the stages with people dressed up as farmers with a duplicator in the back of the car. They were making instant notes and the notes would be brought back to the drivers just before the start of the stage. We were the first to do this on the RAC and there was a hell of a row about it!

The RAC Rally cars had major problems with the production rubber drive-shaft couplings, which had to be changed regularly. This was also the first event in which the Minis ran with full-length dural sump guards, and used single-filament quartz-iodine bulbs fitted on long range lamps.

The Mini from Minsk

With the 1,071, the mechanics, and the drivers – Paddy Hopkirk in particular – on top form, things were shaping up for the team and the Mini's first big-time win. The efforts of the Abingdon team could not have been better rewarded than with their first Monte Carlo Rally victory in 1964.

The six car Mini team (running now with the smaller Mini-Moke sump guards, radiator muffs, and Triplex heated windscreens) included Group II 1,071s for Hopkirk (33 EJB) and Pauline Mayman (277 EBL) and Group III 997s for Timo Makinen (570 FMO), Rauno Aaltonen (569 FMO), South African Jack Thompson (18 CRX), and the BBC's Raymond Baxter (477 BBL). Raymond was a Monte regular with the BMC team, driving Minis and an MG 1100, usually finishing well-placed in addition to handling his demanding broadcast schedules. Raymond was later to serve as BMC's Director of Publicity.

Paddy's win was a closely fought battle against the opposition and the handicap system. Starting from Minsk in Russia with co-driver Henry Liddon, Paddy by no means had the easiest run or the best of the weather. The navigation in Russia was not easy and Paddy recalls one nasty moment when they went the wrong way and had to do a very quick handbrake turn when faced by an unfriendly military gentleman described as a 'tea cosy with a sten gun poking out'!

Paddy was also in trouble in France, when by mistake he shot up a one-way street. An

Top British finisher in fourth place on the 1963 RAC Rally, Paddy Hopkirk gave the leading Scandinavians (Tom Trana, Erik Carlsson, and Harry Kallstrom) a run for their money.

BBC commentator Raymond Baxter was an enthusiastic rally competitor and a regular member of the BMC team. He was later a popular PR Director for BMC.

Victory on the 1964 Monte Carlo Rally by Paddy Hopkirk and Henry Liddon was the first major international win for the works Minis and probably the most publicized rally victory of all time – albeit not so popular with the French!

angry gendarme appeared on the scene and demanded that he presented his road book for the breach of the traffic regulations to be recorded, an entry which would have undoubtedly disqualified him from the Rally. But the quick-thinking Irishman declared that he had not got his road book because he had retired from the Rally and was hurrying home to attend the funeral of a close relative. The gendarme looked disbelieving, recorded Paddy's name and details of the car, and finally sent the crew on their way. Paddy was always dying to see the expression on that gendarme's face when next morning he read that a certain Monsieur Hopkirk in a car registration number 33 EJB had won the Rally!

The popularity of the first Monte victory was heightened by the David and Goliath battle between the diminutive Minis and the massive team of Ford Falcons, who had openly declared that they were going to conquer rallying's greatest prize. Despite the performance of Ford's racing drivers – Bo Ljungfeldt, Jo Schlesser, Henri Greder, and Graham Hill – plus the ever-present threat of Carlsson's Saab, Paddy led his Finnish team mates to a marginal but glorious victory and the Abingdon team again took home the Team Prize. It was the first British win on the Monte since 1956.

It was a great achievement not only to beat the handicap formula, and the big capacity opposition, but also to gain victory over mainly dry roads which gave little advantage to front-wheel drive cars. The results were, however, very close and Henry Liddon recalled that victory really took them unawares.

> We had sat on a wall at the finish in Monte with Bohringer, who we had met up with during the event; he was really a sort of father figure to us. We worked out a few stage times and I mentioned to Paddy that we had beaten him by a couple of minutes on some of the stages – so we thought that we must have done quite well!

So close was the result that when Paddy awoke from his slumbers and heard he had won, he took a great deal of persuading that he had won outright, and not just won his class!

Paddy's car was flown home to go on the *Sunday Night at the London Palladium* TV show with Bruce Forsyth, where everyone stood up and sung 'Land of Hope and Glory'. It was a great moment but not without some behind the scenes dramas. Just before the car was due to be driven onto the revolving stage it failed to start. Mechanic Brian Moylan was hauled out of the audience and quickly diagnosed that the starter motor pinion was not functioning and needed cleaning. Fortunately for Brian the rally tool kit was still in the boot and the starter was whipped off and cleaned just in time!

The team could not have asked for a better result than victory in the most famous rally of all to support their demands for yet more power, to help the Mini maintain its winning ways.

Interior of the 1964 Monte-winning Mini.

Chapter 5

1,275 Mini Power

The 1,071 Mini-Cooper 'S' was designed with yet further engine developments in mind, and in March 1964 two new models became available. By fitting a long-stroke crankshaft and a taller block a 1,275 cc (75 bhp) version was provided, while with a short-stroke crankshaft the capacity was reduced to 970 cc (68 bhp).

The smaller-engined car was originally conceived with the 1-litre class of the European Touring Car Championship in mind but was later used on a number of rallies where there were advantages in running in the smaller class. The 970 Cooper 'S' was a very smooth and refined motor but it was only produced in limited quantities for the purposes of homologation for competitions. The 1,275 version was the obvious evolution of the 'A' series unit within the limitations of the 1,300 cc class, for both racing and rallying. Later improvements to the 1,275 included a diaphragm-spring clutch, toughened crankshaft, oil cooler, twin fuel tanks, hydrolastic suspension, and improved reclining seats.

John Cooper recalls the decisive meeting at Longbridge when the important go ahead for the 1,275 was given:

> When I was at a board meeting at Longbridge we were discussing the two new Mini-Cooper variants and they said we can't do this, it would mean altering the boring machines and things like that. The engine was originally designed as an 850 and how can it possibly be 1,300 cc? I thought that I had wasted my time coming up to Longbridge that day but, as we went out of the door, Harriman turned to me and said, 'We are bloody well going to do it though!'

Winning first time out

The new-found power of the 1,275 was immediately put to good effect. First time out, and with the new model only just homologated, Timo Makinen (AJB 66B) claimed outright victory on the Tulip Rally, just beating a Ford Galaxy driven by Henri Greder. It was a clean sweep for the BMC team, with the Morleys winning the GT category in the big Healey and the Minis once more taking the Manufacturers' Team Prize with the assistance of privateers Peter Riley and Julien Vernaeve. This was the first of many occasions that Julien, the popular Belgian privateer, was to support the works entries to win a class or the team award. Julien was a BMC Dealer who prepared his own race and rally cars and was a particularly successful Group I exponent.

Regulations for the 1964 Alpine Rally favoured the Group III category, so Rauno Aaltonen drove a lightweight car (AJB 55B) with aluminium doors and boot lid. Rauno consolidated the Mini's growing reputation when he collected a Coupe des Alpes and won his class. Pauline Mayman, in a 970 car (AJB 66B), returned from her nasty accident on the Monte to win the Coupe des Dames.

The ultimate development of the Mini came with the 1,275 Mini-Cooper 'S', offering over twice the power of the original Mini-Minor with vastly improved transmission, suspension, and brakes. With basic competitions preparation it was to prove an instant rally winner. Timo Makinen on the 1964 Alpine Rally.

First time out for the new 1,275 Mini-Cooper 'S', Timo Makinen and Tony Ambrose won the 1964 Tulip Rally (with some verbal advice from Stuart Turner!).

Marathon Mini

Until 1964 no Mini had ever survived the horrors of the Spa–Sofia–Liège Rally, although privateer David Hiam very nearly made it in 1963. The honour of being the first and only Mini to finish the gruelling Marathon fell to the lone works entry (570 FMO) of John Wadsworth and Mike Wood, their achievement being somewhat over-shadowed by the big Healey win of Rauno Aaltonen in what was to be last of the Liège Marathons. John, son of Edgar Wadsworth, a well known north country motor sport personality, was a successful club rallyman of the time and earned his Marathon drive by being the only private entry to gain a Coupe des Alpes on the 1964 Alpine Rally.

Although John only drove once for the team before retiring from motor sport to rejoin the family business, his Liège co-driver Mike Wood began a long association with the team, principally as regular co-driver to Tony Fall. The partnership, Fall the Yorkshireman and Wood the

Lightweight Group III car for Rauno Aaltonen and Tony Ambrose on the 1964 Alpine Rally winning a Coupe des Alpes and the class.

John Wadsworth and Mike Wood look relaxed at the start of the 1964 Spa–Sofia–Liège – they looked even happier, but not quite so relaxed, once they had become the first and only crew to get a Mini to the finish of the gruelling non-stop four-day Marathon.

Lancastrian, provided a surfeit of north-country humour and the pair were to become known as the 'Morecambe and Wise' of the international rally set. Mike was a legendary club navigator, having started rallying in the early 1950s both as a driver and co-driver. One of the great characters of British rallying, Mike was renowned for his 'rallymanship' and was once described as the only person who could actually make a printing clock produce the time that he wanted!

Mike recalls the Marathon drive:

This was to be my first works Mini drive, having navigated in the previous year with Timo Makinen on the Alpine and the RAC Rally and done the 1963 Liège with Logan Morrison in big Healeys.

Rauno Aaltonen had done a Liège recce with John Wadsworth and as John, therefore, was well prepared for the event, Stuart Turner decided to run a Mini in company with the already large entry of three big Healeys and three MGBs. The seven car entry strained the availability of co-drivers so, as I knew John well, Stuart asked me to co-drive the Mini.

The large and varied entry made the logistics of the spares and service schedule somewhat difficult and, being the only Mini, we did not have too many spare wheels and tyres.

Inevitably, once the event got under way it was not too long before we were running miles behind Rauno in the big Healey, who was in the lead and, of course, went on to win the event. Running almost last, and at times some five hours behind the leaders, this meant that in the early stages of the event some of the service crews simply could not wait for us. This problem resolved itself in the latter stages of the event as the service crews could not catch up anyway on the homeward run and, apart from Rauno, we were then the only other BMC car still running.

The Liège was really a two driver event and really hard going in a Mini. It is difficult to describe how rough the roads were and what it was like to drive almost non-stop for four days and four nights in those conditions. John and I have talked about our adventure many times since and clearly we were so tired at the time there are bits of the event which we simply cannot remember at all.

I did some of the easier driving on the way down to Yugoslavia, then the organizers sprung a route alteration on us and actually the extra time allowance for this was the only thing that kept us in the event. When we set off from Sofia on the way home, having done two days and two nights with the same to come, John was pretty well on his last legs. We really only got about an hour or so of rest in Sofia.

By the time we got to Bulgaria we were going slower and slower. I do remember us struggling along at 20 mph at one point, and this was renowned as the fastest of all rallies! I simply could not keep John awake. In the middle of the night, when we had almost ground to a halt, I looked at the route notes and saw that there was a section coming up of about 15 miles where we did not have to worry about any junctions. I said to John that I would take over, he got his head down for about 20 minutes and that just about kept him going through Yugoslavia and into Italy. He cannot remember to this day moving over and letting me drive!

When we got to Sofia we had 20 minutes left of our time allowance before we were out of the event and there seemed no way that we could continue from there as we were constantly losing time. Twenty minutes could have been lost on any section. Morale was pretty low and at the Sofia control I was working with the service crew and John went to clock in. When he came out John was almost in tears because the officials had issued a notice saying that an additional two hours had been given for the following section because of route diversions. Rather than rejoicing because we were still in the event, John was really hoping that we could have retired there and then but now realized that he had to go on!

Even with the additional time allowance it would be touch and go if we could make it. There was a saying that if you came out of Yugoslavia with anything less than 30 minutes in hand you would never make it to the finish. We left the Yugoslavian border with a mere six minutes to spare and so it became a road race across Germany and Italy all through the night and over the four dreadful passes – the Croche Domini, the Gavia, the Vivione, and the Stelvio. Somehow we and the Mini kept going; when we did get service and had to stop for fuel it was like a racing pit stop. At one time on the German autobahn John tucked in behind an ambulance and a police car who eventually got so annoyed that we were following them that they stopped and were going to summons us if we went any further!

Actually, the motivation of having to race to the finish probably kept us going. We had a nasty moment when we could not find a passage control in a town. We had it clearly pin-pointed on our route notes on a particular avenue in the centre of the town but there was nothing there, and no other cars around – we were so far behind that we had not seen another rally car for ages. We spent about five minutes there and decided to carry on. All the way back to Liège my mind was tortured with the thought that if we made it to the finish we might be disqualified for missing this control.

Underbonnet of a 1964 works Mini-Cooper.

Up to this point, amazingly, the Mini had not suffered serious mechanical problems other than when we had run very short of good tyres and the sump guard had taken an incredible battering, and we had run for a long time with it dangerously roped up to the front bumper. By the last night, however, the Mini's Achilles heel at the time – the dreaded drive shaft couplings – started to make an awful racket and we knew we had trouble.

After the last of the Italian passes, the Stelvio (which was run downhill through the notorious 48 hairpins), the drive shafts were almost wrecked. Stuart Turner and Doug Watts were servicing at the bottom, but there was no time to spare so we had to keep going. Stuart said that he would follow us all the way in the service car and be ready to change the drive shafts if necessary.

Out of Italy and on to the long run up to Belgium the drive shafts got worse and worse and they finally gave out right in the middle of a little town. It was early Sunday morning, traffic was just starting to move around and we ran the Mini off the road into an open area so that it would be clearly visible when Stuart arrived.

It was at this point that I believe I made a significant contribution to future works Mini servicing procedures by suggesting to John that to make the job as easy as possible we should tip the car on its side. This was to become a regular sight on future events at BMC service points. The reaction of the locals on this occasion was typical of what usually happened in future – fuel gushed out of the filler caps and ran down the gutters, people stood around in total disbelief and must have thought that the British were quite mad. This time a police car arrived on the scene but by then Stuart had arrived, Doug did a lightning drive shaft change and we were away again before they had time to really understand what was going on.

And so we made it to the finish, 20th and last but one, to receive our garland and champagne from Monsieur Garot the organizer. With trepidation I immediately pointed out to him our problem with the passage control and it was typical of this sporting gentleman whose club ran one of the most professional events on the calender, that he apologized to us that the control officials had left early and did not expect anyone to be running so late – no problem. Had that been the Monte Carlo Rally there would have been hours of protests!

For the first and only time a Mini had finished the Marathon!

Paul Easter

Another new co-driver made his works Mini debut on the next event for the team, Paul Easter joining Timo Makinen for the Tour de France (BJB 77B). Paul had been a successful Mini privateer in national events but had more recently turned his hand to competing overseas.

Paul Easter (left), who was to become Timo Makinen's permanent co-driver from the 1964 Tour de France, gets some words of wisdom from deputy shop supervisor Tommy Wellman (centre) and Henry Liddon.

In British events I had spent all of my time bouncing off banks on narrow Welsh roads, then driving like a lunatic to catch up again. I had come to the conclusion that unless you had a genius as a navigator who knew where every gate was and the name of every sheep in Wales, you did not stand a chance. So I switched to foreign rallies instead. It did not cost much more and it was certainly less damaging to the car.

The Tour was not a happy event for the team, with three out of the four Minis retiring and only Pauline Mayman (AJB 6B) salvaging a 970 class win.

For Paul Easter his first ride with Timo was a co-driver's nightmare. Coming into Grenoble on the last day of the event, when they were lying well-placed, Paul was driving with Timo stretched out asleep in the passenger's seat. A taxi shot out of a side turning, Paul swerved across the road, hit the kerb, the Mini darted back across the road and ended up wedged against a kilometre post. Timo woke up with a grunt, surveyed the wreckage, turned to a quivering Paul and said, 'I think we go find nice pub and you buy me big drink!' Clearly there were no repercussions to this incident for the Makinen-Easter pairing went on to become one of the closest partnerships in rallying.

Terminal destruction testing was held in Wales to try and find out what would break first on the Mini and what would be the next component to fail. There was always close liaison with Longbridge following such trials to see whether production modifications could be made. Tony Fall was volunteered to see how far he could make the Mini fly!

Longbridge liaison

The growing competition achievements of the Mini at this time helped to strengthen relationships between the Abingdon team and the design and development departments at Longbridge.

The evolution of hydrolastic suspension on the Mini during 1964 was a good example of the co-operation between the two departments and how Longbridge used the Competitions team to carry out final evaluation and testing. Jack Daniels (Mini project engineer at Longbridge) made an early hydrolastic prototype available to Abingdon and this was tested by Paddy Hopkirk, Timo Makinen, and Don Morley over some bumpy roads in France, British pot-holed farm tracks, and circuit tests at Snetterton by Timo Makinen in a Don Moore race car. Later, Rauno Aaltonen and John Wadsworth used a hydrolastic car for their recce of the Spa–Sofia–Liège and then the Tour de France. Further testing in an English forest was carried out by Paul Easter, Barrie Williams, and John Wadsworth.

The results of these tests found Longbridge fitting modified hydrolastic units and making further alterations to the standard specification when the units were found to 'sag' after prolonged use on rough roads. Further modifications had to be carried out when an interaction was found between the hydrolastic units and the suspension, which caused drive shaft coupling problems and later steering arm failures.

Despite the fact that these cars had been sent to us fully tested and signed-off by the Longbridge testers, it was good that the Abingdon team, by simulating competition conditions, had been able to make a real contribution to the final production specification. This feedback to Longbridge improved relationships with the people who ultimately signed off the Competitions budget and to whom regular requests were made for production line changes to comply with homologation requirements.

Driver tests

Testing the drivers was as important as testing the cars, and Stuart Turner was keen on running regular circuit test days offering various drivers the opportunity to sample a variety of cars. This was seen as a good opportunity for the established stars to show that they were still on the pace while giving up-and-coming names a chance to pit themselves against the works stars.

One such test day took place at Silverstone during the summer of 1964, with a race and rally big Healey, an MGB, one of the Donald Healey race Sprites, and a selection of 1,275, 970, race and rally Minis. It was notable that Paddy Hopkirk was consistently amongst the fastest in every car while a young Jackie Stewart (then driving the Formula 3 Cooper for Ken Tyrrell) showed Rauno Aaltonen and Timo Makinen a thing or two about how to handle a Mini on a race circuit.

The late Geoff Healey caused some light relief on this occasion by regularly lifting the bonnet of the Sprite every time a driver finished his run, ostensibly to check the oil. The drivers had all been given a strict rev limit and what they did not know was that the wily Geoff had fitted a tell-tale rev-counter under the bonnet and had been carefully writing down all the readings! There were a few red faces afterwards when Geoff calmly announced to the assembled company his findings!

The 1964 season finished with the RAC Rally and an eight-car BMC team entry of BMC Sweden-prepared Minis for Harry Kallstrom (AGU 780B) and Carl Orrenius (AJB 44B), a pair of Abingdon cars for Paddy Hopkirk (CRX 90B) and Rauno Aaltonen (CRX 89B) plus pairs of big Healeys and MGBs. The Minis, all Group III, were running with raised suspensions, not only to improve ground clearance but also to reduce the load on the rubber drive shaft couplings. The cars also used adjustable roof-mounted Lucas spotlamps.

The Minis showed early promise, with the quick Harry Kallstrom actually leading at one stage, but it was a bad event with only the two big Healeys staggering to the finish. Kallstrom went out with a broken differential, Orrenius crashed, Hopkirk went off the road, and Aaltonen retired with a broken gearbox when challenging Tom Trana's Volvo for the lead.

While the team held regular driver test sessions, it must have been pretty disheartening for the up-and-coming privateers to be pitched against the team's ultimate array of talent – (left to right) Rauno Aaltonen/Henry Liddon, Tony Fall/Mike Wood, Paddy Hopkirk/Ron Crellin, Timo Makinen/Paul Easter, and Lars Ytterbring/Lars Persson.

Privateers

If the RAC Rally finished on a low note, the successes of private owners and other teams during the year showed that the Mini-Cooper 'S' was now really making its mark on the worldwide motor sport scene. Barrie Williams won the Welsh Rally and Ronnie McCartney the Circuit of Ireland. Warwick Banks and John Rhodes led a Mini victory in the Mallory Park Three Hours' Race. John Handley and Ralph Broad led another Mini 1–2–3 in the Brands Hatch Six Hours'. Paddy Hopkirk and Julien Vernaeve won the 1,000 cc class in the Spa 24 Hours' Touring Car Race. John Fitzpatrick was overall runner-up and 1,300 class winner in the BRSCC National Saloon Car Championship, while Warwick Banks was winner of the European Touring Car Championship.

This fork-lift truck was used at a service point close to the start of the 1964 RAC Rally as a publicity stunt. It could have served a useful purpose assisting the mechanics further along the route when the tough going eliminated all four works Minis!

Harry Kallstrom won the Nordic Rally Championship (four top rallies in Norway, Denmark, Finland, and Sweden), Picko Troberg was Swedish Ice Racing Champion, Borje Osterberg Swedish Speed Racing Champion, and Timo Makinen Finnish Ice Racing Champion.

Bonus Scheme

While Abingdon offered various levels of support to many of the above teams and drivers, one of the team manager's most frustrating jobs was fending off the persistent overtures from up-and-coming private owners in search of support and even a works drive. Some applicants may have been well known, and the team manager had probably been keeping an eye on the event results columns in the motor sporting press for names that consistently achieved good placings. Many, however, would be total strangers – some of whom may not even have had a car or have ever done any competition driving. Clearly, there was seldom an opportunity to offer these people a test drive and only very rarely could the most experienced and successful privateers be offered a works drive, or, more likely, a modest supporting budget for a specific event.

BMC was the first to set up a Bonus Scheme which offered cash rewards to private owners using their own BMC cars in a listed range of events (racing and rallying). This was not only an eminently fair system, whereby success was well rewarded, but it also meant that the team manager could respond to the persistent phone calls from young hopefuls by sending them details of the Scheme and basically wishing them the best of luck in applying for support. The payouts through the Scheme gave a good indication of who the top privateers were in the various categories and it was generally these people who went on to receive further support. Above all it went a long way towards ending the team manager's worst nightmare, the over-enthusiastic privateer who, calling unannounced at Abingdon, offered to take you out to lunch (which may have been pleasant) and, on the way to the pub – or, worse still, on the way back to Abingdon – demonstrated just how fast he could drive!

Special Tuning

Up to this time BMC private owners and dealers wishing to purchase competition parts had to do so through BMC Service at Cowley. This was not an entirely satisfactory arrangement because, inevitably, the staff there were not always geared up to handle competition technical enquiries from enthusiasts, while ordering special competition parts through local dealers was a tedious route.

During the summer of 1964 the BMC Special Tuning Department was set up alongside the Competitions workshops. Initially the range of parts was limited, but in time it came to include the homologated parts for all BMC models used in competitions. Tuning kits were also supplied, and later Special Tuning was to open up its own workshops where customers' cars could be prepared to works specification. As a training exercise for their mechanics, Special Tuning also prepared and entered selected cars in international events when the Competitions shop found themselves overladen.

Special Tuning was first run by Glyn Evans from the MG Service Department but later Basil Wales took over from Customer Liaison at Cowley. Former Sprite racer Mike Garton joined as customer technical correspondent and Maurice Burton of the Mini Seven Club also worked in the department for some time. Later Ron Elkins was appointed to head up the technical section.

While the initial objective of Special Tuning was to provide a better service to private owners, in the longer term the profits from parts sales and customer car preparation were to go some way towards off-setting the financing of the overall competitions programme. Its existence also eased the burden on the Competitions office in handling private owner enquiries. Certainly there would be little time to handle such enquiries in the coming year, when the team launched a concerted and successful attack on the European Rally Championship.

Chapter 6 _____

Aaltonen European Champion

Created in 1953, the European Rally Championship had first undergone German domination by Mercedes, Auto Union, and Porsche, then from 1957 to 1959 the Swedes had taken over, with Volvo and Saab. For the next three years there had been a close struggle between Mercedes and Saab, but by 1963 BMC were coming to the fore: Eugen Bohringer's Mercedes won the title, but BMC achieved four Championship rally wins.

For the first time for many years, the 1965 Championship presented a sensible, straightforward and worthy contest. There was a better geographical spread of 12 qualifying rounds and some 20 works and semi-works teams competed for the major honours. BMC, like most manufacturers, did not start the year planning to chase the Championship title but, by mid-season, it was clear that Rauno Aaltonen had a very fair chance of success and the later programme was geared to assist his win.

Makinen's Monte

It was Timo Makinen, however, who hit the headlines at the start of the season by putting up a truly sensational performance to win the Monte Carlo Rally with Paul Easter who, after his first drive with Timo on the Tour de France had ended with a crash, did not expect to be asked again: 'While Timo wanted me to partner him again, not everyone in the team was that enthusiastic, perhaps feeling that an experienced navigator would have been a more sensible choice than someone who had previously been a driver. However, Timo as usual got his way, I am pleased to say!'

Makinen (AJB 44B) and Rauno Aaltonen (CRX 88B) had Group III cars with lightweight aluminium doors, bonnet and boot, perspex side and rear windows, rear seat pan and bulkhead drilled with lightening holes, underfelting and most of the interior trim removed, a modified radiator grille, alloy wing extensions, and improved Triplex heated windscreens. Lucas spot lamps served as dipped headlights, allowing the use of the non-dipping quartz-iodine bulbs in the main headlamps. Power output measured 75 bhp at 6,500 rpm at the wheels.

The other four Minis were Group II cars for Paddy Hopkirk (CRX 91B), Don Morley (CRX 90B), Harry Kallstrom (AGU 780B), and Raymond Baxter (8 EMO). The entries were spread from various starting points, Paddy and Timo from Stockholm, Rauno from Athens, the Morleys and Baxter from Minsk, and Harry Kallstrom from Paris. Makinen chose to start from Stockholm so as to run up on the snow-ploughed main roads and avoid the worst of the tedious and dangerous French routes. Paul Easter did more than his fair share of the run-in driving.

> I had driven the bulk of the way from Stockholm. Timo had done a bit of day driving, but I had done the four nights on the road to keep him well rested. In view of what was to come in the way of bad driving conditions, this may well have contributed to our success because when the blizzard came, Timo was fit and fresh. But the run-in was not entirely without incident.
>
> We were running through Luxembourg with Paddy up ahead in formation, when a car com-

Timo Makinen's 1965 Monte Carlo Rally victory has been claimed as one of rallying's greatest drives.

ing the other way suddenly lost control, rolled, and shot between the two Minis and disappeared off the road. That could have been the end of our Monte. Then at the Luxembourg time control when it was our time to leave, the officials could not find our road book and they said that we had not handed it in. The control was in the entrance to a hotel with a table set up in the foyer which had a large table cloth on it reaching down to the ground. After searching everywhere and starting to panic, I lifted up the table cloth and there was our road book on the floor!

At the Gap control we could not find the service crew so I started to change the wheels while Timo took the road book into the control to get the time stamped. When we got to Monte we found that we had been penalized two minutes at Gap for booking in early. Timo had not checked the time and that took a bit of sorting out!

An incident at the Frankfurt control was another heart-stopping moment. The big Finn was asked for his autograph by a pretty girl and, of course, he obliged and then dashed off for a quick snack before his due time out. Panic ensued when he realized that the girl had taken his road book as well as her autograph book by mistake. Timo recovered it just in time!

Timo and Paul ran into the notorious blizzard just before the merging points of the concentration run at Chambery. With plenty of time in hand, most competitors bumbled along in the bad conditions, but not Timo. He drove the final miles flat out so that, before setting out on the competitive run-in to Monte, he had fully tested the performance and handling of the spiked tyres in bad conditions.

From Chambery onwards, the blizzard was really monstrous and crews had to fight their way through the blanket of snow, so bad that all the quartz lamps in the world, heated windscreens, two-speed wipers and spiked tyres could hardly cope. Many crews got lost, went off the road into ditches, or struck obstacles buried in the snow. Navigation was incredibly difficult because snowdrifts had covered many of the landmarks and mileage recorders were highly inaccurate because of constant wheel-spin.

Timo, running as leading car in the Rally, was acting as pathfinder for the rest and Paul Easter recalls the conditions:

> The snow came right over the roof and the weight of it cracked the windscreen. We only knew where the road was because the snow dipped a little between the sides. You could not see signposts or anything. The drifts were deeper than the bonnet. It was a lonely night and once we left Gap we never saw another rally car for the rest of the night.
>
> I must admit that it was a bit forbidding sitting next to the fastest rally driver in the world and with the prospect of winning the most important rally of them all, and this was only my second

Stuart Turner tries to calm the ever-exuberant Timo Makinen while Ford competitions manager Henry Taylor (left) wonders what he has to do to beat the works Minis!

time in the hot seat. The mileages were up the slot because of wheel spin and the old single Halda distance recorder was not much good. Service was difficult because we either missed them in the snow, there was not time to stop, or the service crews had been forced back by the conditions. However, we never had any panics, we never had to rush into a control, and there were always one or two minutes in hand in the end.

Timo's judgement was superb, in the deep snow he just aimed for the middle of the dip. His driving skill was absolutely fabulous. He was so good that he never seemed to be making any great effort, and it was hard to believe that we were the fastest car in the Rally most of the time.

That only 35 of the 237 starters reached Monte after the 2,000 mile run-in, within the hour of lateness permitted to qualify for the final Mountain Circuit run, was almost unprecedented, and gives some idea of the severity of the conditions. That Timo's Mini was the only car to finish without any lateness penalties at all was amazing. That he made fastest time overall in three out of the five special stages on the final run-in to Monte was astounding, especially being number one on the road.

The 35 runners then had to take part in the 400-mile Mountain Circuit with six flat-out special stages timed to the second. At the start Timo had the equivalent of a 10 minute lead over his nearest rivals, Lucien Bianchi (Citroën) and Eugen Bohringer (Porsche). He could have taken things easy but Timo preferred to set his usual pace so that he could keep fully alert and strengthen his position, setting the fastest time on five out of the six stages.

On the one stage that he was not fastest he lost time, and very nearly the Rally, when the contact breaker spring in the distributor snapped. That Timo and Paul diagnosed the fault and changed the spring in the remarkable time of only four minutes is almost unbelievable – that would be a good effort for a skilled mechanic with all the tools ready in a well-lit garage. To do it by the side of the road in the middle of the night in a snowstorm is the work of a truly professional rally crew.

Of the 35 finishers who took part in that Mountain Circuit, only 22 returned to Monte, Makinen scoring a dominating victory over Eugen Bohringer (Porsche) and Pat Moss (Saab). Of the other works Minis, Paddy Hopkirk (CRX 91B) won the Group II class despite damaging his suspension after hitting a snow-covered kilometre stone near Gap. The Morleys (CRX 90B) were runners-up in the class. Rauno (CRX 88B) went out with a loose condenser in the distributor, Kallstrom (AGU 780B) had clutch failure, while poor Raymond Baxter (8 EMO) never even made the start when his car put a rod through the block on the way to Minsk. The Russian Embassy refused permission for a private plane to send a replacement engine.

Finally, when Timo and Paul piled into the Mini to go to collect their trophies at the prize-giving the car refused to start. After a quick look under the bonnet, mechanic Nobby Hall was called in and, finding no spark, he changed the coil and the sparking plugs to no avail. On closer examination of the distributor it was discovered that when Timo had replaced the contact breaker spring, he had dropped the little fibre insulating washer off the base plate. Somehow, the spring had stayed in place for the rest of the Mountain Circuit tests but, when the engine had cooled down, it had moved and shorted to earth. Rallies are not often won by such good luck!

Timo's Monte win has been described as probably the greatest single rally drive of all time. Paul Easter would agree.

> Timo's performance was just unbelievable. Head down, leaning forward over the wheel, trying to peer under the snow and the driving blizzard as it hit the screen. We never once had a moment. We never once drove other than absolutely flat out. He was amazing.
>
> The only other occasion when I was totally spellbound by Timo's driving was on the snowy RAC Rally in 1965 in the big Healey when, in similar conditions and after getting a maximum penalty at the Perth control, I ended up doing some of the stages standing on the rear bumper and hanging on to the hardtop to try and get more traction. Doing a special stage on the rear bumper of a works Healey with Makinen at the wheel must be the ultimate co-driver's experience!

The Mini's second Monte win was given worldwide acclaim by the press and no doubt it

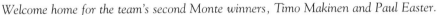

Welcome home for the team's second Monte winners, Timo Makinen and Paul Easter.

With his regular Irish co-driver Terry Harryman wishing the rock face was not always on his side, Paddy Hopkirk uses all of the road to keep ahead of the works Lotus Cortinas and win the Circuit of Ireland.

was the margin of Timo's crushing victory that set Monagasque minds thinking of ways and means of preventing further Mini domination.

Swedish cold comfort

After such a brilliant Monte it seemed sensible to send the Abingdon trio to another winter classic, the Swedish Rally. Paddy Hopkirk (AJB 33B), Timo Makinen (DJB 92B), and Rauno Aaltonen (DJB 93B) were joined by Harry Kallstrom (AGU 780B) entered by BMC Sweden. This, however, turned out to be the first of what was to become an annual abortive attempt by the team to win with the Mini in Sweden. On this occasion all four cars retired with broken differential pinions due to lack of lubrication caused by the intense cold. Paul Easter recalls that it was so cold, (minus 42°C), that when they were towing the stricken Minis back to the ferry after they had broken down they could not run the engines, so to keep warm the crews lit their camping gas stoves in the passenger footwells!

Better fortune came on the Circuit of Ireland, the event falling into line with the RAC Rally format with speed tests and special stages taking over from the traditional driving tests. Paddy Hopkirk (CRX 89B) won outright after a tremendous battle with the Ford Cortinas of Vic Elford and David Seigle-Morris. Hopkirk made it a hat trick of BMC wins in Ireland, with Ian Woodside winning with a Sprite in 1963 and Ronnie McCartney winning with a 1,071 Mini in 1964.

Snowy Tulip

The unusually severe winter conditions in Europe persisted for the Tulip Rally, much of the southern route becoming impassable so that many stages had to be cancelled. The BMC team, however, were alone in being prepared for such conditions and the wily Stuart Turner had studded tyres laid on for the lone works Mini (AJB 33B) of Timo Makinen.

Setting off from Holland's seaside resort of Noordwijk, the first of 19 speed tests was at the Nürburgring, where Timo was joint fastest with Peter Harper's Sunbeam Tiger followed by the Morleys' big Healey. Moving south, to the first of the timed climbs, Timo and the

Talking point on the 1965 Tulip Rally was the battle between the Morleys' big Healey and the Mini of Timo Makinen. At the finish the Mini was only eight seconds behind the big Healey on scratch times!

Morleys increased their lead on scratch, the pair having their own private battle.

A Monte-type blizzard in the Vosges mountains caused havoc, particularly amongst the private owners, 33 of whom were running BMC cars and most of whom were quite unprepared for winter motoring conditions. Monte winners Timo and Paul had to push their car while the Morleys had to virtually carry their Healey over the summit of one climb. Privateers Julien Vernaeve and Henry Liddon were observed reversing up one climb with Henry sprawled on the bonnet in an endeavour to improve traction over the driving wheels.

On scratch times over a hastily modified route, the Morleys finally took the advantage over the Minis, finishing just eight seconds ahead of Timo with Julien in a creditable third place. Then came the usual re-classification of the entry according to the class improvement system, which not only took into account a competitor's performance in relation to the others in his class, but also a comparison was made between the performance of the other class winners in the categories. Thus Don Morley was placed no higher than eighth overall, while Timo's brilliant performance earned him nothing better than sixth overall. Julien Vernaeve came off best by winning his class in the GT category.

All Greek to Timo

Sometimes you can retire from a rally quickly and quite painlessly when the car stops with some incurable mechanical problem, or is perhaps too badly damaged to continue following an incident. More often, however, one small mechanical difficulty leads to others until, finally, you are staggering around the route with the car slowly falling to pieces as drama follows drama.

The 1965 Acropolis Rally turned out to be just such an event for Timo Makinen in a lone Mini entry (DJB 93B) with Paul Easter, who at first had a job persuading Stuart Turner to enter the event: 'Timo and I wanted to do the event, but as it was not down on the schedule, Stuart said that he would only agree if this was a one car entry and that we used my own Mini as a recce car and Stuart would come out with just two mechanics.'

The exhaust falling off caused the first problem. There was not time to put it back on so they had to carry it in the car, Paul clutching the hot and battered pipe. It was on the next section that they smelt burning and discovered that the lack of the exhaust system had set fire to the carpets. Paul now had to fight the fire on the move and must have caused some alarm to the locals by throwing pieces of burning carpet out of the window!

Arriving at a ferry crossing it was found that the rubber drive shaft couplings needed replacing. Once the car was on the boat, Timo and Paul tipped it on its side and started to dismantle the drive shafts. Meanwhile the ferry captain was going mad as petrol gushed out of the filler cap, ran down the decks and into the bilges. Arriving at the other side of the crossing, the Mini was righted and wheeled on to the sloping ramp; a donkey pulled it up onto the roadway, where it was then rolled onto its side again to finish the repair. By this time the locals were convinced that their fellow boat passengers were quite mad!

With the Mini mobile again Timo set off, still maintaining his lead when the rear sub-frame began to break up. A holed sump shield was now added to their problems, which Paul removed prior to a time control, taking the car through the control and changing the drive shaft couplings again after the out control. Meanwhile Timo, who had decided that this was the end of his rally, had disappeared into a local bar to drown his sorrows. Paul had to drag him out, and with the loose sump shield in the back they were off again.

Next the rear sub frame damage got so bad that the tyres began to puncture as they rubbed against the bodywork. Welding was called for at the next service point and the Mini was again tipped on its side. Despite attention to the overflowing fuel, a spark from the welding torch started a small fire and within seconds the Mini was ablaze. While Timo fought to retrieve his passport and money from the glove pocket, bystanders got the fire under control, the repairs were completed, and the charred Mini again took to the road.

With only 15 cars still running, there was a chance that Timo could hold his slender lead. Sadly, however, the fire had melted one of the carburettors and the engine was soon only spluttering along. It finally stopped and refused to start again as the bearings had seized, prob-ably as a result of the frequent displacement of oil during the 'tip-up' service stops. With just 60 miles to the finish, an exhausted Timo and Paul sat by the roadside and watched the sur-vivors go by in the dust. To add to the tale of woe, Stuart Turner, in his attempt to keep pace with the ailing Mini, had a monumental head-on accident with a lorry and had completely wrecked his service car!

By mid-season, Rauno Aaltonen and Tony Ambrose were hot on the trail of the European Rally Championship title with a run of outright wins on the Geneva Rally…

Championship trail

Better fortune came to Rauno Aaltonen (EBL 55C) when he scored a runaway win on the Geneva Rally, despite some pretty serious works opposition from Standard-Triumph, Lancia, Alfa Romeo, and DKW. The Morleys in their big Healey were fastest on scratch but the premier award was won on handicap. The Morleys were fastest on five out of the 13 stages while Rauno was fastest on the rest.

Rauno then claimed an equally convincing victory on the Czech Rally and by now was clearly well and truly in line for the European Championship title. Of the 83 starters only 12 lasted the 1,200-mile route. Driving a Group II hydrolastic car (EJB 55C), Rauno beat the two Lancias of Rene Trautmann and Giorgio Pianta into second and third places.

A feature of the event was the high speed road sections which forced the crews to wear crash helmets for most of the event – really a glorified road race. Fortunately it was all made reasonably safe by excellent crowd control, with police and marshals manning virtually every junction.

Co-driver Tony Ambrose recalls the event:

> The Rally started and finished in the town of Liberec, due north of Prague. As we left in the early evening a light rain made the roads (mainly smooth cobbles) extremely slippery, and with a required average speed of 50 mph, the countryside was soon claiming imprudent victims.
>
> For us the Rally went according to plan, the excellent policing of the route giving us more opportunities than we had foreseen for changing drivers. Once, a dark object, about the size of a large dog, shambled its way across the road. We were both awake at the time and together in amazement remarked – a bear. Deer in various sizes frequently crossed the road, sometimes alarmingly close to the car.
>
> No servicing was allowed and a maximum of six wheels and tyres was permitted. Consequently after a puncture the amusing scene was witnessed of Rauno changing an inner tube, accompanied by the ribald comments and verbal bastinado of our mechanics.
>
> As we arrived at the finish we were hailed as the likely victors but the final test, which was a race around the streets and alongside a lake at Liberec, was still to come. This was run in heats of

...and the Czech Rally (where Rauno gives one of his customary and impromptu press conferences).

about eight cars and again much of the surface was cobbled. The crowds lined the pavement and surged forwards into the road to get a better view of the leading car. This was frightening as Rauno was really motoring and to watch from the passenger's seat as the crowd parted to make space – only just enough space – for the drifting Mini-Cooper was quite alarming.

After this our win was assured and that night we were toasted in vodka by the Russian Volga Team and a variety of other potent liquids were mixed in the traditional two-gallon tasting-glasses which formed a large part of the awards. We left Czechoslovakia with a greater feeling of warmth towards the people than I had anticipated. We made friends not only with other competitors in the Rally, but also with a number of likeable citizens of Liberec who regarded the hotel where we stayed as their only source of close contact with visitors from the West.

German grumbles

Paddy Hopkirk had a less rewarding outing on the German Rally, the Nordrhein-Westfalen. Although between them his Mini (DJB 92B) and the MGB of team-mate Andrew Hedges won every special stage, the handicap system gave victory to a locally-entered Opel Rekord. The road sections were highly confusing and were so arranged that only with local knowledge could one find the well-hidden controls which were placed up farm tracks and dubious country lanes. The only timed tests included driving tests, slalom sprints, hill climbs, and even a timed 'Le Mans' start.

Paddy was pretty outspoken against the organizers and swore that he would never compete in the event again. The organizers retaliated by saying that they would not accept his entry. The only good thing to come out of the event was that the team won a barrel of German beer, which was duly transported back to Abingdon and quickly consumed.

Alpine clean sweep

Only 1.7 seconds separated Timo Makinen from Rene Trautmann's winning Lancia on the 1965 Alpine Rally but, despite this disappointment, the BMC team collected just about every other Alpine award that it was possible to win. They brought home no fewer than 27

The BMC team took home 27 major awards on the 1965 Alpine Rally, including a Coupe des Alpes and a coveted Coupe d'Argent (for three non-consecutive Coupes), won by Paddy Hopkirk.

major trophies, probably the largest and most impressive array of silverware ever won by a works team.

Only eight Coupes des Alpes were awarded that year and only four went to British cars, three going to the Minis of Timo (AJB 33B), Paddy (EBL 56C), and privateer Tony Fall, competing in his first Continental event. Timo ran a dry suspension car, the rest running hydrolastic. All used a new 'export' six-bladed cooling fan and these Alpine cars produced 84 bhp at 6,800 rpm.

Paddy realized a personal ambition by winning his Coupe des Alpes, for he gained an even more coveted Alpine trophy, the Coupe d'Argent for completing three non-consecutive unpenalized Alpine runs. Another member of the team scoring a personal hat-trick was Pauline Mayman, who with Val Domleo won the Coupe des Dames in the touring category for the third year running. Pauline had retired the previous year but returned to gain her Alpine hat trick – her car (DJB 93B) being prepared by Special Tuning.

The girls had a worrying time when the fan belt began to slip, eventually causing a temporary engine seizure. They came to a halt close by a small mountain stream, built a dam, filled the radiator from the windscreen washer bottle, and pressed on to the control to arrive mere seconds late, thus losing their Coupe des Alpes. These were the only road penalties that they suffered on the whole event.

Timo was involved in an amusing incident when he smashed his off-side rear lamp glass, to find that the service crews had used up their spares on another damaged Mini. Stuart Turner therefore suggested that when Timo got to the end of the stage at Grenoble, if he went back to the hotel being used as the Rally HQ, he would find a Mini parked outside. This belonged to a private entrant who had crumpled the rear of his car and retired. Timo was told that it would be okay if he borrowed the lamp glass until the end of the event. When Timo arrived in Grenoble he located a Mini outside the hotel and started to remove the lamp glass when he was apprehended by an important looking gentleman who was not impressed by the Finn's actions. There just happened to be two Minis parked outside the hotel and this one belonged to one of the senior Rally officials!

Rauno Aaltonen and Tony Ambrose had the harrowing experience of being directed by a gendarme up the wrong road just after a time control. By sheer coincidence the roadbook instructions fitted the wrong route and it was not until after some six miles that Tony spotted the error. They retraced their steps just as fast as a 1,275 Mini with 7,000 rpm on the clock would go but reached the next control just 67 seconds late. They lost their Coupe but, more serious, Rauno lost his Coupe d'Or, the most precious of all Alpine awards presented for three consecutive penalty-free runs.

Finally, top honours in the Team Prize went to the Minis, all six of the Abingdon-prepared cars finishing amongst the 32 survivors.

Polish points

Amassing a healthy score of Championship points, Rauno's brilliant form continued with victory in the Polish Rally – three outright wins within a couple of months. Rauno drove a lone Group II Mini (CRX 89B) and was the only driver to finish unpenalized on the road.

Tony Ambrose reported on the event:

> Our recce did not last long because the car we were using had done the Alpine Rally, had taken a very severe pounding and expired on the third night. That evening we were fortunate to bump into Rene Trautmann and Claudine Bouchet who were driving a Lancia. At this time they were just ahead of us in the Championship, so we were particularly impressed by their sportsmanship when they offered to take us in the back of their car to complete our reconnaissance. This we enjoyed very much, for it was interesting to see how our principal rival went about the task of preparing for a critical Championship event.
>
> On the Rally all went according to plan, a highlight being a circuit race at Krakow airport

where Rauno was most impressive, putting up fastest time of all. After this, disaster nearly struck us on two occasions.

When driving through a village on wet cobbles, Rauno swerved to miss a cat, clouting the kerb in the process and bending a rear suspension arm and wheel. However, we changed the wheel and completed the Rally with a slightly deformed car.

The second occasion was when we suspected a shortage of water in the engine and Rauno undid the radiator cap to be drenched in a shower of boiling water. His right arm suffered and was immediately raw and painful. Had it been slightly worse we would have been forced to retire immediately. Fortunately among a small crowd of spectators was a competent nurse who dressed his arm in a most expert manner. I took over the wheel for a short time but the tough and wiry Finn was soon ready to demonstrate once more his skill and determination at the wheel.

The best section came on the last night in the form of a very tight road section run in rainy conditions at an average speed well in excess of 50 mph. This took place near the Czech frontier and it seemed strange to see the same searchlights which we had seen on the Czech Rally only five weeks previously but from the other side of the barbed wire.

In fact there were three consecutive road sections which were really tight. The critical one we managed to do with four seconds to spare, being the only car to do it without penalty in spite of the fact that the cars of smaller capacity, such as the diminutive Fiat-based Steyr-Puch of Zazada and the Saab of Carlsson, were allowed two minutes more. This, together with some very fast times on the special stages, resulted in our third outright win of the year.

Timo's 1,000 Lakes

The team's winning ways continued with the 1,000 Lakes Rally, when Timo Makinen (AJB 33B) won for the second year in succession with Rauno (EBL 55C) runner-up. Paddy Hopkirk (EBL 56C) finished sixth overall, ahead of all the visiting Swedes, one of the few 'foreigners' to successfully challenge the locals on their home ground. In Paddy's own opinion, that 1,000 Lakes result was one of the most satisfying of his rallying career. Minis took

Timo Makinen, on home ground, started an impressive run of victories on the 1,000 Lakes Rally in 1965.

five out of the top 10 placings and won the Team Prize.

With a healthy score of points for the 1965 European Rally Championship, Rauno Aaltonen and Tony Ambrose set off for the penultimate round, the Munich–Vienna–Budapest Rally. Rauno (CRX 89B) scored a lucky win, for it was his principal Championship rival, Rene Trautmann, who led the Rally all the way until 30 miles from the finish when he had the bad luck to have piston failure on his Lancia.

Originally the regulations for the Rally indicated that the results would be on the class improvement system. Furthermore, it was ruled that no servicing would be allowed. Crafty Stuart Turner rounded up some privateers to run to team orders behind Aaltonen, namely Tony Fall/Ron Crellin (AJB 55B) and Geoff Halliwell/Mike Wood (CRX 90B) plus a co-drivers crew of Paul Easter/Henry Liddon (in Paul's own car). The last crew were really there to unofficially service Rauno and swap tyres and wheels, Paul having to drive with racers through the forest and Weathermasters on the tarmac. They also carried 21 gallons of fuel, the luggage for both crews, and an enormous kit of tools and spares.

As things turned out the organizers had the last laugh when, just before the start, they changed the regulations back to scratch classification. However, the Easter/Liddon support crew enjoyed a good run and, despite regularly stopping to swop tyres and service Rauno, finished and helped win the Team Prize.

Tony Ambrose reports:

> The Rally was a poor relation to the other two behind the Iron Curtain. Restrictions imposed by the police in Germany and Austria did not permit interesting road sections and the special stages were too short to be a satisfactory means of deciding the Rally. In Hungary our route led around Lake Balaton, but before we reached there we raced over a special stage on which such high speeds were possible that we averaged 75 mph to achieve fastest time by more than a minute.
>
> The rest of the roads in Hungary were extremely dull until our arrival in Budapest when we competed in the final hill climb. Results showed us winners, clear Championship leaders with one event to run.

The retirement of European Rally Championship leader Rene Trautmann's Lancia some 30 miles from the finish of the Three Cities Rally gave Rauno Aaltonen an unassailable lead for the title.

Mike Wood recalls how he and Geoff Halliwell spent the prizegiving in hospital!

Geoff was general manager of the Tillotson Group where I worked at the time and we had bought quite a lot of cars from Abingdon. We had done some club events together and were really entered to support Rauno's challenge for the Championship.

We were not having a very good event and came to this stage which was a hillclimb, where we were using pace notes which we were definitely not used to. Halfway up the climb either Geoff got into the system, or perhaps we got over confident – anyway we had a big accident.

I would have been alright but I had not fastened my seat belt properly and was quite badly concussed. The next thing I remember was that I was in an ambulance on the way to hospital in Vienna.

Geoff seemed to be okay and came to see me the next morning, by which time I was fine but he was starting to feel very groggy and could hardly stand up. I discharged myself from the hospital and we staggered off to get the first plane home. Not one of my better results!

Championship finale

Rauno's win on the Three Cities Rally put him at the top of the Championship table and only a really outstanding drive by Rene Trautmann on the RAC Rally could now rob BMC of the Championship title. Trautmann, however, was to withdraw his Lancia before the start, so the interest really centred within the BMC camp as to whether Timo Makinen – who chose a big Healey – would beat his Mini-mounted team-mate, Rauno Aaltonen (DJB 93B). The fact that both were in different classes did not jeopardize Rauno's chances for the Championship, and the struggle between the two Finns proved to be the main interest of the event.

The 2,500-mile route was now truly the 'Rally of the Forests' with some 500 miles of forest stages, and this was the first year that pace notes were banned and there was no pre-start practising. It was to be a rough, tough event with only 62 out of 162 finishing.

Rauno had the strongest possible support team, works Minis being in the hands of Paddy Hopkirk (EBL 56C), Harry Kallstrom (EJB 55C), and two newcomers to the team, Tony Fall (CRX 89B) and the dapper little Finn, Jorma Lusenius (DJB 92B).

Tony Fall got his place with the team after winning a Coupe des Alpes as a private owner earlier in the year in his first Continental event. From Yorkshire, where he worked as a car salesman for the legendary Jaguar rally driver Ian Appleyard, Tony only started rallying in 1964 but immediately impressed with a string of fine results.

Tony Fall had his first drive with the team on the 1965 Munich–Vienna–Budapest Rally following his Coupe des Alpes winning performance on the Alpine Rally the previous year.

The two BMC Finns had a battle royal on the RAC Rally, the final advantage going to Rauno Aaltonen when the Mini's front-wheel drive reigned supreme over Timo Makinen's big Healey on a decisive snowy Welsh stage.

Tony recalls his feelings at joining the team:

The BMC team was an exciting place to be in the 1960s but compared with rallying today it was all very simple. The testing that we did was for reliability and durability more than performance. Assessing new wheel and tyre combinations normally comprised Timo driving the car round the car park at Abingdon and saying that he either liked it or he did not like it. Obviously, we set up the car a bit, but basically we just used to drive the cars as they were given to us. I certainly never did any back to back testing and I don't think I knew what development was.

Jorma Lusenius had earned his works drive as a result of his performance on the 1,000 Lakes Rally in a Mini entered by BMC Sweden, when he gave Makinen a run for his money. Jorma enjoyed a good run on the RAC, winning the 1,300 GT category. Lars Ytterbring showed his pace in a private Mini, finishing seventh overall after starting as a late entry at the back of the field. Hopkirk, third overall in the early stages, was slowed by mechanical problems. Sweden's Harry Kallstrom was up amongst the leaders when the snow was at its worst but was forced out when he swept the exhaust system off on a rough Scottish stage and then broke the gearbox. Tony Fall had climbed up to second place overall when he went off on a Scottish stage.

With the snowy weather conditions and studded tyres not allowed, the ever-resourceful Stuart Turner got his service crew, Bill Price and Pete Bartram, to supply make-shift snow chains for the Minis, made from dog-lead chains and leather collars bought from a local village store!

Timo in the big Healey and in typical style, set off to establish an incredible lead until an

Final qualifying round of the 1965 European Rally Championship was the RAC Rally, with Rauno Aaltonen all set to take the honours.

European Rally Championship victory for Rauno Aaltonen and Tony Ambrose and, at last, Championship success for a British car.

off-the-road episode on one of the snowy Yorkshire stages put him right out of the running. But he fought back to such good effect that he was back in the lead by the time the Rally reached Wales. Meanwhile, Rauno had been playing a waiting game and such was the pace of the Healey and the Minis led by Rauno, Lusenius, and Hopkirk that most of the works opposition had dropped out.

Now all interest centred on the contest between the two Finns as the cars tackled the steep snowy slopes of the Welsh stages. Timo had set the fastest time on 31 out of 53 stages over conditions which most of the time favoured the nimble front-wheel drive Mini rather than the heavy low-slung sports car. On the last night, with five stages to run, Timo had a six-minute lead over Rauno, but an icy stage in Wales was to decide the outcome when a steep slope slowed the Healey and only a lot of pushing got it going again. Aaltonen stopped in the same place but his Mini was able to re-start and beat the Healey to the end of the stage by seven minutes. On the next stage Timo was to lose more time when the distributor filled with water and, despite going flat out on the final stages, Rauno was to win by three minutes.

So, for the first time a British car had won the European Rally Championship, the Mini being the first British car to win the RAC Rally for six years – a fitting reward for the Aaltonen/Ambrose partnership, which claimed five out of the team's eight wins of the season. Without doubt it had been the busiest and most successful year for any works team.

Rauno was quick to acknowledged the support of the team:

> By the mid-1960s nothing could stop us from winning. This was not only because of the fantastic car but because of the unique BMC team from Abingdon. I do not think that any team since has reached, relatively speaking, the same high level, which has to do not only with the mechanical aspect of the cars but also includes things from strategy to perfect gentlemanly manners.

As an amusing postscript, before going home to celebrate after the event, Rauno used his rally-winning Mini to take his British driving test. Just before he was about to leave Abingdon the test centre phoned to say that would Mr Aaltonen mind if the tests were postponed for an hour or so because some of the roads on the test route were still a little bit frosty and probably not suitable for a learner!

The Monte Fiasco

Over the years there have been some pretty major international confrontations concerning the rules and regulations of motor sport but none have caused quite so much acrimony or publicity as the disqualification of the Minis which finished 1–2–3 on the 1966 Monte Carlo Rally.

Problems really started in June 1965 when the FIA published the general rally regulations (known as Appendix J) for all events in 1966. This included definitions of different categories of cars and listed the modifications permitted in each category together with the minimum production numbers that had to be met to qualify for each category.

In previous years there was the additional requirement that 1,000 identical cars had to have been built in 12 consecutive months to qualify for Group I (standard) or Group II (modified), but only 100 were required for Group III (sports prototypes). The details of these regulations ran to several pages of small print. The only significant change that appeared in the 1966 Appendix J was that the Group I production requirement was now 5,000 units, Group II was still 1,000, and Group III was raised to 500. This did not at first cause concern because the 1,275 Mini-Cooper 'S' entries had always run in Group II or Group III trim.

However, the big surprise came when the Monte Carlo Rally regulations were issued in November. The Monte had in recent years been run on various handicap systems, designed ostensibly to give a fair and equal chance of victory to any kind of car. This year it was immediately apparent that only a Group I car would stand a chance of winning at all. Group II and III cars would run under such severe handicaps that it would have been a total waste of time entering cars in these categories.

In retrospect it was quite obvious that the Monegasque organizers were fed up with little foreign cars winning their Rally outright twice in succession and were determined that they should not do it a third time. They were convinced that 5,000 Mini-Cooper 'S' cars could not possibly have been built in the previous 12 months and they believed that a virtually standard Mini-Cooper 'S' could not possibly win the Rally anyway.

Late regulations

The Monte regulations were late in being issued and the closing date for entries was uncomfortably near. Both Appendix J and the Rally regulations were full of ambiguities and the team managers for all the major manufacturers ran around in small circles trying to find out for certain if the cars they wanted to use would, in fact, be eligible to run. Volvo and Saab, who had been regular competitors for many years, gave up the problem as insoluble in the time available and decided not to enter the Monte that year at all.

Stuart Turner believed that he could sort this one out and the entries were made. What the Rally organizers did not realize was that successful rallying sells cars and the year's production figure for the Mini-Cooper 'S' stood at just under 5,000. By stepping up production just a little, 5,047 identical cars were built within the specific 12 months and the model was homologated as a Group I car. However, the details of exactly what modifications

Preparations for the 1966 Monte Carlo Rally were fraught with the late publication of the regulations and with constant last-minute rule changes.

were permitted were still far from clear in many respects, particularly as no less than three revised versions of Appendix J were issued by the FIA during the last few weeks before the Monte.

In December Stuart Turner and Henry Taylor (then competitions manager at Ford, who was in a similar position) flew to Paris to try and sort out the matter with the FIA, taking with them a questionnaire of over 100 points that were not clear to them. They returned satisfied that their cars complied with the regulations in every respect. It is significant that the matter of the headlamp modifications did not appear on this questionnaire, for this was one matter about which there appeared to be no doubt whatsoever.

It was obvious that the regulations were going to be strictly enforced this year and that the

Although running to 'production showroom' Group I regulations for the 1966 Monte Carlo Rally, there were no restrictions on interior fittings and instrumentation.

Group I regulations were stricter than usual anyway. There was far too much at stake for either team to take the slightest risk of infringing the regulations and when the cars were eventually prepared both team managers sincerely believed that their cars were 100 per cent in accordance with both the word and the spirit of the regulations. BMC at least dared not do otherwise. They were setting out with the intention of winning the Monte again – and the winning cars are always fully scrutineered.

Even so, never before had they had so little time in which to prepare cars for an event and never before had the preparations been carried out under such difficulties. The specification of the cars had to be changed three times as revised versions of Appendix J were issued with changes to permitted modifications and, in fact, the final version was not received at Abingdon until after Paddy Hopkirk's car had been sent to the Warsaw start!

The four-car works Mini team comprised three Group I cars for Timo Makinen (GRX 555D), Rauno Aaltonen (GRX 55D), and Paddy Hopkirk (GRX 5D), with a Group II car for Raymond Baxter (GRX 195D). Demonstrating the rising popularity of the Mini, out of the 245 entries, 34 were Minis (12 of them with British crews).

Hostile reception

The late Wilson McComb, then BMC Competitions press officer, arrived in Monte Carlo before the start and went to Rally Headquarters and was immediately button-holed by a senior official and asked to arrange for BMC mechanics to be standing by at scrutineering after the Rally took place, for they would be needed should the scrutineers wish the cars to be completely dismantled for inspection. This was a reasonable request, but the manner of making it showed that scrutineering was uppermost in the organizers' minds as far as the BMC cars were concerned.

Furthermore, it soon became apparent that there was an atmosphere of real hostility towards the British team, both from the Rally officials and the French press. In the latter's sports pages there was much talk about the unnamed 'cheats'... 'The cheats have had their day' ...'The cheats will be exposed'... and so on. The pro-British manager of a Monaco restaurant, where the team members regularly dined, said: 'Ah, monsieur, I regret that you will not win this year; victory will go to a French car – it is arranged.'

Allowing for a certain amount of local partisanship and even exaggeration, it seemed that the French were gunning for the BMC team. The conscience of the team was as white as the snow on the mountains above Monaco, but down in the town the atmosphere was unpleasant to say the least.

So the Rally began and the first section – the converging run from the various starting points to Monte Carlo – passed without much incident and no loss of road marks for most competitors. Makinen arrived in particularly good shape, having had an extremely comfortable journey from Lisbon, recalls his chauffeur, Paul Easter:

To overcome the discomfort of having to use the standard Mini seats in Group I on the 1966 Monte Carlo Rally, these somewhat elaborate 'seat covers' were devised to provide an instant bucket seat. However, Paul Easter recalls that for the long run-in from Lisbon his man Makinen removed the passenger seat and built himself a fully reclining bed!

Opposite *Classic Timo Makinen Monte action before the fiasco of the team's disqualification for the alleged lighting regulation infringement.*

The Group I regulations meant that we had to have standard non-reclining seats in the car so when we arrived in Lisbon, Timo got the local BMC agent to construct a special bed because he wanted his usual relaxing run-in. The standard passenger seat was taken out and placed upside down on the back seat behind the driver, then a full length wooden bunk was set up in the passenger space, covered in foam and was extremely comfortable although, of course, you could not sit up. We left Lisbon armed with goodie bags of sardines and bottles of port wine and so Timo spent the whole journey to Monte eating, drinking and sleeping in that order while I drove. He was in good nick when the rally started!

The second section was the start of the really serious stuff – a 24 hour mountain circuit of some 900 miles, with six special timed stages on closed roads. Timo, who started as number two, was soon leading on the road but he had some frightening experiences. On the Col de Granier, which was supposed to be closed to traffic, he found that in fact it had not been cleared and that non-competing cars were still using it. He had to go the whole climb with the horns blowing and was unable safely to use the whole of the road. When he reached the end of the timed section the marshals were not ready for him and he was delayed for some time before being clocked in. Similarly, at the top of the Mont Ventoux hill climb, there was no control to be seen and Timo and Paul had to drag the marshals out of a near-by cafe before getting their time card stamped!

In spite of these needless delays, on this section Timo was clearly in the lead, followed by Rauno Aaltonen (Mini), Roger Clark (Lotus Cortina), Bengt Soderstrom (Lotus Cortina), and Paddy Hopkirk (Mini). The French press in particular were amazed at Timo's performance on the special stages, on several of which he had been fastest on scratch out of the entire entry – the hottest Group III sports cars included. They were so amazed, in fact, that they frankly disbelieved that such a performance was possible with a genuine Group I car. Hostility towards BMC increased and thinly veiled hints reflecting deep suspicion flew about.

Lighting regulations

Then a notice was posted in Rally Headquarters suggesting that some cars might not be complying with the international highway regulations (not the Rally Regulations be it noted) in respect of their headlight dipping system. A special scrutineering session was arranged for the next morning and all cars were checked by the scarcely scientific method of holding a cardboard hatbox in front of each car and observing the light pattern on main and dipped beams.

As a result of this a curious notice was then posted to the effect that all cars had to have a driving beam and a passing beam and that the following cars did not comply with this regulation. There followed a list of all the British cars that were subsequently to be disqualified with a description of the dipping system in each case. It then said that the acceptability of these dipping arrangements would be decided at the final scrutineering – no more than that.

With this vague but worrying pronouncement hanging over them, the top 60 crews set off on the final section of the Rally – an 11 hour run at night over some 380 miles of mountain roads with six special stages included. As in the previous tests, Timo put up a magnificent performance and by the unofficial reckoning of the press afterwards (subsequently confirmed) he had won outright, with Rauno second, while Paddy had beaten the Lotus Cortinas into third place.

So to scrutineering, where the BMC cars were subjected to a technical inspection that lasted for eight hours! The power units were stripped completely to the last nut and bolt and measured in every dimension. The parts were even weighed as well, with a pair of bathroom scales bought at a local hardware shop – scarcely a precision instrument! Combustion chamber spaces were measured for volume, suspension parts checked, and even the wheels were de-tyred and weighed. Dynamos were checked for standard output. Nothing at all could be found to be at variance with the homologated specification even though their measuring methods were crude in the extreme.

Several times the scrutineers claimed to have found discrepancies, and BMC mechanics had to point out that they were measuring things the wrong way. Once the scrutineers announced that the combustion chambers were the wrong volume, but they were found to be referring to an homologation form for an 850 Mini-Minor instead of a 1,275 Mini-Cooper 'S'. Finally, they declared that the front wheel track of Paddy's car was wider than it should have been by the monstrous amount of 3.5 mm. This discovery was released to the French press who crowed with delight at this 'victory for truth'. When it was pointed out that a rubber-suspended car was bound to settle a little in the course of a tough 3,000 mile rally and the track measurement was meaningless unless related to the ground clearance, they were persuaded to measure again and found that at the declared ground clearance the track was the correct width.

The organizers, therefore, issued a very grudging apology, without withdrawing the allegation. The matter of the headlights had not been raised again since the special inspection of them earlier.

Disqualification

However, when the results were announced, the British contingent were appalled to see that the four top names were simply not there, and that first place had gone to Pauli Toivonen's DS21 Citroën. No reason was given for the disqualification of the three leading works Minis, Roger Clark's Escort in fourth place, and the other works Escorts of Bengt Soderstrom and Vic Elford. Rosemary Smith (Hillman Imp) was disqualified from winning the Coupe des Dames and the award was given to a ladies' crew who technically did not even qualify as finishers. No explanations were given until nearly an hour later, when an announcement was made that they had all been disqualified because the lights did not conform to Appendix J (not be it noted to international highway law as before).

The Minis had two different headlight dipping systems operating between the two single-filament quartz iodine headlamp units and the two quartz iodine fog lamps (only two additional driving lamps were allowed in Group I). To dip the lights the driver could either extinguish the headlamps totally and light the fog lamps, or dim the main headlamp beams through a resistor. It was possible to run with full headlamps and fog lamps on the stages.

After the organizer's announcement, no less than 32 formal protests were immediately lodged with the organizers and the battle was on. The protests were rejected and appeals lodged with the Automobile Club de Monaco. These were rejected too and the protests were finally re-submitted to the FIA as the international governing body. All rejected the protests.

It was quite obvious that the organizers themselves had no great confidence in the matter of the lights as grounds for disqualification. All but the organizers believed them to be entirely acceptable; but even if they were not, it was a minor technical anomaly of no importance whatsoever to the performance of the cars. The organizers were obviously quite certain that no standard Mini-Cooper 'S' (with power two-thirds that of the previous Monte winners) could win against such tough European opposition, and that thorough scrutineering would reveal how the 'cheats' had made them go so fast.

Their chagrin at finding not a trace of cheating at all must have been great, particularly in view of the widely publicized suspicions before the event. To save face they had to find something – anything – however trivial and irrelevant. The fact that the organizers had to constantly change their attack from one complaint to another suggested firm determination to find something wrong.

The French press, of course, were now even more hostile and went on to declare that clearly an ordinary car brought from the dealer could not be anything like the cars used by Makinen, Aaltonen, and Hopkirk. The answer to this was to mount an exercise with the co-operation of the French sports paper *L'Equipe*, which had been consistently critical and suspicious. A completely standard demonstration Mini-Cooper 'S' was selected from the local BMC dealer's showroom in Monte Carlo and matched up a steep hill climb course, chosen by the paper, with Paddy's rally car. Both cars were driven up the hill against the watch alternately by Timo and Alain Bertaut, a French journalist with considerable racing experience. In this test both Bertaut and Timo put up better times in the showroom car than in the rally car thus showing, once and for all, that in all important respects, the cars that really won the Monte Carlo Rally were genuinely the same as you could buy!

While it was true that the team received a whole lot more publicity by the disqualification than by winning, and the team's reception upon returning home was some consolation, the drivers were bitterly disappointed at failing to take home the considerable financial rewards of rallying's richest prize fund.

The final snub for the organizers came when their declared winner, Pauli Toivonen in a Citroën, refused to accept his award at the official prizegiving.

Stuart Turner summed up the whole sorry affair:

> We got thrown out, I passionately believe, because the cars were so quick that people thought that we had swapped cars. The organizers looked at the times and simply did not believe them. The logistics of trying to change cars and cheat in the middle of the Rally is ridiculous anyway. People blamed it on the French just trying to fake it for a French car to win. I don't accept that. I think it was the French trying to chuck out the English who they thought had been cheating.
>
> I think if they had not thrown us out on the lighting they would have throw us out on the colour of Paddy's socks!

It was, indeed, a sorry affair.

The team do not look too disappointed at having been disqualified from their 1–2–3 finish. Left to right on the roof, Paul Easter, Henry Liddon, and Tony Ambrose, and on the bonnet Rauno Aaltonen, Timo Makinen, and Paddy Hopkirk.

Protest Year

Afﬁter the fiasco of the 1966 Monte Carlo Rally disqualifications, everyone hoped that the season would continue on a happier note. But with further wrangling at many other events, 1966 went down in the record books as the year rallying hit the headlines, mostly for all the wrong reasons.

For what was hoped would be a little light relief after the Monte, Timo Makinen (DJB 92B) and Rauno Aaltonen (GRX 310D) were dispatched to Scandinavia with their usual Group II cars to see how they fared on the Swedish Rally. But it was a fruitless effort, Rauno retiring early on when a rock smashed the radiator against the fan and the boiling engine finally seized. Timo was put out with a broken drive shaft when leading.

Flowers rumpus

While the Finns were in Sweden, Paddy Hopkirk and Tony Fall fared no better on the Italian Flowers Rally, the event that produced the second international rumpus of 1966.

Paddy, now partnered by Ron Crellin, set some very competitive stage times in a Group II

From the 1966 Italian Flowers Rally, Paddy Hopkirk was to begin a new partnership with Ron Crellin.

Beating the works Lotus Cortinas, Tony Fall dominated the 1966 Circuit of Ireland.

car (GRX 309D), but a succession of punctures and an overheating engine finally dropped him way down the leader board. Tony Fall in a Group I car (GRX 5D) got no further than the end of the run-in section, when he was disqualified for having removed the paper air cleaner element to the carburettors as a temporary adjustment to the mixture. Despite the fact that he was carrying the element in the car, the officials refused to let him continue.

But the most publicized incident of the Rally was the exclusion of the winning Lotus Cortina of Vic Elford, which was thrown out at scrutineering because there was a discrepancy between the number of teeth on one of the gears and the total listed on the homologation form (subsequently proved to be a misprint!). Another much publicized and highly unsatisfactory end to an international rally.

With disastrous Monte, Swedish, and Flowers rallies behind them, 1966 was turning out to be a grim year. But in typical fashion, this spurred the team on to even greater effort and the next three events on the programme brought three worthy victories.

On his third drive for the team, Tony Fall (DJB 92B) gained his spurs in fine style to win the Circuit of Ireland after a superb battle with the works Lotus Cortinas of Vic Elford, Brian Melia, and Roger Clark. For a change Paddy Hopkirk (GRX 55D) did not win his home event, rolling three times!

The Finns then had a dominating run on the Tulip Rally, having tossed before the start to decide who would drive Group I and Group II. Aaltonen claimed the Group II car and won outright from Elford's Cortina by 45 seconds, while Makinen won the Group I category from Bengt Soderstrom's Cortina by eight seconds, despite his engine developing a vast thirst for oil which required the crew to carry gallons of Castrol on board and change oiled-up plugs frequently. This was the first year that the Tulip results were awarded on a scratch basis and to round off a successful trip to Holland, the Minis won the Team Prize along with private entrant the late Bob Freeborough.

Following his win the previous year with a big Healey, Paddy Hopkirk tackled the Austrian

Left *The Finns had a field-day on the 1966 Tulip Rally, having tossed to decide who would drive Groups I and II. Rauno Aaltonen drove Group II to win outright while Timo Makinen won the Group I category.*

Right *Repeating his victory on the Austrian Alpine Rally the previous year with a works big Healey, Paddy Hopkirk returned to win again in 1966, this time with the Mini.*

Alpine again, this time in a Group II Mini (DJB 93B), along with Tony Fall (GRX 310D). The main opposition came from the works Porsches. No service was allowed during the event, body damage was marked at scrutineering, and the cars had to carry the same number of spare wheels throughout, these being secretly marked overnight in the parc ferme before the start.

Fall hit early problems with a puncture and lost 10 minutes after running some two miles on the flat tyre and then the bare rim, which finally ended up with the steel wheel wrapped around the brake drum. He later retired after hitting a pile of logs. Paddy had a good event, beating all the opposition to win outright, and came away with a pile of trophies but rather frightening memories of the event, which was run on ultra-fast road sections in broad daylight with the hazards of local traffic.

Acropolis acrimony

Everyone was now on top form for an all-out attack on the Acropolis Rally, but it seemed that others were still equally determined to put a stop to the run of Mini wins.

But for the protests at the finish, the 1966 Acropolis could well have been one of the most sporting events of the year. Just about every rally-minded manufacturer sent works teams to Greece, except Citroën who declared that the event was too rough!

Three hydrolastic cars were entered for Paddy Hopkirk (GRX 311D), Timo Makinen (HJB 656D), and Rauno Aaltonen (JBL 172D), with special attention paid to under-body protection and the fuel tanks. The full-length Dural sump guards were used again but this time skid plates were fitted under the battery box and the leading edge of the silencer. Guards also protected the front of the brake callipers to stop rocks damaging the flexible hoses, and the latest Hardy Spicer drive shaft couplings were fitted in place of the troublesome rubber units.

From the start under the shadow of the famous Acropolis, the 105 crews set off into the rough and very soon it was evident that this was to be a Ford versus BMC affair, the Abingdon Minis against the works Cortinas of Elford, Clark, and Soderstrom. Stage times gave the advantage first to one team and then the other and there were no holds barred, including a bit of doubtful short-cutting, recalls Paul Easter:

> There was one section where we remembered from the previous year that a little rough track
> led through a village and cut off quite a bit of the route. We had checked it out during our recce

The 1966 Acropolis Rally ended in acrimony when Paddy Hopkirk and Ron Crellin, having been declared the winners, were thrown out for servicing in a crowded and badly defined control area.

but the organizers had threatened to block it off on the event. So as to be sure that we could get through, we sent the BMC press officer Wilson McComb up there with a recce car and told him to check whether the road was open, park at the start of the track and direct us down the track or along the main road depending upon the circumstances.

We arrived on the scene with a broken rear suspension trailing link bracket, leading the Rally but urgently needing repairs. I got out and removed the bracket from Wilson's recce car and I remember that it took ages using open-ended spanners and no socket set. Poor Wilson was left with a non-runner and was not amused. We told him to stop the next donkey cart that passed and get a tow to the nearest garage and get it welded up – which is exactly what he had to do!

Elford lost his gears and a lot of time, while Rauno dropped out with engine trouble leaving Paddy to battle against the Fords. Timo recovered to lend support although his car was to expire during the final circuit race at Tatoi with a blown head gasket. At the finish Paddy was a clear winner over the Cortinas of Soderstrom and Clark. Everyone seemed delighted with the results, with the possible exception of Ford. A delighted Paddy, with co-driver Ron Crellin, posed for pictures, the results were posted, the pressmen spread the news and that seemed to be that.

Then the trouble started. Just four minutes before the hour was up for protests, a statement was posted by the organizers saying that Paddy had been penalized for arriving 14 minutes too early at a control in the early stages of the Rally and for servicing in the control area. This had the effect of dropping the Mini behind the two Cortinas. According to the statement this decision had been made by the Stewards acting on information supplied by the officials at the control in question.

Stuart Turner immediately lodged a protest but the Stewards refused to change their minds and the matter was passed forward to a National Board of Appeal. After an all-night sitting, they too rejected it so Stuart then gave notice of intention to ask the RAC to raise the matter at the next meeting of the FIA. They eventually upheld the Stewards' decision on the evidence supplied by the officials and finally the Fords were announced as victors.

The reason for Stuart's insistence in protesting was that the action of the Stewards was not in accordance with the international rally regulations, that the control area in question was not satisfactorily defined owing to considerable traffic congestion, and the control warning sign was obscured by parked vehicles. Most significant, it was agreed by the control marshals at the time that no penalty was called for and the official road book was marked accordingly. Finally, quite a number of other competitors found themselves in the same situation at this control but Paddy was the only driver singled out for penalization.

Everyone left Greece with bitter feelings and, as far as BMC was concerned, even more determination to win – particularly over Ford. That was to happen in the very next event.

Fall supreme

As a consolation for missing the Acropolis, Tony Fall was entered with a Special Tuning prepared car (DJB 93B) for the Scottish Rally, which he won (his second win in two months) after a tremendous battle with Vic Elford's Cortina and the Saab of Jerry Larsson.

Straight from Scotland, Tony flew off to the Geneva Rally to compete in a Group I car (EBL 56C) and he was joined by Paddy Hopkirk, who drove Group II (JBL 495D). It was not a happy event for Paddy, who retired with gearbox failure when in the lead, but Tony drove well to bring the Group I car into second place overall behind Gilbert Staepelaere's Cortina. Again the Minis won the Team Prize in company with private owners Georges Theiler and David Friswell.

Returning to England for the London Rally, Tony proved that he was on top form by leading all the way until three stages from the end, when he rolled the car (DJB 93B) on a treacherous stage which the organizers were forced to close after the incident.

There was no stopping Tony Fall and Mike Wood in 1966 as they added the Scottish Rally win to their achievements.

Co-driver Mike Wood remembers it well.

> The London Rally was a big time event in its day with a route equalling the RAC Rally for length and toughness. We were in the lead and I remember that we had high hopes of collecting the £1,000 prize money, which was quite good in those days.
>
> Tony had already put the car on its side without too much damage. Then we came to this stage in the Forest of Dean. There was a long, fast straight which looked okay, but what you could not see was a disused single-track railway line that cut across the road. We did not have notes, there were no danger signs and we hit it at full bore and rolled end over end.
>
> We jumped out and I shouted to the marshals to help us get the car back on its wheels but the only trouble was the car did not have any wheels! It was a total write off.

The Finnish war

By this time what was to become known as 'The Finnish War' between Timo Makinen and Rauno Aaltonen was beginning to brew quite splendidly. The two Finns were really quite good friends but there was always determined rivalry between them. Unquestionably, Timo was always a little bit faster – in any car and in any circumstances – but the crafty Rauno knew that he could probably beat him if he saved his car just that little bit.

Timo was probably mildly jealous of the publicity that Rauno received upon winning the European Championship in 1965. While both the Finns were national heroes back home, there was no doubt that Rauno realized that his team-mate probably had the bigger fan club, perhaps because the public favoured the fun-loving Makinen rather than the more studious Aaltonen. Clearly such rivalry within the team was a very good thing, with each co-driver spurring his partner on to even faster performances. It did not really matter if either of the Finns broke their cars, providing Paddy Hopkirk or Tony Fall were waiting in the wings to take up the challenge – and this was often the case. The Finns' co-drivers, Paul Easter and

The bitter rivalry between the team's two Finns, Timo Makinen and Rauno Aaltonen, became known as the 'Finnish War' and was at its height in 1966, when the pair continually tried to out-manoeuvre each other – usually introducing exclusive and highly secret technical tweaks for their own cars!

Henry Liddon, always rose to the occasion and could be relied upon to wind up their opponents. This usually involved the exchange of exaggerated super-quick stages times between crews, which had the inevitable effect of making them both try even harder!

The 'war' also encouraged the Finns to think a lot about detailed improvements to their cars, which was also a very good thing. Timo would arrive at Abingdon armed with some demon engine or suspension improvement that he had tried on his ice racing Minis back home. Strict instructions were given that Rauno was not to have it fitted on his car! Rauno would do the same, which produced some interesting little situations for the mechanics!

Aaltonen 2 – Makinen 2

The next four events on the 1966 programme took the two Finns to the Czechoslovakian, 1,000 Lakes, Alpine, and Three Cities Rallies – successes being shared equally. On the Czech Rally the lead alternated between the Group II cars of Timo (JBL 493D) and Rauno (JBL 494D) as first one and then the other set the fastest times – the Finnish war at its best according to Paul Easter: 'This was one of the most bitter battles between Timo and Rauno. It got to the point that Timo even did one forest stage on racing tyres when he found out that Rauno was on Weathermasters, just to be different. A totally illogical tyre choice, but he was so determined to prove that he was right and that he was the faster!'

Timo lost time on the Czech Rally with fuel starvation troubles, then Rauno had a slight accident on a stage which put Timo back in front. Finally, it all rested on the round the houses race in Prague and, after a bumper to bumper battle, Timo had a rocker break on the last lap. Rauno was the victor but Timo was able to struggle across the line and make third place ahead of Bengt Soderstrom's Cortina. With the Group I car (EBL 56C) on loan to Sobieslaw Zasada, the popular Polish Champion who had done wonders with his little Steyr-Puch and was now leading the Group II Championship table with a Porsche, the Team Prize again went to the Minis.

Despite the threats of the previous year when Paddy swore that the team would never again compete in the German Rally (and the organizers were equally determined not to

The 'Finnish War' continued on the 1966 Czech Rally, when victory went to Rauno Aaltonen, who just beat Timo following the final and highly entertaining round-the-houses race in Prague.

No doubts about Timo Makinen's repeat win on his home event, the 1,000 Lakes…

accept a BMC entry in future), the 1966 event had a slightly different format, was centred on San Martino de Castrozza (which is not in Germany anyway!) and offered speed tests at the Rossfeld Hill Climb, Hockenheim, and the Nurbürgring. Paddy (GRX 311D) and Tony Fall (JBL 172D), however, had a disastrous outing when both cars retired early on with blown pistons caused by seized gudgeon pins.

…nor on the Munich–Vienna–Budapest Rally.

Polish one–two

Tony Fall claimed his third international win of the season on the Polish Rally, when he finished just ahead of Timo Makinen. Tony, driving a 970 car (GRX 309D), was assisted by the handicap formula against the 1,275 of Timo (GRX 555D), who was given an incorrect stage time which caused a major incident, recalls Paul Easter:

> We were leading on the road, had passed everyone and set fastest time on most stages. On the final stage they were using electronic timing, which gave us a finishing time which showed that we had finished before we had started. We queried this and they switched to hand timing and at the end of the Rally the organizers asked me to write out a little note of explanation and then off we went to do some local sight-seeing.
>
> When we got back the results showed that Timo had dropped to second overall and Tony had won. Stuart Turner refused to protest saying that it did not matter what the results were as the Minis would finish first and second overall anyway. But Timo went bananas, there was an awful row, he refused to attend the prizegiving and never set foot in Poland again.

Returning to his native Finland, Timo (JBL 493D) was able to turn the tables on Rauno (GRX 310D) on the 1,000 Lakes Rally when he beat him to a close one–two victory, the pair leading Tom Trana (Volvo) and Bengt Soderstrom (Cortina) by a comfortable margin. There were five Minis in the top 10, Jorma Lusenius (JBL 494D) coming sixth.

Alpine attrition

While Timo always found the 1,000 Lakes to his liking the long, hot, fast, Alpine Rally never suited his temperament. His performances in this French classic usually found him back on the beach at Marseilles, or the night spots of St Tropez, pretty soon after the start and the 1966 event was no exception.

Timo (JMO 969D) stormed off into a dramatic lead but was out after only the first seven mile stage with a glowing engine and four totally bald tyres. Paddy Hopkirk (GRX 311D) soon retired with differential trouble. Tony Fall (GRX 195D) had an equally unhappy Alpine, recalls Mike Wood:

> Our first problem came at the top of the Mont Ventoux hillclimb test when a wheel sheared off and we were stranded just short of the control. We managed to fit a spare by pinching one wheel nut off each of the remaining three wheels but lost a lot of time. After this we had a slight navigational problem near Lake Annecy and finally the car ground to a halt with mechanical problems on the Col d'Allos.

The serious Mini retirement rate left Rauno with Henry Liddon (JBL 495D) to uphold Abingdon's honour and contest the lead with Gunther Klass (Porsche), Roger Clark (Cortina), and Jean Rolland (Alfa Romeo). Then, with a certain category win in sight and on the final run-in to Cannes, Rauno's Mini suffered a mysterious and complete electrical failure. By virtue of some hastily contrived wiring held in place by Henry, they finished third overall but sadly lost their Coupe des Alpes by some 20 seconds.

The Alpine cars were running with modifications to the brakes in an endeavour to overcome overheating problems, particularly on the Finns' cars with their preference for continuous left-foot braking. In conjunction with Lockheeds, the front discs were cooled with asbestos blocks fitted into the piston callipers, while on the rear drums there were cooling holes in the backplate which now had the wheel cylinder bolted directly to it to dissipate the heat.

For the Munich–Vienna–Budapest Rally it was Timo's turn to take the honours (HJB 656D), and this win brought him within four points of the European Championship and to the all-important final round – the RAC Rally.

Celebrity RAC

The line up of works Minis for the 1966 RAC Rally, no fewer than seven Group II cars, was the biggest ever for the Abingdon team if not the most successful. In addition to the regular quartet of Makinen (GRX 5D), Aaltonen (GRX 310D), Hopkirk (JMO 969D), and Fall (GRX 195D), cars were also provided for Harry Kallstrom (JBL 494D), Simo Lampinen (JBL 495D), and Grand Prix star Graham Hill (GRX 309D). Rauno also persuaded Stuart to prepare a car (EBL 56C) for his sister Majietta, who certainly added a little glamour to the team and drove well to finish on this, her first overseas event.

With Jim Clark joining the Ford team for this event, Stuart Turner – determined to have his share of publicity – had signed up Hill, who was partnered by motoring correspondent Max Boyd. Despite a few driving lessons by Paddy at the team's favourite tank-testing course in Surrey, Graham was the first to admit that he did not take to the Mini or to rallying and he was probably quite relieved when he retired with transmission troubles in the Lake District.

Paddy took Graham for a bit of tuition before the start and commented:

> Graham was a very good pupil, very willing to listen and learn what he could, although I think he would probably have done better learning the ropes from Timo or Rauno. Driving a rear-wheel drive Grand Prix car on a billiard table surface is a very different thing from driving a front-wheel drive Mini-Cooper through the rough forest tracks, and Graham had to learn an entirely different technique. He put up some pretty impressive practice runs although I thought Jim Clark would have a better advantage because he was driving a car which he had been racing before and, as a farmer, I expect he was used to driving on rough roads!

Stuart Turner commented after the event: 'The impression you got was that Graham gritted his teeth and did not really enjoy it. Jimmy, on the other hand, was in the hunt and when he retired he kept on turning up everywhere at service points. The old rally mechanics at Boreham still talk about him.'

Timo Makinen did not have a good RAC Rally, for after an incredible run of fastest stage times that put him in the lead by a comfortable margin, what seemed like a winning run

Amongst the record entry of seven works Minis for the 1966 RAC Rally was a car for Graham Hill, to counter Ford signing Jim Clark in a Lotus Cortina. Graham (left) is seen here with co-driver Max Boyd, Paddy Hopkirk (who had been giving him some driving lessons), and Paul Easter.

BMC Sweden's Harry Kallstrom (right) with Ragnvald Haakansson, who had not enjoyed a very successful previous season, were in top form for the 1966 RAC Rally, finishing runners-up to Bengt Soderstrom's Lotus Cortina.

came to a sad end on the Yorkshire moors with a blown engine. 'No oil pressure, no clutch, and no gears,' shouted Timo as he free-wheeled his mud-spattered Mini into the service area at the end of the special stage. 'Apart from that, she's going like a bomb,' added the jovial Finn as he heaved himself out of the car and slammed the door, asking where the nearest pub was. Any doubts that this was another of Timo's jokes were soon dispelled when the mechanics tried to start the car – the tortured scream of seized bearings and the howl of the disintegrating clutch confirmed Timo's diagnosis. So ended another of Timo's brave attempts to win the RAC Rally and, on this occasion, his chances of the European Championship title.

Paddy Hopkirk was also unlucky – he was the leading British driver until he overshot a junction on a stage, reversed back and the transmission broke beyond repair. Simo Lampinen also had quite a short rally when he rolled in Wales on the notorious Dovey stage. It was Harry Kallstrom who proved that he was the man of the moment as far as the BMC team was concerned and, after a none too happy showing in previous events with the works Minis, he really justified his place in the team this time with a rousing second place overall behind Bengt Soderstrom's winning Cortina. Aaltonen could make no better than fourth. Tony Fall might have finished higher than fifth had he not been distracted when the over-large alternator warning light came on right in the middle of the stage and, momentarily losing concentration, the car shot off the road up a fire break. It was a long time before willing hands appeared to put the car back on the road.

1966 had not brought the team the victories of the past season and it had not been a vintage year for international rallying. The opposition was beginning to get to grips with the Mini domination and clearly 1967 was to require a tremendous effort by the Abingdon team if they were to stay on top.

For Stuart Turner is was not a bad moment to move on, to work in the public relations business for Castrol and, later, to return to the sport as head of Ford's UK motor sport programme.

It was not going to be easy for me to follow in his footsteps.

Hopkirk Victorious

It was just before Christmas 1966 that MG boss John Thornley called me into his oak-panelled office and sat me down in one of the big leather upright chairs by the bay window overlooking the MG works. John paced up and down the room in his usual manner in front of the stone fireplace beneath a classic oil painting of MGs racing at Brooklands. He poured the traditional glass of sherry and I knew that I had either got the sack or that something serious was in the air!

'Got a new job for you,' he said. 'Stuart Turner is leaving us and you're going to be the new competitions manager.' That was the only time that I ever had any disagreement with John Thornley. I protested that I really did not think I could do the job but, of course, I lost the argument. Stuart and I would do the Monte Carlo Rally together and then I would be on my own.

Certainly I felt that my qualifications for doing the job were somewhat slender. I had gone to Abingdon first as general secretary of the Austin-Healey Club in 1960 and later joined the staff of the BMC sports car magazine, *Safety Fast.* Having been an active RAC timekeeper in the past, Stuart had already entrusted me to look after the pit organization of the MG entries in one or two events and I had been fortunate in having been to Sebring, Le Mans, and the Targa Florio with the team. Stuart, at the time, was busy winning rallies and he was probably quite pleased to have a keen youngster take charge of the racing side, which clearly did not interest him so much.

Later I worked as competitions press officer under Wilson McComb, which had given me the opportunity to go on more events and, in particular, to learn more about the international rally scene. It was on these trips that I got to know the drivers and mechanics in the team, as well as those who served with the all-important trade support teams, Castrol and Dunlop in particular. No doubt I got the job on the strength of these experiences rather than because of any technical know-how about competition cars or first-hand knowledge of the international sporting scene. Still, I was able to start by having a lot of friends who made the job much easier and I will always be grateful to them for the help and guidance that they gave me.

It was, therefore, with some trepidation that I moved over the road from my Austin-Healey Club office to the hallowed Competitions Department and squeezed in alongside Stuart in his diminutive office. Preparations were in full swing for the 1967 Monte and it was an awesome experience to be thrown in at the deep end and try and catch up with the organization of this, the most complex event of all. I shudder to think now of the responsibilities that were thrust upon me for that event.

In his marvellous book *The BMC/BL Competitions Department*, which tells the complete story of the team's achievements over 25 years, my deputy Bill Price revealed one of my worst moments during my indoctrination into the complicated Monte service schedule. Having sat through a whole morning's briefing session on the service schedule, which included refuelling points and, in particular, the incredibly detailed tyre service plan, Stuart gave me the master plan and asked me to take it next door and make a copy. To my horror I failed to let the copying machine warm up properly; it chewed up the original and spat out half-burnt offerings onto the floor. It took me ages to piece it together again and produce a new original document!

The author (left) gained most of his international rally experience as BMC's competitions press officer in the early 1960s before taking over as competitions manager in 1967.

Monte revenge

This was perhaps the hardest fought Monte of all and the one that the BMC team so desperately wanted to win to avenge the disqualification of 1966. Many people thought that we should not have entered the event again after the treatment that we received the previous year but that would have seemed like surrender. I am sure that it was right to go back, win or lose, and put up the hardest fight to prove the point.

Though perhaps the Monte organizers' tyre regulations for 1967 were intended as a new handicap against the Minis, they were designed to reduce the mounting costs of competing in this event and to narrow the gap between private owners and works teams. Unfortunately the regulations had exactly the opposite effect. They offered two options – a free quantity of tyres accompanied by a 12 per cent handicap on times, or eight tyres per car for each of the two main sections of the route. All spare tyres had to be carried on the car. The 12 per cent handicap was considered too severe so, like most works teams, we went for the eight tyre option.

This resulted in using the lightweight aluminium Minilite wheels for the first time. The four spare tyres and wheels were carried two in the boot and two mounted on special brackets on the back seat. Roof racks were used for two wheels on the run-in section but discarded for the Mountain Circuit to improve the aerodynamics and handling.

Most teams, in fact, took more tyres to Monte that year than for previous events, to provide their crews with the best possible choice. A vast amount of tyre testing went on before the event and Dunlops offered us an unprecedented selection of compounds and constructions. As for the private owners, they had to make do with the best selection of tyres that they could carry and afford and, with the restrictions on the works crews, there was no

The 1967 Monte Carlo Rally Minis sported front mud flaps to protect their now 'legal' lighting system!

The Monte Carlo Rally tyre regulations for 1967 restricted the crews to the use of only eight tyres. The works Minis carried two spares in the boot, and two on a roof rack on the run-in sections, the latter pair being stowed on special attachments on the back seat for the final stages.

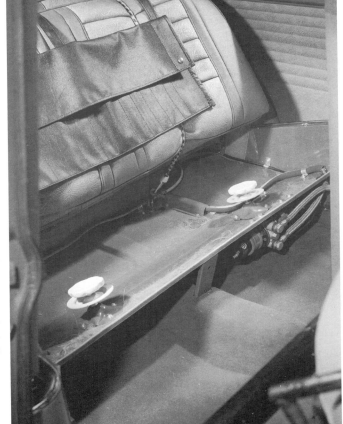

chance of the usual tyre service for them along the route and therefore no opportunities to pick up spares on the way if the crew found themselves running short of rubber. The new regulations, therefore, were not very popular, since asking a crew to drive quickly on ice and snow with worn tyres was pretty irresponsible.

There were few dramas for the five-car Mini team on the run-in sections, all of the works cars of Hopkirk (LBL 666D), Makinen (LBL 66D), Aaltonen (LBL 6D), Fall (LBL 606D), and Lampinen (HJB 656D), arriving in Monte in good shape. Only Paddy, who started from Athens, had met bad weather and he had to do some snow shovelling through Yugoslavia.

Tony Fall reported overshooting a junction in the fog and demolishing a petrol pump in a French garage. He was then over his time limit at a time control and looked like being out of the Rally. 'I opened my wallet and starting laying down 100 franc notes until the official gave in and stamped our card!' recalls the ever-resourceful Yorkshireman.

Careful selection of the eight tyres, aided by the work of the ice note crews surveying the stages in advance of the Rally, found the Minis well placed after the Monaco-Chambery-Monaco leg. Paddy was lying second to Vic Elford's Porsche 911S with Timo and Rauno not far behind, ahead of the Lancias of Ove Andersson and Leo Cella.

With conditions remaining critical, with patchy ice and a lot of dry roads, the Minis opted for almost dry-weather tyres after the Mountain Circuit, Rauno gaining the advantage over his team-mates by going for plain and only partly-studded Dunlop Weathermasters. This selection, with a well-judged drive and sparing use of his studs, expertly guided by Henry Liddon, paid off, and Rauno returned a classic performance to win by only 13 seconds from Ove Andersson's Lancia after several recounts of the times, which was as heart-stopping as the 1966 scrutineering sessions.

Henry Liddon recalled Rauno's brilliant drive over the Turini:

> It was at the start of one of the last runs over the Turini when someone had gone off the road or something, delaying the start. So we had to sit there waiting on the line and, as we waited, more snow began to fall. This meant that instead of having a clear road we should be doing the Turini in soft snow. It is at that sort of time and that sort of occasion when a driver rises above

Monte victory for Rauno Aaltonen and Henry Liddon, avenging the disqualifications of 1966.

himself and performs miracles. It is the peak of a lifetime. I have felt it just once or twice – a supreme moment. And that is where we won the Monte.

Paddy did not seem to be able to maintain his previous supremacy and he could finish no higher than sixth. Simo Lampinen almost fell foul of the tyre regulations when he had a puncture on the Mont Ventoux test and kept on motoring, which totally destroyed the tyre. Co-driver Mike Wood was concerned that the Monte organizers may have disqualified them at the finish if they did not carry their full compliment of marked tyres, so he retrieved what was left of the chewed up canvas and put it in the boot. Sure enough there was a major incident and much explaining to do at the finish when the organizers were very suspicious that perhaps 'again' the Minis had been cheating!

Timo, when running mere seconds behind Elford in the lead, dropped way down the field when he hit a great boulder that mysteriously fell into the middle of the road just as he was passing, smashing the starter motor, distributor, and oil cooler.

The timing of that rock fall was the subject of much light-hearted suspicion by the British contingent and, during the celebrations for Rauno on the plane coming home, the Abingdon mechanics, led by Brian Moylan, composed this little ditty to be sung to the tune of 'Clementine':

> On the Monte in the Mountains
> Racing onwards through the night,
> Was a little Mini-Cooper
> With its lights all shining bright.
>
> Red it was and oh so eager
> And its crew was eager too,
> Faster, faster and still faster,
> Showing all what they could do.

If someone did cause that rock to fall in the path of Timo Makinen's car as he was running mere seconds behind the leading Porsche of Vic Elford, it was a good shot, and the damage was certainly terminal!

Welcome home for the third of the BMC crews to have won the Monte Carlo Rally and…

…thanks to Roy Brown (left) and Brian Moylan (right), the mechanics who built the winning car.

Timo driving, Paul beside him
Reading pace notes as a guide,
Then disaster came and struck them
Hurtling down the mountainside.

No-one knows who shoved the rock down,
But Timo said he thought
Must have been the 'little people'
Giving Paddy their support!

Rauno's Monte win was the sweetest revenge and the perfect leaving present for Stuart Turner, who had now provided a Monte victory for each of his three top drivers.

A Swedish finish

After the Monte, the two Finns were dispatched to contest the Swedish Rally and, for the first time, a works Mini actually finished the event! The cars ran with a special Makinen-designed super-strong sump guard. Timo (JMO 969D) was forced to drop out with brake trouble on only the second special stage, while Rauno Aaltonen (JBL 495D) lost time after a spectacular accident. While progressing well up the leader board in pursuit of Simo Lampinen's Saab and the eventual winner, Bengt Soderstrom's Cortina, Rauno collided with a snow bank on a stage and the Mini rolled end over end, finally finishing up back on its wheels and driveable. During the incident, however, the rear window had fallen out, scattering the contents of the car along the stage. Rauno and Henry Liddon lost time collecting their belongings and stuffing them back into the battered Mini, but gamely struggled on to finish third overall, despite the cold and the effects of exhaust fumes which came in through the windowless car.

On the journey back to the start after they had retired, Paul Easter was convinced that he and Timo were going to have a mighty serious accident.

We had retired with the front brake cylinders burnt out and were driving back to the start on snow covered roads with only the handbrake operational, which in itself made things pretty exciting with Timo behind the wheel. Driving conditions were bad and we came to a long, fast, undulating Swedish road and noticed in the distance that a car was coming towards us. As he got

Despite a dramatic roll into a snow-drift, Rauno Aaltonen and Henry Liddon did at least claim the team's first ever finish on the Swedish Rally in 1967.

closer we noticed that he was going from side to side of the road, just as we were doing the same trying to slow the Mini down using our handbrake. As we approached each other at an alarming speed it was rather like the situation you get when two people meet up in a corridor and one goes to the right and the other goes the same way! Just as we were about to meet head on the other car dived across the road, over the hedge and into a field. Two very drunken Swedes emerged and looked pretty violent so Timo and I made a hasty exit!

Pushing our luck

Just a few weeks after the dramatically close 13 second finish in Monte Carlo between Rauno Aaltonen and Ove Andersson's Lancia, the leading teams were back in the Cote d'Azur fighting neck and neck in the Italian Flowers Rally. This time the winning margin was 15 marks between eventual winner Jean Piot in his Renault and Paddy Hopkirk's Mini (LBL 590D). But that second place was achieved by some rather dubious tactics!

The tiny village of Badalucco sits perched high in the mountains behind San Remo. The road down from the village to the coast takes a tortuous route through the vineyards. You could describe the narrow road as 'downhill all the way' – some might even believe that it would be possible to free-wheel the 12 miles from the village into the town below.

It was at Badalucco that the final special stage of the Flowers Rally finished and, less than a mile from the end, Paddy's Mini – holding a slender lead from Jean Piot – broke a drive shaft coupling. Paddy was able to summon help from a tractor and, with a push over the final brow, he coasted down to the service point at the end of the stage, where Doug Watts and I were waiting.

Paddy had lost his lead but he would be sure of second place if he could reach the final control at the bottom of the hill in San Remo. Although we had a spare drive shaft on board the service car, that final road section was very tight and there was no time to change it. 'Push me down the hill with the service car,' Paddy suggested. 'Hang back if there are any photographers around. I'll keep the engine going and pretend to be driving it normally.'

Doug and I leapt into the service car, one of our faithful 4-litre Princess 'Rs', and began the long push. Fortunately, the bumpers were near enough the same height and we did not do too much damage, despite the fact that co-driver Ron Crellin was worried about the time and continually encouraged us to go faster. Doug drove the big heavy car like a demon, down through the hairpins, although Paddy had a more alarming ride with no power to control the free-wheeling Mini. On many steep stretches he was able to run away from the lumbering Princess and then we would meet up again with a resounding crunch which would propel the little Mini onwards.

There was a passage control in a village half way down the hill, fortunately on a steep

Nail-biting finish on the 1967 Italian Flowers Rally for (left to right) Ron Crellin, Paddy Hopkirk, mechanic Dudley Pike, and Tony Fall.

Bristling with Rauno Aaltonen-inspired special equipment, the only works Mini entered for the Safari Rally finally choked itself to death with dust in the carburettor filters.

incline, so we were able to give the Mini a big push, back off and let Paddy 'drive' into the control while we motored sedately by and waited for him around the next corner. Feigning violent clutch slip, Paddy slowly gathered speed out of the control and soon we were on our way again, without anyone being aware that the Mini was not struggling home under its own power.

As we approached San Remo, more photographers were out to get a picture of what they thought was the winning Mini. Doug was always able to back off just in time, leaving Paddy and Ron to give them a cheery wave while blipping the engine to simulate gear changes.

Our main fear, however, was the traffic on the San Remo coast road, but Doug did a magnificent job in nudging the Mini through the jams. Not even the traffic policemen waving the Rally cars through really appreciated what was going on.

The final drama came a few hundred yards from the control, which was situated in a big car park at the exit to a long tunnel. Doug got up to about 60 mph in the tunnel and backed off just in time to eject a terrified Paddy into the daylight! With lights ablaze and horn blaring, Paddy performed a neat handbrake turn around a bewildered policeman on a traffic island and had just enough momentum to free-wheel into the control area. This final episode was watched by many hundreds of spectators, local TV film crews, and the entire organizing committee, who welcomed Paddy as a worthy finisher.

Although we fully expected that our little game would have been detected, and we would have had to admit it if we had been challenged, nobody murmured a word and Paddy and Ron duly got their second place. The only man who I felt was just a little bit puzzled as to how Paddy had either had time to replace the drive shaft or had managed to free-wheel all that way was John Davenport, co-driver of the third placed Lancia driven by Ove Andersson!

Safari Mini

As a prize for winning the RAC Rally, Rauno Aaltonen took a Mini on the East African Safari over Easter (HJB 656D). The car bristled with Aaltonen-type gadgets and special Safari modifications, including hand-operated screen wipers, handles for lifting the car out of the mud, foot-plates for bouncing it along muddy roads, exhaust extensions for fording rivers, petrol pump mounted high in the cockpit, wing-mounted spotlamps to allow maximum air flow through the radiator and for easy cleaning on the move, fly screen on the radiator, front and rear winch points, and a hydrolastic pump built into the system and mounted on the rear seat so that the ride height could be quickly adjusted.

A Mini was never really a suitable Safari car and, despite Rauno's Safari expertise, the car suffered from overheating and finally expired when dust got into the engine through the inadequate carburettor air filters.

Sebring racing

Straight from his fifth win on the Circuit of Ireland with GRX 5D, albeit this time against little opposition, Paddy Hopkirk flew off to Sebring to drive a Mini in the Four Hour Saloon Car Race with John Rhodes.

On our previous trips to Sebring with the MG and Austin-Healey teams, we had been frustrated spectators in the 'sedan' race which preceded the 12 hour World Sports Car Championship classic. The standard of competition and driving, particularly in the 1,300 cc class, was pretty pathetic and BMC in America suggested that it would be fun to demonstrate the Mini in the hands of Hopkirk and Rhodes. For the 1967 race, therefore, we entered one of our old Group II rally cars (GRX 309D), which proved competitive and gave the crowd a fine opportunity of seeing how a Mini should really be handled on a race track.

The start, with some 70 cars on the grid, was an absolute shambles, with the drivers at the back unable to see the starter's flag. As the cars were lined up according to engine size, the Mini was right at the back but Paddy, who took the first spell, made a great start and was already half-way through the field before he passed the starting line!

The car ran faultlessly and maintained a good overall placing while leading the 1,300 cc class. Then, after two hours, Paddy came in to refuel and hand over to John Rhodes. The pit stop went as planned, everything was running according to plan, then Rhodes came in for an unscheduled stop after only a further one hour's running, John complaining of fuel starvation. The car was quickly refuelled again, when it was discovered that the gravity fuel tank in the pits was pumping in both air and fuel. This had completely thrown our fuel consumption figures. After the second stop the Mini had now dropped to second in class behind a works Lancia, but by the closing laps the Mini was back in the lead by half a lap.

The finishing arrangements at Sebring were unusual in that the timing line was situated on the corner before the pits yet the actual finishing line, where the chequered flag was displayed, was half-way along the pit straight. Rhodes crossed the timing line just before the end of the four hours with the Mini completely out of fuel again and spluttering to a halt in the pit road, not having taken the chequered flag on the circuit. There were large groans from the BMC supporters as the Lancia swept past the flag but all was not lost. More fuel was poured in and John set off to complete another lap, fighting his way through the crowded pit lane. He finally crossed the line four minutes inside the time allowed to complete the last lap.

Then it was announced that the Mini had been beaten by the Lancia and, as I was time-keeping for the team, I took my lap charts and time sheets to the race timekeepers and we were able to prove that, in fact, the Mini had qualified as a finisher according to the race rules and had won the class (the results being taken across the timing line and not the finishing line). Not surprisingly, the Lancia team were furious – it was just like old rallying times again!

Porsche chasing

Hot favourites for the Tulip Rally that year were Porsche, as the results were again to be decided on scratch times, the going was dry, and most of the tests were uphill, which suited rear-engined, rear-wheel drive cars. Nevertheless, Vic Elford's 911S only managed to beat Timo Makinen (LRX 827E) by 46 seconds, and Rauno Aaltonen in the second works Mini (LRX 829E) was right behind his team-mate, the two Finns making it a 1–2 in the touring category, with Julien Vernaeve finishing fourth to bring the Minis the Manufacturers' Team Prize.

Timo's performance was the more remarkable because a piston broke up half-way through the event and, as Paul Easter recalls, they had plans to retire:

Doing battle on the 1967 Tulip Rally against the now threatening Porsches, Timo Makinen/Paul Easter who were only beaten by Vic Elford's Porsche 911 by some 46 seconds. The Minis finished 1–2 in the Touring Category.

Just south of Geneva we were determined to retire because we assumed that a piston had burnt out and before every stage we had to jump out, pour in a gallon of oil, change the plugs and do it all over again at the end of the test. We were sure that we were not going to finish – besides, Timo had some good friends in Geneva!

Then we came to a service point where Doug Watts was in command; he would not have any of that and gave us both a big lecture, saying that if the car was still running we were to drive it to the finish. We set off suitably admonished with gallons of oil in the back and packets of sparking plugs. Timo was now suitably fired up and drove like crazy. The final test was a comic obstacle course around some huge concrete pipes, Elford hit one of them and very nearly lost his lead so we could have won after all.

Having threatened to retire halfway through the Tulip Rally when a piston broke up on his Mini, requiring regular plug changes and gallons of oil, Timo Makinen was told to carry on and drove so fast in an effort to terminally destroy the engine that he finally won the touring category and very nearly caught the leading Porsche!

David Benzimra, son of the Benbros Motors boss in Nairobi who had helped us so much on the Safari, was loaned GRX 5D along with co-driver Terry Harryman for the event but went out near the finish with clutch failure. Indicating the popularity of the Tulip amongst the private owners in those days, of the 108 starters 45 were British privateers, and amongst them were 21 Minis.

Paddy's Acropolis

Of the wins that the team scored during my time as competitions manager I have always felt that the 1967 Acropolis Rally was one of the most rewarding. The Minis, having campaigned in Greece for four years and dropped out every time when in the lead (or, as in 1966, being disqualified from first place) it was fitting that Paddy Hopkirk, the moral victor in 1966, should come through to final victory. But this was no easy win.

From the start, the Abingdon trio of Makinen (GRX 195D), Aaltonen (LRX 828E), and Hopkirk (LRX 830E) set the pace against the main opposition, Ove Andersson (Lancia) and Bengt Soderstrom (Cortina). Then Rauno was involved in an accident with a non-competing Volkswagen which was going the wrong way on a stage that was supposed to be closed. (The driver was actually a doctor going to the rescue of another crashed competitor.) Rauno was hospitalized with mild concussion and co-driver Henry Liddon suffered some big bumps and bruises. However, they both recovered in time to join the victory celebrations. This left Timo Makinen to take up the challenge, but soon he was out too after troubles with a broken rear sub-frame and a grumbling gearbox.

So it was Paddy, with co-driver Ron Crellin, who soldiered on to the finish, with a well-judged drive. The event ended with a comic driving test, the Parnis hill climb, and a race around the Tatoi airfield. On the driving test Paddy showed that he had forgotten nothing of his old 'pylon-bashing' skills and on the hill climb he made quite sure of victory by beating his nearest rivals, Andersson and Soderstrom, by some three seconds, despite being baulked by a car that had set off four minutes ahead of him.

The final circuit race, which did not affect the results provided you finished, was a great

After the protests of the previous year, the team were determined to win the 1967 Acropolis Rally and Paddy Hopkirk/Ron Crellin obliged with a very satisfying victory.

spectacle as the three leading cars diced together. But then the Mini gave up the ghost with no bearings and Paddy wisely stopped just short of the finishing line and, at the end of the 30 minutes race, restarted, to take the flag a very popular winner.

Lars Ytterbring

It would be a foolish competitions manager who was not always on the look-out for up-and-coming driving talent and who did not give them the opportunity of a works drive if the budget and programme allowed. One of the young Swedes who impressed me, both as a driver and as the sort of man who would slot well into the team, was Lars Ingvar Ytterbring and his equally pleasant co-driver Lars Persson. They formed a good relationship with the boys in the Special Tuning Department, who prepared several cars for them to rally both in Europe and at home in Sweden.

The pair drove for us on several occasions, their first performance being on the Scottish Rally in 1967 when they finished second overall in GRX 311D to Roger Clark's Lotus Cortina – a result which they repeated on the same event the following year.

Geneva confusion

The 1967 Geneva Rally finished in some confusion. The Geneva Rally itself counted only for cars in Groups I and III, so the entries for all the other Groups were put into a separate classification and entered under the name of another Rally – the Criterium de Crans-sur-Sierre. When it was all over two completely different sets of results were announced which put Vic Elford's 911S first in the Geneva Rally with the Minis of Tony Fall (LRX 827E) and Julien Vernaeve (LRX 829E) first and second overall in the Criterium event. The confused results did no justice to the brave performance of the Mini crews against the more fancied Porsche opposition.

Belgian Group I exponent, Julien Vernaeve, regularly joined the team to add class and team awards to the list of achievements.

Although this was Julien Vernaeve's first drive in an Abingdon-prepared Mini he was no stranger to the team, having helped us to win several team prizes in the past. Julien, who came from Ghent in Belgium, was equally at home rallying or racing. He won the Belgian Rally Championship in 1962 and 1963 and their Saloon Car Championship in 1964, driving his own Minis, mostly with engines prepared by Don Moore. When he drove for the BMC team he never failed to achieve what was demanded from him – indeed, he often produced some exceptional results. He was a driver who always seemed to go best on tarmac events which he had practised – his Tulip Rally results being particularly notable. Julien was famous at Abingdon for his regular appearances with a scruffy Mini van into which he would pack as many scrap parts as he could scrounge to keep his own Minis competitive! In return he never failed to reciprocate this assistance with generous hospitality whenever the team passed through Belgium.

Danube disqualification

Any rally, particularly if it ventures through faraway countries, can be won or lost on documentation. A team manager's nightmare is to have a potential winner fail because someone has not got the right piece of paper in the right place at the right time. That's what happened to Rauno Aaltonen (LRX 828E) on the 1967 Danube Rally.

At the start in Prague, there was considerable disagreement between Rauno and the officials as to what visa was necessary for the Finn to enter Hungary. It was finally agreed that he did not need one but we were told that if this was wrong information, he could easily obtain one at the frontier. When Rauno reached the border, he found that he did need a visa but that the officials, of course, refused to give him one on the spot. The Mini was therefore out of the Rally. My frustration and disappointment was only redeemed by the fact that the Austin 1800 driven by Tony Fall and Mike Wood won the Rally on this, its first international outing.

After a tremendous battle with the Saabs of Simo Lampinen, Tom Trana, and Carl Orrenius, Timo Makinen (GRX 195D) just won the 1,000 Lakes Rally for the third year running. But the event produced a spectacular drama when the bonnet flew open on a stage. The car had been overheating so Timo had removed the spot lamps and was running with the bonnet slightly open, held closed only by the rubber safety straps. But on one enormous 'yump' the bonnet flew up and Timo had to drive on for some six miles peering out of an open door. Even so he dropped only 19 seconds on the fastest man. It was later rumoured that when Alec Issigonis saw the dramatic picture, he banned the BMC Photographic Department from issuing any further prints!

Nothing stops Timo Makinen when he is in full flight on his favourite 1,000 Lakes Rally!

Marathon Minis

In 1966, the second year when the old Spa–Sofia–Liège Rally became the 84 Hours Marathon de la Route at the Nurbürgring, we surprised everyone – including ourselves – by winning outright with an MGB driven by Andrew Hedges and Julien Vernaeve. When the rather complicated regulations appeared for the 1967 event, it seemed that a 1-litre car would stand a very good chance of beating the handicap formula. We therefore entered a pair of Group VI 970 cc cars, the driving teams being Andrew Hedges/Julien Vernaeve/Tony Fall (GRX 5D) and Clive Baker/Roger Enever/Alec Poole (LRX 830E).

The cars ran with Group II engines for reliability but with lightweight bodies. The only mechanical novelties were the auxiliary forward-facing water radiators and an electric pump which enabled the drivers to top up the oil in the sump on the move from an auxiliary tank in the cockpit.

The rather complex nature of the event deserves some explanation. Firstly, it was run upon the combined south and north circuits of the 'Ring, which totalled 17.5 miles. Each lap was therefore the equivalent of a 15 lap race on the club circuit at Brands Hatch! After 12 laps cars were allowed an extra three minutes for refuelling, after 75 laps an extra 10 minutes was allowed for servicing. A bogey time was set for each lap and exceeding this time earnt penalties. The bogey time was set according to the car's seating capacity and the size of the engine. Minis in the 1,000 cc class with four seats were allowed an 18 minute lap time, the Porsche (also four seats) 15 minutes. Exceeding the bogey time by just one minute resulted in a penalty of one complete lap, the general classification being worked out on distance run. The Minis lapped in about 15 minutes so we had about two and half minutes per lap available for emergencies – but this was not cumulative. The three drivers in each car did three hours at the wheel and then had six hours' rest.

The event started well for us and after six hours the Minis were running in eighth and tenth places, three laps down on the leading Porsches, the main opposition driven by Jochen Neerpash, Vic Elford, and Hans Herrmann. Also fancied were the Alan Mann Ford Mustangs of Jackie Ickx and Gilbert Staepelaere.

After nine hours we had crept up to fifth and sixth overall. By midnight on the first day, after 12 hours' running, we were up to third and fourth, the Enever/Poole/Baker car running

One of the more unusual outings for the works Minis was on the 1967 84 Hour Marathon at the Nurbürgring, when the team entered a pair of 970 'racers'. The author and Clive Baker running-in the Marathon cars at Castle Combe.

Routine pit stop for the Andrew Hedges/Julien Vernaeve/Tony Fall car, which finished second overall and raced non-stop for some 5,500 trouble-free miles.

a lap ahead of Hedges/Vernaeve/Fall. Into the second day only 26 of the original 43 starters were running and only five were completely unpenalized, including the two Minis.

During the early evening the circuit was shrouded in fog and visibility at times was down to some 10 yards. The Minis continued to buzz around on a 16 minute lap but, just before midnight, Clive Baker went missing and crawled back to the pits 20 minutes late reporting that the throttle cable had broken. Clive had stopped on the circuit in a very dodgy position in the dark and the fog, threaded the broken cable through the bulkhead and adjusted the throttle cam so that it could be controlled from inside the car. Clive looked suitably harassed and later described how a Tatra driver went the wrong side of the Mini in the fog and disappeared off the circuit into the hedge. Six further minutes were lost fitting a new cable and then the Mini was away again, just inside the maximum 30-minute allowance. The car was clearly out of the running so I instructed Alec Poole, who took over, to forget our carefully planned schedule and rev limits and go flat out to try and catch up with the leaders.

Tired but happy after 84 hours on duty, (left to right) Mick Hogan, Tommy Wellman, the author, Pete Bartram, and Robin Vokins.

Midnight came with 48 hours run (two Le Mans!) and still the two Minis were in the running, indeed there were two other private 970s and a 1,275 still going. Alec made excellent progress until he misjudged one of the Nurbürgring's deceptive bends in the fog. The car went off the road in the early hours of the morning and ended up on its roof, out of the event. Alec was unhurt but very annoyed!

Conditions and visibility at the time were unbelievable, as witnessed by the sight of an ambulance joining the circuit, driving straight across the track instead of along it and crashing head first into the wall on the other side, backing up and then motoring off down a slip road, the crew confident that they were travelling on the circuit!

As daylight dawned the surviving Mini was hanging on to third place, 12 laps behind the Elford Porsche. When the latter came in with brake disc problems the Mini moved up to second place, running right behind the leading Porsche, driven at the time by Terry Hunter. By this time the Mini was the only car running unpenalized, an honour which we were to hold until 70 of the 84 hours had elapsed.

Elford rejoined, determined to make up his deficit, but he was still behind the Mini when Hunter came into the pits with the leading Porsche's engine making very expensive noises. A broken valve was diagnosed and the mechanics decided to try and change the engine within the 30-minute time allowance. They took 40 minutes and the car was disqualified, so the Mini took the lead. While it did not take Elford long to catch and pass us, we managed to hold onto second place to the finish, despite a last-minute scare when a front wheel bearing started to show signs of trouble, five minutes being lost when this had to be changed and the stubborn hub took a long time to budge.

Only 13 cars finished, the Mini covering some 5,500 virtually trouble-free racing miles in the 84 Hours. We were particularly proud to take home the special reliability award based on penalties for the minimum time spent in the pits. Not bad for the smallest cars in the race.

Fastest Alpine

With the Alpine Rally open this year to cars from Groups I to VI this was going to be the fastest-ever running of the summer classic, with its flat-out stages and 40 mph selectifs. We therefore entered three Group VI 'racers' for Hopkirk (LRX 827E), Aaltonen (JBL 172D), and Makinen (GRX 311D) and a Group II car for Tony Fall (GRX 310D). The Group VI cars used a single twin-choke Weber carburettor, ultra-lightweight bodies, fibreglass bonnets, aluminium doors, and perspex side and rear windows, and the bumpers were removed, all this saving nearly 1 cwt over a Group II car. The cars also had an auxiliary cooling radiator fitted alongside the oil cooler and a somewhat crude but legal dual braking system (necessary for Group VI), which used the normal hydraulic system and a cable link from the brake pedal to the handbrake lever. The Alpine Minis produced some 90 bhp at the wheels.

The Abingdon cars were hardly competitive entries from the start and the crews knew that they would be outclassed by the opposition and could only really win on reliability against the Renault-Alpines, the lightweight 911 Porsches, Alfa Romeo GTAs, works Citroëns and Imps. Thus, from the traditional starting point in Marseilles, it was the Porsche of Vic Elford that made the running, along with the Renault-Alpines of Gerard Larrousse and Jean Vinatier.

The first BMC casualty was Tony Fall, who went off the road at Sigale and hit a wall. Not far up the road, Rauno Aaltonen stopped with gearbox failure. Timo Makinen seemed to be having a longer Alpine than usual but, by the end of the first stage at the Alpe d'Huez ski resort, he was in trouble with an overheating engine, although lying third behind the leading Renault-Alpines. Paddy's car, however, was in perfect shape and lying in a reasonable seventh place.

On to the second leg, Timo moved up to second place with the retirement of Jean Vinatier only to lose time with a broken throttle cable then drop out after the final descent of the Col d'Allos with brake troubles requiring new callipers more often than pads.

With a carefully judged performance and, in particular, superb pace note work by Ron Crellin in the fog, Paddy slowly overhauled the leaders – actually overtaking Larrousse on one foggy stage. With the later retirement of the flying Renault-Alpine, Paddy gained the lead and, after a classic drive, was able to return to Marseilles with a three minute margin over the GTA Alfa-Romeos of Bernard Consten and Jean Claude Gamet – all that remained of the serious opposition. Our Alpine Rally celebrations were enhanced by Brian Culcheth's performance in winning his class with the lumbering 1800 on his first works drive with the team.

Those Corsican fan belts

To return home from an incredibly expensive sortie like the Tour de Corse and have to tell the senior management that your two cars retired on the very first stage with a fault as elementary as slipping fanbelts is not a very happy experience! But that's what happened on the 1967 event.

The BMC team had never been to Corsica with a full scale entry before and in the 12 year history of the event a British car had never got anywhere near winning. So we were really going into the enemy camp and the Tour was very much a French preserve. It was becoming an event which also carried great weight in terms of publicity and sales to the French market – the main reason why we went. However, we were made extremely welcome by the locals and our European rivals, particulary Renault, who had dominated the event for so long. They were genuinely delighted that we had come along to challenge them on their home ground. They sensibly realized that one-make domination of the event could in time jeopardize its future standing and they were intent on winning yet again, but this time in the face of some real opposition.

To describe the Tour de Corse one must first describe Corsica and that is not easy, for it is difficult to convey in words the unique terrain and nature of the island's roads. As Paddy Hopkirk said: 'I thought I had seen every sort of rally – the Safari, the Acropolis, the Monte – but the Tour de Corse is something different again.'

Practically every mile of the island's roads is made up of a tortuous sucession of bends,

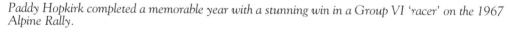

Paddy Hopkirk completed a memorable year with a stunning win in a Group VI 'racer' on the 1967 Alpine Rally.

twists, turns, and ups and downs through the mountains. They called it the 'Rally of 10,000 Bends' but we worked out from our pace notes that there must be at least 23,000 bends in the 23 hours of the event over some 800 miles. It is rather like driving from London to Edinburgh and back in and out of the cat's eyes all the way!

I went for a five-hour practice run with Rauno Aaltonen and Henry Liddon one evening and we cannot have got into even third gear on more than a dozen occasions, and this for a mere five or ten second burst. For the rest of the time the Mini was screaming along in second gear, Rauno sliding the car left, right, left, right through the bends. It was quite hypnotic and rather like one of those 'white-knuckle' fair-ground rides!

The route comprised one complete lap of the island, covering just about every road starting and finishing in Ajaccio, a little fishing port on the south-west coast. The time schedules were quite impossible so it was virtually a road race over closed roads. The police and public were tremendously enthusiastic and everything on the island virtually came to a complete halt so that the event could be run.

Our two Group VI Minis for Paddy Hopkirk (GRX 5D) and Rauno Aaltonen (JBL 172D) lasted only a few miles over the first stage when slipping fanbelts caused immediate and irreparable overheating troubles. This was despite the belts being run-in, checked, and adjusted before the start. The event turned out to be a Lancia benefit with victory going to Sandro Munari.

It was little consolation to discover afterwards that the manufacturers had supplied a batch of faulty belts. It was just our luck that storeman Neville Challis had to pick those two belts from the bin at Abingdon – specially as a belt from the same batch had been fitted to the fuel-injection recce car that had covered some 3,000 trouble-free miles.

The year ended with the last-minute frustrating cancellation of the RAC Rally because of foot and mouth disease – fuel-injection Group VI Minis having been prepared for Timo Makinen, Tony Fall, and Paddy Hopkirk.

The year, however, had been a profitable one and against all odds the works Minis were still winning, having claimed victory in three great classics in one season – the Monte, Acropolis, and Alpine.

Prepared for the cancelled 1967 RAC Rally, the potential of this rare fuel-injection car was dramatically demonstrated by Timo Makinen on a TV spectacular.

Chapter 10 _____

Luckless Year

Traditionally, the Monte Carlo Rally opened the 1968 season and once again the Abingdon Minis were entered in force for the winter classic. Again, there was a determined effort from drivers, mechanics, and supporting trade personnel to try and bring home another Monte victory. Everything went according to plan except the weather for, apart from awful blizzards in Yugoslavia which had caused the Minis to run for the first time ever with chains, this was to be the first of a run of 'no-snow' years on the key sections, which was to make the contest against Porsche and Renault-Alpine in particular almost impossible.

Under these conditions the Minis were really handicapped out of the running, for while front-wheel drive gave a certain advantage on snow and ice, particularly on the downhill sections, the advantage swung dramatically to rear-engined, rear-wheel drive cars when conditions were drier – especially uphill. Furthermore, the outright power and speed of the new generation of rallying sports/racers was now starting to put the Minis a long way behind on performance.

Although the results of the 1968 event were disappointing, everyone realized that in the circumstances we could not have achieved a better result. Rauno Aaltonen (ORX 7F), Tony Fall (ORX 707F), and Paddy Hopkirk (ORX 777F) finished third, fourth and fifth overall behind the Porsches. They won the Team Prize and were placed 1–2–3 in the category. Timo Makinen's car (ORX 77F) was the only one to have any trouble when the crankshaft pulley came loose. He arrived at Monte after the run-in sections with a white-hot engine and failed to re-start for the Mountain Circuit or, as Paul Easter explains, they failed to leave the Principality!

> We thought that as the car was actually still driveable we had better be seen to make an effort to start the Mountain Circuit, so we arrived at the re-start dressed up with our racing overalls and all the gear but underneath we had our ordinary clothes on. The car started, we roared off up the road, parked outside the Tip Top bar, took our racing overalls off and spent the rest of the Rally there!

Although I said that everything went according to plan, that was not entirely so because this was the year of the carburettor controversy that very nearly caused as much of a rumpus as those headlights in 1966. For the first time we were using the twin split-Weber carburettors in Group II, developed and built at Abingdon from a prototype that Timo Makinen had seen in Finland. Basically by cutting a pair of standard Weber carburettors in half and fitting the two left-hand 'halves' on to the standard Group II inlet manifold, it was possible to gain Group VI Weber-type performance in Group II (around 92 bhp at 6,500 rpm). Cliff Humphries was responsible for this new development.

Having studied the Group II regulations very carefully I was confident that the use of these carburettors was permissible. Nevertheless, I wrote to the FIA in Paris and to the Monte

Opposite *Outclassed by the Porsches and not helped by mainly dry weather conditions, Rauno Aaltonen and Henry Liddon still took the touring car category on the 1968 Monte Carlo Rally.*

Tony Fall and Mike Wood put up a brave fight to get on terms with Rauno Aaltonen, finishing second in the 1968 Monte Carlo Rally touring car category.

organizers many weeks before the event sending them details and photographs of our new carburettors. They thus had ample opportunity to raise any queries and, to indicate that we had no intentions of cheating, we passed on details of the new engine specification to the press. Nobody said anything about it until we arrived in Monte.

After the Concentration Runs I was asked to attend a meeting of the Sporting Commission for, following the initial technical inspection of the cars upon arrival in Monte, the Technical Commission had informed the Sporting Commission that they had doubts about the eligibility of the carburettors. They wished to discuss my interpretation of the regulations covering this point.

It was clear from the start that they were doing this in a genuine attempt to safeguard BMC and the Rally from a repetition of the 1966 fiasco, when they were aware of what they thought was a possible infringement of the regulations at an early stage in the Rally and yet they permitted the Mini crews to finish the event before disqualifying them. I was told that there

The use of the Abingdon-designed and built split-Weber carburettors on the 1968 Monte Carlo Rally caused almost as much of a rumpus as the great headlight controversy of 1966.

was no doubt that a protest would be forthcoming from other competitors if we continued using the new carburettors and they wanted to discuss the matter at the earliest opportunity.

I began by thanking them for the opportunity of this early discussion and we all agreed that for the good of the Monte and rallying in general we should do everything possible to prevent a repetition of the 1966 incident.

The English translation of the French regulations covering the alterations permitted to carburettors said: 'The carburettors provided by the manufacturer may be replaced by others providing that the number be the same as that fitted by the manufacturer and that they can be mounted on the inlet manifold of the engine without using any intermediary device and by using the original attachment parts.'

The Technical Commission began by suggesting that we had fitted an 'intermediary device' between the carburettors and the manifold. I replied that this was not so and I explained that this was a prototype carburettor which, according to our interpretation of the regulations, began at the point of junction with the manifold and continued through the main body of the carburettor to the end of the inlet pipe. I pointed out that the small additional inlet stud on the carburettors was not bolted to the carburettor but was welded to it as a complete unit.

While the Sporting Commission were clearly divided over this point, the original French regulation was read and it was found that there was a discrepancy between the English and French texts. In the French text the interpretation of the final wording of the regulations read: 'The carburettors must be mounted on the inlet manifold of the engine *without modification or deformation* and without using any intermediary device, and by using the original attachment parts.' The words in italics were omitted from the English text.

While there was concern about the discrepancy in the text on a very significant point, we agreed that only the French text could be accepted as the official code. The Commission then felt that the carburettors were not eligible because we had modified them to make them fit the standard manifold. Again I pointed out that we had not modified them because, although we had used basic Weber principles and some Weber design features and components, this was an entirely new prototype carburettor which we had designed and built in England. There could, therefore, be no question that we had modified them to make them fit the manifold – they were designed to fit it in the first place. After one hour the meeting was adjourned for the Technical Commission to make its decisions.

I was later asked to join the meeting and the verdict of the Commission was that in the event of a protest they felt that they would have to uphold it as they were still not satisfied that the carburettors were in accordance with the regulations.

In view of the fact that we had discussed matters in such a friendly and frank atmosphere and, bearing in mind the discrepancy of English and French texts, they then made the remarkable proposal that we should change the carburettors before the Monte–Vals–Monte leg. I said that this would be quite impossible because even if our crews could make up enough time to have the work done, we had not got any other carburettors with us. Furthermore, I said that I thought that it would be a scandalous thing to do as it would be totally against the event regulations and this would undoubtedly give rise to justified protests from other competitors. It was also putting the organizers into an even more embarrassing position which, having allowed us to start, now wanted us to 'secretly' change the specification of our engines.

The atmosphere was now getting somewhat strained and the Commission then offered us the opportunity of changing the carburettors in parc ferme overnight. This proposal was even more stupid than the first and I reminded them that the whole purpose of our discussion was to try and avoid a repetition of the dramas of 1966, not to create an even bigger fiasco!

The tone of the meeting was clearly demonstrated when I was then presented with what was clearly a bogus telephone message reporting that Paddy Hopkirk was in the parc ferme at this very moment trying to change the carburettors on his car. What had I got to say about that? I looked across the table at the RAC Steward, our good friend Jack Kemsley, in sheer amazement and it was he who suggested that we all go down to the parc ferme right away to witness that Paddy was as good a mechanic as he was a driver! The humour was not appreciated by the French but I think we won that round, as the subject was quickly dropped!

Continuing the argument, I was adamant that our cars complied with whatever translation of the regulations one chose. I again refused to change the carburettors and, in such a clearly hostile atmosphere, I said that I must now consider withdrawing the team. Following long discussions with the drivers, opinions were divided as to whether they should stick their necks out on the Common Run and the Mountain Circuit only to face the chance of disqualification, or withdraw now and save the cars for another, more worthwhile event. It was a difficult decision and it was by no means unanimous that, after yet another meeting with the Technical Commission, we decided to press on. That final meeting had at least indicated that the Monte organizers would not raise any objections or disqualify us but they would have to carefully consider the reasons presented by anyone who lodged an official protest. We thought this was fair enough, and that it would be the end of the matter because it was clear that all of our rivals agreed with our interpretation of the regulations.

With the Rally over, the cars were taken to the usual scrutineering but our suspicions were aroused when instead of asking for just the class-winning car, the scrutineers demanded to see all three Minis. Heading the scrutineering team was the same gentleman who had been officiating in 1966 and clearly he was still very anti-BMC. He certainly did not agree with the Sporting Commission's decision that the carburettors complied with the regulations. The carburettors and the manifolds were torn apart to try and find some slight discrepancy with the regulations or the homologation sheet. It was an unsuccessful exercise which took so long that, by the time the scrutineers' session was over, there was not time to give the winning Porsche even a cursory going over!

There were happily no protests from other competitors so the results stood and the matter was finally resolved by sending formal applications to the FIA who ultimately agreed that our interpretation of the regulations was correct and that the carburettors were quite legal.

End of another controversial Monte – this time the power of Porsche and the weather had beaten us.

Rauno Aaltonen and Tony Fall took their 1968 Monte Carlo Rally cars on the Italian Flowers Rally, but both cars were out-paced and failed to finish.

Challenging the Twin Cams

After a disappointing Flowers Rally, when both Rauno Aaltonen (ORX 77F) and Tony Fall (ORX 777F) with their Monte cars retired, came the Circuit of Ireland and the hope that Paddy Hopkirk could gain another 'home' win. Ford, however, had now got the new Escort Twin Cam and with Roger Clark at the wheel not even the combination of Paddy with a Group VI 'racer' (JMO 969D) could succeed and the car retired when the differential disintegrated.

Two Group II cars were entered for the Tulip Rally, Makinen (LBL 66D) and Julien Vernaeve (ORX 707F). Julien won the Touring Category and finished third overall in dry conditions behind the Twin Cam Escorts of Roger Clark and Ove Andersson. Makinen made a rare driving error and went off the road in a big way on the Col de Brabant, the Mini ending up some six foot down a bank in a muddy field. Timo and Paul set off down the hill to try and find a tractor but when they returned there were enough Frenchmen around to manhandle the car back onto the road. Time lost was 69 minutes, yet in true Makinen style he got to the end of the section within the time allowance. But for this incident, and time lost with a puncture, Paul reckoned that they could have won the event by a mere second.

Paddy Hopkirk (GRX 5D) led the Canadian Shell 4000 Rally for three days and then had serious overheating troubles which, although cured by the emergency fitting of an auxiliary radiator, brought disqualification on a technical infringement.

Returning to the Acropolis Rally, Rauno Aaltonen reckoned that his car (RBL 450F) was the fastest Group II Mini he had ever driven, yet the little Finn could only make fifth place behind the flying opposition, Clark's winning Escort Twin Cam and the Porsche 911s of Zasada and Toivonen. Timo Makinen (GRX 310D) was an early retirement with overheating – a sad ending to what was to be his final drive with the team.

With the main players in Greece and on the Shell 4000 in Canada, Lars Ytterbring was our sole entry on the Scottish Rally, his car (JMO 969D) being prepared by Special Tuning. The Swede drove a fast and consistent rally to finish second and, but for a puncture on a critical stage, might have got closer to Clark's winning Escort Twin Cam.

BMC Canada invited Paddy Hopkirk and Tony Fall to try their luck on the Shell 4000 Rally. (They tossed for which one got the girl and which one got the horse!) Paddy led the event for three days but was then disqualified for fitting an auxiliary cooling radiator to try and solve serious overheating.

Sweden's popular Lars Ytterbring drove for the team on several occasions and established a good relationship with the Special Tuning Department, who regularly prepared his car. Lars very nearly won the 1968 Scottish Rally before having to concede victory to Roger Clark's works Escort Twin Cam.

Euro finale

The Portuguese Rally in October was to be the final European Championship outing for the works Minis, where Paddy (LBL 606D) had to be content with second place in the very last minutes of the event when fog prevented the service crew from reaching their service point to provide racing tyres for the last crucial stage.

While many of the disappointments of 1968 could be fairly blamed upon bad luck, undoubtedly many of the retirements – and there were lots of them – could be attributed to the fact that the Minis were now being considerably overstressed to keep pace with the opposition. While in 1967 reliability had often won through, with the demand for more power to keep up with the new generation of specialist rally cars, the Minis now added unreliability to a non-competitive performance on many events.

Undoubtedly another reason for the lack of continued Mini success was that a great deal of Abingdon's time was now being directed to the testing and development of the BMC 1800s in preparation for the London–Sydney Marathon to be held at the end of the year. This meant, particularly in the latter part of the season, that there was a complete stop on all Mini development and testing at a time when it was most necessary.

It was more than unfortunate that the British Leyland merger should have come at this time, when the team's fortunes were at their lowest ebb and our only competitive rally car was clearly coming to the end of its international career.

Chapter 11

Anatomy of a Monte

In the opening chapter I mentioned that back-up support and behind the scenes organization was one of the team's key ingredients for success. Having the right mechanics in the right place with the right equipment at the right time was always vitally important. Nowhere was this more significant than on the Monte Carlo Rally, when the BMC support plan for servicing, refuelling, tyre changes, and the work of ice note crews resembled a military operation. There is no doubt that the effective execution of the plan by everyone involved contributed to the team's success.

In this chapter I have detailed the BMC movement schedules and service plan for the 1968 Monte Carlo Rally when the team entered four works Minis and two Austin 1800s.

First, however, a brief introduction to the team's key mechanics who played such an important part in the plan.

Doug Watts – team leader

The man who, more than anyone, inspired Abingdon's team of mechanics to winning

Doug Watts (left), the team's stalwart shop supervisor, with (left to right) Henry Liddon, Ron Crellin, Paul Easter, Tony Fall, and Mike Wood.

form and who was involved with the Competitions Department from its earliest days was the late Doug Watts, the shop's first foreman and later its supervisor.

Like practically all of the mechanics in the team, Doug was a local man and his first job was as a clerk in the local Morland's brewery. Even at this early age his lifelong dislike of paperwork was apparent and he soon moved on to the carpenter's shop, where he showed a remarkable aptitude with the tools of the trade. He later became a fitter in the metal shop, making barrels, and after a few years had done just about every job at Morland's including serving as a drayman.

In the war Doug got a job at the MG factory working on armoured cars and tanks but then left to join the Royal Engineers, where he passed out as a top-class fitter which gained him a posting to North Africa, working on the railways. This led to a spell as an engine driver in Italy, and those who knew Doug can just imagine how his talents would have kept old trains on the move under challenging circumstances. It was these experiences which nurtured the qualities of determination and improvisation that he was to display to such good effect in his later years at Abingdon.

Returning home post-war, Doug was welcomed back at MG where, after a time as a rectification fitter on the MG 'TC' line, he was promoted as one of three road test inspectors. In those days the testers took the cars straight from the line, went for a drive around the local lanes and, if anything was wrong, they had to put it right with their own bag of tools at the roadside. Excellent background for a rally mechanic!

One of Doug's greatest qualities was that he was a fine judge of a man's character and ability. It was he who picked the mechanics and established how the team should work together – something that was to prove so vital to moulding that all-important team spirit. Above all he was able to transmit his unbounded energy, enthusiasm, and loyalty to those around him. When Doug died in 1993 after bravely fighting a long illness, Stuart Turner commented, 'Doug simply was the team.'

The mechanics

In its early days the Competitions workforce comprised a selection of the top mechanics from the Development Department – Cliff Bray, Jimmy Cox, and Harold Wiggins. There was also a shy tea-boy by the name of Gerald Wiffen, later to become one of the team's longest-serving and most experienced mechanics.

Tommy Wellman was one of the earliest recruits, coming from the Service Division at MG. Tommy was soon to become charge hand and to follow Doug up through the ranks as his faithful deputy. Tommy was a great improviser, a talented schemer for new ideas, and never happier than when given a seemingly unsolvable project – like how to design and build an indestructible side exhaust system for a big Healey tucked up into the driver's door sill. Tommy had a wide circle of chums in important positions in neighbouring factories who he could always call upon for help.

The late Doug Hamblin was another early recruit, this time from the Rectification Department. He was a bold, brash character but a hard and efficient worker who very soon earned his title as deputy foreman. It was a sad day for the team when Doug lost his life in a road accident on the 1964 Monte.

Den Green was ready and very able to fill the vacant post of deputy foreman. He was a brilliant mechanic who came to Abingdon from an Oxford garage. Den, particularly in the later years of the Department, gained the growing respect of the team's drivers as one of the most resourceful operators in the field. He inherited from Doug the spirit of adventure and determination and, unlike some of his colleagues, was able to keep abreast of the office paperwork (which he too hated) while losing none of his skills as a practical worker.

Soon the growing Competitions team was encroaching too much upon the space of the Development Department and was moved to its own premises just a few blocks away. They took with them a very important member of the team – its storeman, the late Neville Challis.

Left *Deputy supervisor Tommy Wellman was never happier than when presented with a seemingly impossible technical problem to be solved.* **Right** *One of the most resourceful and respected mechanics in the team, deputy foreman Den Green.*

A good storekeeper is a secret weapon in any Competitions Department and Neville was one of the best. He had a remarkable capacity to produce just what you wanted 'off the shelf' or, if he could not, then he knew just where to go and get it.

With the move to new premises, a new tea-boy was found – Bob Whittington, who progressed to became a meticulous worker. His place was filled by young Johnny Lay, who was one of the very few in the team who did not stay, emigrating to the United States where he set up in business on his own. Another old-timer was Brian Moylan who, unlike his team-mates, was not a local man but came to Abingdon from London during the war years. Brian was always serious and a great 'thinker' who later served as Shop Steward. Nobby Hall was one of the original Abingdon road testers. Nobby was a craftsman rather than a mechanic, one of the finest metal workers and welders in the business.

Following his brief trip to America, the team was happy to welcome back Cliff Humphries, who was a superb all-rounder. In later years his acknowledged skills as an engine builder led him to become chief technician, responsible for the development and testing programme of new projects and new models.

The Department attracted people with the widest possible interests – Johnny Organ was a

Left *Cliff Humphries was the team's technical guru, later responsible for the development of new projects.* **Right** *John Smith from Lucas was the resident electrician at Abingdon. He personally hand-wired all of the works cars and has subsequently helped many owners of ex-works Minis with the restoration of their cars.*

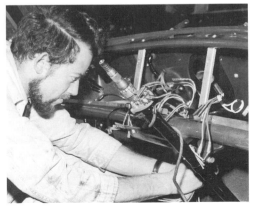

professional boxer, Roy Brown a lay preacher. For the rest of the team, Doug selected a succession of MG apprentices who passed through the Department as part of their training and
who showed particular ability. Amongst those who stayed to become long-serving fitters were
Peter Bartram, Dudley Pike, Tommy Eales, Robin Vokins, Mick Legg, Mick Hogan, and
Gordon Bisp. From the former Service Department came Johnny Evans, Frank Rudman, and
their chief tester, Eddie Burnell. Completing the team were panel-beater Stan Bradford and
electrician Derek Argyle. John Smith of Lucas must also be considered as a fully-fledged
member of the team, for he was almost a permanent resident at Abingdon, wiring up all the
race and rally cars.

To assist Marcus Chambers in the office a young commercial apprentice by the name of Bill
Price came to Abingdon. Bill was a tower of strength to Marcus, Stuart Turner, and later myself,
his speciality being the technical paperwork within the office and, in particular, the all-important homologation of new parts and models. In his later years he took on more responsibilities
and led the team on many events as assistant competitions manager, commanding respect from
everyone in the team. When the Abingdon Department was closed down, Bill worked for a
short time in the motor trade and then, when Competitions was re-established under British
Leyland at Cowley, he returned to his old job working under John Davenport.

Last, but no means least, were the long-suffering secretaries who somehow managed to
keep pace with not only the ever-changing travel schedules on events but also the always elusive competitions managers. Margaret Hall and Jane Derrington worked for Marcus
Chambers, Diana Kirkby survived the whole of Stuart Turner's reign, while Mary Smith and
Sandy Lawson made my spell in the 'hot seat' a great deal easier.

There have been many tributes to the team from drivers, but Paddy Hopkirk's is probably
the most appropriate:

> I would categorically say that the Abingdon team was the best in the world. Those guys
> worked incredibly hard, when they were cold, when they were sick, in all the difficult conditions.

*Competitions Department personnel: left to right, Brian Moylan, Nobby Hall (kneeling), Bob
Whittington, Tommy Eales, Neville Challis, Cliff Humphries, Tommy Wellman (seated), Johnny
Lay, Pete Bartram, Jean Stoter, Harry Carnegie, Johnny Organ, Doug Watts (seated), Roy Brown,
Jane Derrington, Den Green, Doug Hamblin (seated), Bill Price, Ernie Giles, and Gerald Wiffen.*

I think the team's success was a combination of things rather than just the car. Mr Issigonis would not like to hear me say that, but I would say it was the servicing, the briefing, making sure the service cars were in the right place, making sure that the drivers had practised enough. It was the combination of all those things.

This, then, was the team that was to make the name of Abingdon as well known in international rallying circles as MG's post-war competition achievements had done through racing and record breaking.

Team spirit

From the team's earliest days a unique *ésprit de corps* was generated between management, staff, mechanics, and drivers which was not always apparent amongst their rivals. This undoubtedly came about when Marcus and Doug established a working environment where everyone in the team played an equally responsible role and was thus treated with equal respect. The BMC team always made a point of travelling together, staying in the same hotels, eating at the same table, and drinking at the same bar. In this way everyone from the number one driver and the team manager to the rawest apprentice mechanic gained each other's respect, friendship, and confidence.

That the mechanics also turned out to be first-class technicians seemed to be taken for granted and yet it is significant that few of them came into the Department with any specialized knowledge or experience in the preparation of competition cars. The majority of the fitters started as tea-boys or apprentices who at first were allowed to clean the cars, change the wheels and tyres, perhaps later strip an old recce car that was to be written off, then slowly learn the art of car preparation by working with senior mechanics who themselves had climbed the same ladder of experience. This is in total contrast to the works rally teams of today, where personnel are drafted in with specialist experience in chassis work, suspension set-ups, engines, or transmissions, and the level of individual high-technology qualifications is amazing.

The procedure for building the cars was also totally different from today, as each mechanic was personally responsible for the complete preparation of his car from a bare bodyshell upwards. The Abingdon mechanics assembled suspensions, hand-built the complete engines, transmissions, body modifications, and interior trim work, and ran in the car and fine tuned

Team spirit was always seen as a significant factor in the team's success and a special working relationship existed between drivers, staff, and mechanics. Here Simo Lampinen discusses his car for the 1968 RAC Rally with mechanic Johnny Organ.

it – they were responsible for everything except the electrics, which were handled by a resident Lucas specialist. Whenever possible the mechanic that built the car also went out servicing on the event so that he could also look after 'his' car.

All the cars were built up according to a carefully detailed build sheet which would be drawn up by the supervisor. With the exception of one or two very minor points, and personal driver preferences, all of the cars on an event would therefore be almost identical.

The team unquestionably benefited from having its operation based within a self-contained factory that was very much pro-competitions, and which was able and willing to supply all the ancillary services that were vital to the operation of the team. The heads of many departments were old timers with happy memories of MG's former racing and record-breaking activities and they did not need much persuasion to help out with requests for odd jobs, often volunteering some overtime if it could not be squeezed in between production line work. The team was constantly calling upon the services of Abingdon's general transport fleet to collect and deliver drivers to the airports; the paint shop, which always saw that the cars appeared in their immaculate red and white livery; the press shop, which fashioned non-standard metalwork; and the trim shop, which ensured that the cars' interiors were always given a professional touch. The team also benefited by the regular technical input offered from MG's Development Department – Syd Enever, Terry Mitchell, the late Roy Brocklehurst, and Don Hayter.

Budgets

Although the BMC team in its heyday probably spent more on competitions than its rivals, the Abingdon team never had unlimited finances with which to operate. Having said that, certainly during Stuart Turner's reign there was little doubt that he was never refused the right financial backing for worthwhile projects. Competition budgets would be assessed at a brief and informal annual meeting when the enthusiastic backing of people like John Thornley, John Cooper, and Alec Issigonis all helped to underline the growing importance of competition successes.

However, the very nature of the team's activities within a production factory also meant that it could not always conform to the everyday working routines, practices, and trade union rules. It was very useful, therefore, to have a strong ally in the factory management, especially if he was also the man who signed the cheques! The team benefited by just such a relationship with MG's chief accountant Norman Higgins, who was always available, day or night, to administer to its often involved financial dealings. Above all he was a genuine supporter of all that the Department did and, in good times and in bad, he was a wise counsellor and good friend.

Recce and practice

Moving now to the team plan for the 1968 Monte and the more detailed pre-start activities, before Christmas 1967 all of the drivers and co-drivers had completed a three-week recce and practice covering the Common Run and the Mountain Circuit.

For the initial recce and making of pace notes they used two completely standard Minis plus two recce Minis (old rally cars) fitted with standard engines. Standard cars were used for this long and tedious part of the recce because they were likely to be both more reliable and more pleasant to drive.

After this first recce, the cars were returned to the BMC agent in Nice, Garage Auber, where with the assistance of one Abingdon mechanic, the two former rally cars were fitted with Group II engines. These were brought down to Nice in the back of the two new Group II recce cars. Thus four Group II cars were then available for the final practising sessions and the two standard cars were available as spares. All of these cars were then left with Garage Auber in Nice to be re-prepared for the use of the ice note crews upon their arrival.

Time to admire the scenery for the recce crews on the 1968 Monte Carlo Rally

Co-drivers' harrowing tales of sordid living conditions, too much work, and no time for meals are somewhat dispelled by this shot of Henry Liddon, Mike Wood, and Paul Easter hard at work on an Acropolis Rally recce!

BMC 'Bible'

The following team instructions (known as the BMC 'Bible') for the 1968 Monte Carlo Rally are presented word for word as they were issued to the mechanics, drivers, co-drivers, the trade support teams and the ice note crews upon their arrival.

Loading for service vehicles

3 Princess 'R's, 1 Wolseley

Full Mini kits and running repair kits for 1800. One small Mini and 1800 running repair kit to be taken to Dover by one car and handed over to Castrol A.60 van (Risdon/Plummer).

Van

Full Mini kit and 1800 running repair kit for own use. Two small Mini kits to be handed on to B. Whittington and K. Bauman/A. Schultz service cars in Monte. One full 1800 kit and Mini running repair kit to be handed on to B. Moylan/D. Plummer 1800 service car in Monte. Four standard seats with covers to be exchanged for full recliners on arrival at Monte. Balance of fuel bags. One fuel drum and pump.

Transporter

One full Mini kit to cover Athens–Monte service points. One full Mini kit to be handed over to R. Stacey at Brindisi to cover Athens–Monte service points.

General

All service vehicles to carry Mini quick lift jacks, hydrolastic pumps, welding gear. Cars should carry four fuel bags each to Monte, the balance will be carried in the van and handed out before the Monte–Vals–Monte leg and the Mountain Circuit as per fuel plans.

Start points to Monte service schedule

Time of First Car	Point	Crew	Car
20 January			
01.30	Dover	Hall/Weal/Moylan	Wolseley
13.26	Boulogne (2nd time)	Wellman/Read	Princess 'R'
10.00	Brussels	V. Vernaeve	Mini, 1100
10.35	Madrid	Price/Wiffen	Princess 'R'
17.32	Belgrade	Green/Whittington/Stacey	A.60
21.55	Bayonne	Price/Wiffen	Princess 'R'
23.40	Poitiers	Hall/Weal/Moylan	Wolseley
21 January			
02.15	Bergerac	Brown/Legg	Princess 'R'
07.49	Millau	Risdon/Plummer	Castrol A.60
14.38	S. Flour	Brown/Legg	Princess 'R'
18.58	Padova	Vokins/Bradford	Transporter
20.20	Bourg	Dunlop	Transporter
21.28	Trento	Green/Whittington/Stacey	A.60
21.42	S. Claud	Hall/Weal/Moylan	Wolseley
22 January			
03.14	Alessandria	Vokins/Bradford	Transporter
05.11	Digne	Risdon/Plummer	Castrol A.60
08.13	Monte	Wellman/Reade	Princess 'R'
		Challis/Hogan	Van
		Price/Wiffen	Princess 'R'

Notes on service from start to Monte

1. Times shown on the service schedule are for the time of arrival of the first car. At most points, however, cars could be 20–30 minutes early.
2. The service cars at Monte will remove the roof racks from the Minis and replace the full reclining passenger seats with standard Mini seats and covers.
3. If service crews could organize a room and washing facilities at hotels near to service points this would be useful in case the crews have a lot of time in hand.

4. Refuelling and servicing on the public highway is prohibited on all itineraries between the arrival and departure points in Monaco and the towns of Menton and La Turbie. However, the organizers confirm that as in previous years servicing can be carried out in garages *off the public highway*. When the cars first arrive in Monte (and after the Monte–Vals–Monte leg) service will be at Esso Service Buckel, Moyenne Corniche, Cap d'Ail (tel. Cap d'Ail 82.23.80).

5. A. M. Almeida Comercio of Lisbon (tel. 320319) and Doucas in Athens (tel. 912.029) have been asked to provide garaging and servicing facilities at the start.

6. BMC Garages have been asked to provide service at the following points and display BMC signs: *Athens start* Larissa, Cuneo; *Lisbon start* Zaragova, Pamplona; *Dover start* Lille, Ostende, Auriac. If crews have time in hand and don't need service please stop and say hello to these people so that they will be encouraged to help us again in the future.

7. If the car is in trouble on the run to Monte drivers or mechanics should phone D. Watts in England (Abingdon 1946) who will fly out with spares to intercept the Rally.

8. It is prohibited for any competitor to park or stop on the highway or the roadside at a distance of less than 100 metres from a time or passage control or on arrival or starting point of the classification test. Mechanics must watch this point and as a general rule work before controls. On the Monte–Vals–Monte leg and the Mountain Circuit mechanics must be prepared to run through the control and work on the other side as well if necessary.

9. D. Green and R. Whittington will have to get the two Minis transferred from their passports on to those of the drivers.

10. D. Plummer to travel to Dover with T. Wellman/M. Reade to meet C. Risdon of Castrol (A.60 van). Take small Mini running repair kit and transfer this to the A.60 at Dover.

11. B. Moylan/D. Plummer to collect 1800 (LMO 391E) from Garage Auber on arrival at Monte and load their service kit which will be carried down in the van.

12. All barges to Monte will carry 2 x ¼ studs.

Fuel plans for Monte–Vals–Monte leg

Because of the very tight time schedules on the Common Run and the Mountain Circuit there is not time for the Rally cars to refuel at garages. Service crews therefore have to provide fuel from full bags (capacity 4 gallons) or from special fuel drums.

Place	Fuel for 4 x Minis and 1 x 1800 Bags per car	Total Bags	Crew
P. des Moilans	4 gallons from drum	20 gallons from drum	F
S. Auban	1½	7	G
Les Grillons	1½	7	A
Chamloc	2	10	C
S. Agreve	3	15	B
Burzet (1st time)	1½	7	D
Burzet (2nd time)	–	–	D
Vals les Bains	2	10	H
Aubenas	2	10	E
Bedoin	2	10	A
Orpiere	2	10	G
Gap	1½	7	C
Selonnet	6 gallons from drum	30 gallons from drum	F
Digne	2	10	B
Montferrat	2	10	A
P. C. Albert	1	5	E
Levens	1½	7	G
Monte	(see note below)		C + D

Crew	Total bags carried	Total fills
A	10	7 + 10 + 10 = 27
B	15	15 + 10 = 25
C	10	10 + 7 = 17
D	7	7
E	10	10 + 5 = 15
F	1 drum	50 gallons

Crew	Total bags carried	Total fills
G	10	7 + 10 + 7 = 24
H	10	10
	72	

If P. Browning has been unable to arrange the Monte service point at a garage, crews C and D should each bring all their bags full. This is to be advised at the final briefing.

Service points Mountain Circuit

TIME	PLACE	POINT	CREW	CAR
25 January				
19.13	Menton	Emergency	Moylan/Plummer	1800
19.36	Sospel	Control Start Stage 1	Wellman/Brown/Bradford	Princess 'R'
19.51	Moulinet	End Stage 1, Start Stage 2	Hall/Vokins/Weal	Wolseley
20.16	La Bollene	End Stage 2	Bauman/Schultz	Mini
20.42	Le Chaudan	Control	Price/Wiffen/Legg	Princess 'R'
21.16	St. Sauveur	Control Start Stage 3	Green/Reade	Princess 'R'
21.38	Beuil	End Stage 3	Whittington/Auber mex	Mini
22.11	Puget-Theniers	Control	Challis/Hogan	Van
23.21	Levens	Control	Moylan/Plummer	1800
23.50	La Bollene	Start Stage 4	Bauman/Schultz	Mini
26 January				
00.15	Moulinet	End Stage 4	Hall/Vokins/Weal	Wolseley
00.30	Sospel	Control	Wellman/Brown/Bradford	Princess 'R'
01.38	D414/N202	Control	Price/Wiffen/Legg	Princess 'R'
02.28	St. Sauveur	Control Start Stage 5	Green/Reade	Princess 'R'
02.51	Beuil	End Stage 5	Whittington/Auber Mex	Mini
03.23	Puget-Theniers	Control	Challis/Hogan	Van
04.33	Levens	Control	Moylan/Plummer	1800
05.02	La Bollene	Start Stage 6	Bauman/Schultz	Mini
05.27	Moulinet	End Stage 6	Hall/Vokins/Weal	Wolseley
05.42	Sospel	Control	Wellman/Brown/Bradford	Princess 'R'
06.19	Monte	Control	Price/Wiffen/Legg	Princess 'R'

Possible time in hand will be given to mechanics at the final briefing; generally most service points will be racing pit stops.

Fuel plans for Mountain Circuit

Fuel for 4 x Minis, 1 x 1800

Place	Available per car	Total available	Crew
Sospel	½ bag (emerg.)	2 bags	B
Moulinet	½ bag (emerg.)	2 bags	D
La Bollene	1 bag	5 bags	H
Le Chaudan	1½ bags	7 bags	A
St. Sauveur	1 bag	5 bags	C
Beuil	½ bag (emerg.)	2 bags	G
Puget-Theniers	6 galls. from drum	30 galls. drum	F
Levens	1 bag	5 bags	E
Le Bollene (2nd time)	½ bag	2½ bags	H
Moulinet (2nd time)	½ bag (emerg.)	2 bags	D
Sospel (2nd time)	2 bags	10 bags	B
D414/N202	1½ bags	7 bags	A
St. Sauveur (2nd time)	1 bag	5 bags	C
Beuil (2nd time)	½ bag (emerg.)	2 bags	G
Puget-Theniers (2nd time)	6 galls. from drum	30 galls. drum	F
Levens (2nd time)	1 bag	5 bags	E
La Bollene (3rd time)	½ bag	2½ bags	H
Moulinet (3rd time)	½ bag (emerg.)	2 bags	D
Sospel (3rd time)	1 bag	5 bags	B

Crew	Total bags carried	Total fills
A	7	7 + 7 = 14
B	17	2 + 10 + 5 = 17
C	10	5 + 5 = 10
D	6	2 + 2 + 2 = 6
E	10	5 + 5 = 10
F	2 bags + drum	30 + 30 = 60 galls.
G	4	2 + 2 = 4
H	10	5 + 2½ + 2½ = 10
	66	

Crews A, B and F should be able to refuel at the Garage between the first and second circuits.

Crew F should always have two bags at the ready in case two cars arrive at the same time and are unable to fill from the drum.

Notes for Ice Note Crews

1. When you arrive in Monte, go to Garage Auber and collect the four best recce Minis. Pick the best selection of tyres and make sure that you have a reasonable running repair kit, some tools and at least one petrol bag on board.

2. Check with Garage Auber to see whether the crews have left their pace notes there. If they are not there they will be at the Helder.

3. Come to the Helder, meet P. Browning, collect your pace notes and any final instructions. You should leave Monte during Saturday afternoon.

4. With so many tyres and so many options available this year, road reports are going to be very useful as a guide to Dunlops as to which are the most likely tyres to be used at the various points. Generally all the Dunlop vans will have available all the options, but they will only have sufficient wheels to offer about five options per car. Your road reports will therefore serve as Dunlops fitting up instructions.

5. Miss M. Smith will be on 24-hour phone duty at the Helder (tel. to be advised) to receive your road reports. You should give your first report on Sunday afternoon, followed by reports on Monday morning, on Monday afternoon and throughout Monday night. A final report on Tuesday morning would be useful.

6. We will have our own weather forcasting service in operation and Miss Smith will be able to give you local forecasts.

7. The Dunlop crews will phone the Helder to receive information regarding your road reports. When you call at the Helder on Saturday afternoon it is hoped that we can give you details regarding time and place for a rendezvous with the Dunlop crews in your area so that you can pass on your reports direct.

8. The crews will have written their pace notes to agree page by page with H. Liddon's master notes. (They have also been asked, where possible, to write their notes to agree line by line with the master notes.) This should assist with the ice note marking.

9. Notes should be marked as follows: underlined in yellow means road wet; underlined in dotted red means patchy ice or snow; underlined in solid red means ice and snow.

Instructions for Ice Note Crews, Monte–Vals–Monte leg

Note: Some of the less important road reporting will be covered by the service cars on their way to their service points.

Crew A A. Ambrose/Mrs. Ambrose (covering Tests 1 and 6)

Do road report from Monte along the route over Test 1 (S. Auban) to junction N211/N85. Give road reports on this section; do ice notes for Test 1 and hand these out at the start of Test 1.

After passage of the Rally go to Test 6 (Chorges) over the route in the reverse direction from Digne and give road reports on this section. Do ice notes for Test 6 and hand these out at the start of Test 6. Go to the end of Test 6 after Makinen and Aaltonen, and get their comments to pass on to Hopkirk and Fall. Return to Monte after the passage of the Rally.

Crew B D. Morley/Mrs. Morley (covering Tests 2, 3 and 7)

Go direct to S. Agreve and cover the route from here over Test 2 and over Test 3 to Vals-les-Bains. Give road reports over this section, do the ice notes for both Tests and hand them out at S. Agreve. Establish a phone contact between Burzet and S. Agreve so that latest reports from Burzet can be passed back. Burzet also to phone back reports from Makinen and Aaltonen for the benefit of Hopkirk and Fall.

After the passage of the Rally go direct to Test 7 (Levens), do the ice notes for this Test and hand them out at the start of the Test.

Return to Monte after the passage of the Rally.

Crew C J. Vernaeve/R. Freeborough (covering Test 4)

Go direct to Bedoin and cover the road reporting from here to Orpiere and over Test 4 (Col de Perty). Give road reports over this section, do the ice notes for Test 4 and issue these at the start of Test 4.

Return to Monte after the passage of the Rally.

Crew D G. Mabbs/D. Mabbs (covering Test 5)

Go direct to Test 5 (Gap), do the ice notes for this test and hand them out at the start of the Test. Go to Gap after Makinen and Aaltonen are through and get their comments to pass on to Hopkirk and Fall.

Return to Monte after the passage of the Rally.

Instructions for ice note crews, Mountain Circuit

All four crews should leave Monte early morning on Thursday.

J. Vernaeve/R. Freeborough to concentrate exclusively on ice notes for Tests 1, 2, 4 and 6 (Turini) handing these out at Sospel first time through. Advise Dunlop crew at Sospel of most likely tyre requirements and phone reports back to Helder thoughout the day. Assist with service at Sospel.

G. Mabbs/D. Mabbs do road reporting *en route* east of a line Nice to S. Sauveur. Advise Dunlop crews at all controls of likely tyre requirements and phone reports back to Helder. Generally float around in this area during the passage of the Rally to assist with service.

D. Morley/Mrs Morley to concentrate exclusively on ice notes for Tests 3 and 5 (S. Sauveur). Establish phone contact between Garage at Beuil and S. Sauveur so that after Makinen and Aaltonen have been through their reports can be passed back for information of Hopkirk and Fall. Advise Dunlop crews at S. Sauveur of likely tyre requirements and phone reports back to Helder throughout the day. Assist with service at S. Sauveur and if possible try and do a run over the Test between the first and second crossings.

A. Ambrose/Mrs. Ambrose do road reporting on route west of a line Nice to S. Sauveur. Advise Dunlop crews at all controls of likely tyre requirements and phone reports back to Helder. Generally float around in this area during the passage of the Rally to asssist with service.

Monte–Vals–Monte leg, road reporting by service crews

The following service crews are asked to phone Miss Smith at the Helder (tel. to be advised) with a report of road conditions on the way to their service points on the Monte–Vals–Monte leg.

D. Green/M. Reade to report on the road conditions along the Rally route from junction N211/N85 to Chamaloc.

T. Wellman/R. Brown/S. Bradford to report on the road conditions from Chamaloc over the Col de Rousset and along the Rally route to S. Agreve.

B. Moylan/D. Plummer to report on the road conditions from Bedoin along the Rally route in the reverse direction to Aubenas.

C. Bauman/A. Schultz to cover the section Vals-les-Bains to Aubenas and report on the road conditions.

General notes

1. Works crews who retire will be expected to assist with service or ice note work later in the event.
2. All fuel bags carried on Rally cars will be handed over to service crews on arrival at Monte.
3. Abingdon service crews will use their normal octagon signs. Dealers *en route* to Monte have been asked to display BMC signs.
4. It is the co-driver's responsibility to say how long can be spared at service points, to say what work is to be done and how much time there is in hand. In view of the large permutation of tyres available please be specific about your requirements and appreciate that the mechanics will not be as familiar as you are with recognising the tyres.
5. Service crews should consult the co-drivers in Monte over the most suitable places to set up their service points on the Monte–Vals–Monte leg and the Mountain Circuit.
6. Mechanics must study the fuel plans carefully in conjunction with the service schedules. Watch the fire risk with the inevitable spectators and always have a fire extinguisher at hand.

7. The four works Minis will always have preference for servicing over the 1800. The two Special Tuning 1800s should be given full works service if there's time and providing the supply of spares does not jeopardize the chances of Culcheth/Syer. Help private owners only if you have time.

8. The Culcheth/Syer 1800 will be running on a special mineral oil. This will be provided in plain Castrol tins marked B204. Each service car will carry at least one gallon tin.

9. On the way to their first service point on the Monte–Vals–Monte leg, W. Price/G. Wiffen/M. Legg collect the BMC transporter from Dunlops in Monte and drive it to the nearest garage to the control at Pont Charles Albert. Lock the transporter and leave the keys with the garage. These will be picked up by B. Moylan/D. Plummer when they arrive to cover this service point. There will be no Dunlop crew here so B. Moylan/D. Plummer assisted by D. Morley and D. Parker (Castrol) will have to unload the transporter and have all the tyres sorted. B. Moylan to bring the transporter back to Dunlops in Monte afterwards.

10. There should be no late night revelry until the Mountain Circuit is over!

11. Remember that our cars will be bunched closer together for the Mountain Circuit. An order of priority for work will be given at the final mechanics briefing.

12. Mechanics will be given their petrol money at the first mechanics briefing.

13. On the Monte–Vals–Monte leg, service cars should leave immediately the five works cars and the two Special Tuning 1800s are through.

14. On the Mountain Circuit most service crews see the Rally through several times at the same place. Study the routes so that you know from which direction to expect the cars.

15. On arrival at Monte for the first time all service crews should check over their kits and make sure that they have the correct number of fuel bags according to the fuel plans. Crews must do the same before the Mountain Circuit.

16. All mechanics must be at meetings at The Helder at *18.00 hrs. on Monday 22nd* and at *18.00 hrs. on Wednesday 24th.*

17. We have three electric impact drills to be used for wheel changing. For the Monte–Vals–Monte leg these should be carried by Wellman/Brown/Bradford, Hall/Vokins/Weal and Moylan/Plummer. For the Mountain Circuit they should be carried by Wellman/Brown/ Bradford, Green/Reade and Bauman/Schultz.

Tyres

As we have more tyres on this year's Monte than ever before, and no less than 13 permutations of tread pattern and studding, it is absolutely essential that everyone is thoroughly familiar with what the tyres look like and what they are called.

The following is a list of all the tyres available:

> R7 Green spot racers
> CR70 Green spot racers
> SP44 Dry compound, plain (un-studded)
> SP44 Wet compound, plain (un-studded)
> SP3 Studded
> SP44 Dry compound, part-stud, graded
> SP44 Wet compound, part-stud, graded
> SP44 Three-quarter studded, graded
> SP44 Full stud, graded
> SP44 Full stud, non-graded
> Chisels (long and short versions)
> Knobs (long and short versions)
> 'Hakka' specials

Graded tyres have their studs protruding at varying lengths in the tread pattern. These tyres are also studded with a greater number of studs in the trailing block of the tread pattern, thus graded tyres are 'directional' and have to be fitted on the correct side of the car.

To facilitate fitting, tyres will be colour coded as follows:

> All dry compound tyres will be painted BLUE.
> All wet compound tyres will be painted GREEN.
> Graded tyres with RED flash must be fitted to off-side of car.
> Graded tyres with YELLOW flash must be fitted to near-side of car.

(Tyre fitters will have to ensure that the colour flash appears on the *outside* of the wheel when the tyre is fitted.)

Service point for Timo Makinen on the 1968 Monte Carlo Rally, with an ominous pool of oil under the engine and the Castrol tin at the ready. Paul Easter (right) is probably checking his hand luggage to find the next flight home from Nice!

A very tough recce and practice schedule for Tony Fall and Mike Wood paid off with the crew's best Monte Carlo Rally result, fourth overall just behind Rauno Aaltonen.

Assistant competitions manager Bill Price (between Henry Liddon and Rauno Aaltonen) supervises a service point before the final Turini tests.

Rauno Aaltonen brilliant over the Turini, fast enough to win the touring category but not to catch the two leading Porsches.

Post mortem

After every event the crews were asked to complete and return a standard report form covering all aspects of the car's performance and the general team organization. These forms were not only circulated unedited within the Department but were also sent to the appropriate Heads of Department within BMC and to all the supporting trade personnel as applicable.

The following report is by Tony Fall and Mike Wood for the 1968 Monte Carlo Rally.

Competition Report Form
Type of car: Mini Cooper 'S' 1275 Mk. II Reg. No. ORX 707F. Group: 2. Event: Monte 1968. Date: 19–26 January. Driver: T. Fall. Co-driver: M. Wood. Approximate mileage covered: 4,750 km.

1. ENGINE

Power satisfactory?	Yes
Carburation and ignition satisfactory?	Flat spot on carbs when braking
Petrol consumption?	Approximately 180 km. per fill-up
Oil consumption?	Negligible
Grade of oil?	Castrol XXL
Oil pressure variation?	Nil
Any oil surge?	No
Max. revs used?	8,000 rpm
Any excessive pinking or running-on experienced?	No
Any overheating?	Yes, when reaching the top of Turini we overheated (100°C) with apparent loss of power
Any work carried out?	Carbs retuned at St. Sauveur by Den Green

2. TRANSMISSSION

Any noise?	Normal
Any vibration?	Yes. Drone at certain revs
Ease of change?	Very good
Clutch satisfactory?	Yes. Clutch slave cylinder replaced
Gearbox and final drive ratios satisfactory?	Yes

3. SUSPENSION AND ROADHOLDING

How was the general balance of the car?	Very good – the best yet with anti-roll bar fitted. Please fit to all future rally cars – except for very rough events
How was the steering?	Very good
Type of tyres fitted?	Racers and full popins non-graded
No. of tyre changes?	Don't know
What was the tyre wear and what pressures?	Wear normal, 40 lb front, 35 lb rear
Any road wheel trouble?	No
Any shock absorber trouble?	No
Any hydrolastic trouble?	No
Number of times suspension pressurized?	None

4. BRAKING

Brake material used?	Ferodo DS.11 front, VG.95 rear
Pedal pressure satisfactory?	Yes. A 425 lb per sq in. limiting valve was fitted. Please always fit this specification on my future rally cars. For my style of driving this proved very satisfactory
Did you experience brake fade and under what conditions?	No

Did you experience any serious wheel
locking?   No
How often were the brakes adjusted?   Twice
How often was brake material renewed?   Once

5. ELECTRICAL SYSTEM
Was the lighting satisfactory?   Yes
Did you have any fanbelt trouble?   Tightened once
Was the intercom satisfactory?   Very good but tended to fade after much use
Did you make any electrical repairs
or replacements?   One fuse kept repeatedly blowing. This was when
                                                 we used the centre spot lamps through the dip switch.
                                                 It was OK when we used them direct

6. BODY
Were there any leaks or draughts?   No
Was the seating satisfactory?   Yes. Please always use drivers' seat brackets on my
                                                 future rally cars
Type of seat fitted?   Full recliners to Monte then lightweight seats
Were the switches and minor controls
in easy places?   Yes
Were the seat belts satisfactory?   Yes
Make and type of seat belts fitted?   Irvin full harness
Did the screen wipers and washers
work satisfactorily?   New Trico washers very good
Was the heating, demisting and
ventilation effective?   Yes
Were the instruments accurate, visible
and well lit at night?   The rev counter was way out
Were rally clocks accurate?   Rally clocks again failed half-way

7. PREPARATION
Was the car handed over to you in
good condition?   Yes
Were the travel arrangements
satisfactory?   Yes
Were the tools, spares and equipment
sufficient and satisfactory?   Yes
Was the hotel accommodation
satisfactory?   Yes
Were the servicing arrangements during
the event adequate?   The best yet – after the pep talk at the end of the
                                                 Common Run!
How did your car compare with its
rally or commercial competitors?   Not fast enough to beat a Porsche!

Publicity

Publicizing the team's successes involved a considerable amount of pre-planning and was an important part of our activities. There was little point in achieving hard-earned and expensive success if the publicity and marketing value was not exploited.

Competition success advertising used to be a lot more popular than it is today and BMC would regularly take full-page display advertisements in the national daily newspapers to announce even a modest class win or a team prize. This would be backed up by carefully integrated support advertising by trade companies like Castrol and Dunlop. These advertisements would also be spread across the motor trade and motor sport publications.

Preparing the success advertisements was a complex business. Firstly, there would be a planning meeting with the publicity director, where we would try and forecast the prospects for success – whether outright victory was possible, a class or category win, the ladies' prize, or team award. Then we would meet with the advertising agency and help them to compile the appropriate copy to ensure that they had all the details correct. There was a very strict code of practice at the time which meant that you could not make sweeping statements such as 'BMC wins again' without qualifying exactly the achievements that had been claimed. You had to be very specific and give the correct, full name of the event and complete details of the awards that were publicized. There were some lively telephone calls between rival manufacturers on Monday morning if someone had not got it right!

The BMC Photographic Department based at Cowley would then be brought in to take reference shots of all the cars on the event before they left Abingdon so that these could be used in the advertisements, which had to be set up well before the start. Very seldom was there the time or opportunity to rush photos from events back to England for this purpose.

Usually there would only be time for a quick, last minute photo session around the local Abingdon lanes, the photographers using all of their skills to try and find a neutral background that would not look too out of place for the event. Inevitably there were some strange success advertising photos of cars supposed to be in exotic locations which were actually a blurred image of the car taken in the Abingdon car park.

Sometimes it was not possible to photograph all of the team cars and there was often a last minute panic to swap number plates, competition numbers, and even Austin and Morris badges when one car had to double for its team-mate. Most likely the cars did not even have their competition numbers or rally plates fixed until after scrutineering at the start of the event, so the photographers sometimes had to do some clever retouching, adding hand-drawn competition numbers afterwards.

A particularly interesting photo session took place prior to the 1966 Monte when, ever confident of achieving the hat-trick, a series of photos was taken at Abingdon before the start with the 1964 and 1965 winning cars alongside what, it was hoped, would be the third winner – one of the 1966 team cars. This picture had to be done three times in anticipation of any of the three team cars claiming victory this time!

Such were the achievements of the works Minis at the height of the team's winning form, it was significant that everyone left Abingdon for the event with such confidence that anything other than outright victory was considered almost a failure!

Cheeky publicity photo taken prior to the 1968 Monte Carlo Rally, showing the winning 1964 (left) and 1965 (centre) cars and what was hoped would be the winner in 1966. Three versions of the photo were taken with each of the 1966 team cars.

Leyland Rule

Towards the end of the 1968 came news of the British Leyland merger and the inevitable rumours that Competitions would be amongst the first departments to be closed down – after all, Lord Stokes had very quickly done the same thing with Triumph's Competition Shop at Coventry.

Being already committed at Abingdon to a massive programme for the London–Sydney Marathon, this was not the best of times to begin a battle for survival. After countless indecisive and time-wasting meetings, and in an atmosphere in which nobody knew to whom they were responsible, I finally managed to gain some guidance regarding the future.

The Department was to stay, but the programme of activities was to be drastically reduced to events in those countries where our winning could give the company both marketing and publicity benefits. This was fair enough, but Lord Stokes had put the emphasis on 'winning', which was now becoming a pretty tall order as far as the Mini was concerned. He had also expressed a significant dislike of rallies, principally because of their cost.

A lot of head-scratching went on as to the plans for the future, for on the rallying side the Mini clearly could only hope to win a few carefully selected events, and then only on reliability rather than in a straight fight against the opposition. Other manufacturers – Porsche, Alpine-Renault, Ford, and Lancia – were now committed to producing a new generation of rally winners by engineering performance options at the design stage, so that highly competitive homologated competition models could then be produced. Apart from fuel injection developments there was, quite frankly, not a lot more one could do with the Mini and there were few other cars in the Leyland range that offered serious competition potential.

Reluctantly, therefore, we were forced to reduce our rally programme and our financial commitments, by terminating contracts with Timo Makinen, Rauno Aaltonen, Tony Fall and their respective co-drivers Paul Easter, Henry Liddon, and Mike Wood. As Paddy Hopkirk was at that time on a two-year contract, he was retained to cover our small future rallying programme along with his new co-driver, the late Tony Nash.

It was sad to have to dismiss three of the best rally crews in the world but it cost a lot of money to retain a top rank team and, with the prospects of little success for the future, they were better off finding more competitive drives with rival teams.

Turn to racing

With little chance of rallying success with the Mini, as well as the need to trim the Department's expenditure and the indication that many of the British Leyland top brass favoured racing, there seemed little option for Abingdon but to try and make the switch from rallying to the race tracks for 1969. Thus a decision was made to prepare and enter a team of two Minis to contest the British Saloon Car Championship and one or two selected rounds of the European Championship. This would not only be considerably cheaper than rallying but it also meant that the company could cease the considerable financial support that they had previously given to other racing teams.

For 1969 the Abingdon team had to make the switch from rallying to racing, and the always spectacular John Rhodes was to lead the works Mini racing team.

The decision for Abingdon to go saloon car racing with the Mini may not have seemed right at the time, but then we did not deserve the continuing bad luck that had dogged the team in the preceding season. But I was sure that, knowing the background to that decision, there was no other alternative at the time that would have saved the Department from instant closure.

The final go ahead for the racing programme was made at a very late stage and when everyone was much more concerned with the preparation of the 1800s for the London–Sydney Marathon. There was very little time to get the new race cars built and properly tested before the first round of the British Saloon Car Championship at Easter. We had a lot to learn about setting up race cars and about fuel-injection engines, which had only been used once before on a rally car. Having decided that we would build our own engines at Abingdon,

The team had a tough job to beat the 1,300 cc Escorts and mix it with the more experienced Cooper Car Company team, led here by Gordon Spice at Crystal Palace.

we then found that British Leyland had very effectively terminated the production of many special parts which we and other teams had previously used.

To drive the racing Minis we signed John Rhodes and John Handley, while Steve Neal and Gordon Spice went to John Cooper's 1,300 cc Britax-Cooper-Downton team, which had decided to continue on its own without the British Leyland support that it had enjoyed for many years. I had tried to persuade John Cooper to run in the 1,000 cc class for the British Championship, for it was clear that a competitive 1-litre Mini stood a very good chance of success. John, I know, would have liked to have done this (even with one car) but I suspect that he was influenced by his two very forceful drivers, Neal and Spice, who were reluctant to drive in the small car class and were naturally keen to prove a point against the 'works' men, Rhodes and Handley! One man who did go the 1-litre route was Jim Whitehouse of Equipe Arden, who prepared and entered the car in which Alec Poole successfully pulled off the Championship.

Fated Brands opener

It was to the team's credit that, despite every problem, the two immaculate red and white race cars were rolled out of the transporter at the opening British Championship round at Brands Hatch in March. Already their performance at a Silverstone test day had shown them to be quite competitive. But the team's hard efforts were not to be rewarded.

The saloon car race was run in two heats and, in the first, John Rhodes's car was completely written off in a starting grid pile up. Then, in the closing laps of the second heat, John Handley went off the road and his car too was completely wrecked. With our shortage of cars and spare parts, we were banking on getting through the first meeting unscathed to allow more development work and testing before the next event, which was in only two weeks time. To have both cars destroyed first time out seriously hampered our plans and the morale amongst the rally boys in the team could not have been lower. The Leyland top brass were not impressed either!

But two more cars were hastily built and, completely untested, ran at the second round of the Championship at Silverstone. Although they went quite well, and Rhodes and Handley were able to split the two Cooper cars, neither Mini team could get anywhere near the faster Broadspeed Escorts.

The Abingdon boys found it hard to adapt to the atmosphere of racing, and even harder to have to come away from a meeting without the success which they knew was expected of them. Only a few people gave them the credit for making the difficult switch from rallying to racing in such a desperately short time and in such difficult circumstances. It was to their credit that they proved that they could build a racing Mini to within a whisker of the incredibly high standards set by the more experienced and established racing teams.

Silverstone's results set the pattern for the season, with the Abingdon and Cooper cars being always closely matched, neither team, however, being able to hold off the Escorts. Certainly both the Mini teams provided some of the closest and most entertaining racing of the season and I am sure that both lost out to the Ford opposition on many occasions because the Mini drivers were racing against each other and not racing together against the Escorts! In front of the pits where John Cooper and I could see what they were up to, the boys behaved themselves but I have seen some very alarming pictures of what was going on around the rest of the circuit!

This point was well demonstrated in the few European events which the Abingdon cars contested, where the team fared very much better against some formidable 1,300 cc opposition. There were worthwhile outings to the Six Hour Race at the Nürburgring and to Hockenheim, while in the 24 Hours race at Spa, John Handley and Roger Enever led their class all the way until the very last hour, when the car threw a rod. At least the season ended on a happy note when John Rhodes and John Handley scored a 1–2 race win at the Salzburg meeting in October.

TV rallycross provided most of the team's successes in 1969 with drivers John Rhodes, Paddy Hopkirk, and John Handley. Here the works Minis successfully fire mud in the eye of an unimpressed Graham Hill driving a Ford Capri.

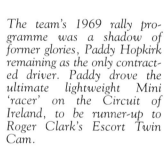

The team's 1969 rally programme was a shadow of former glories, Paddy Hopkirk remaining as the only contracted driver. Paddy drove the ultimate lightweight Mini 'racer' on the Circuit of Ireland, to be runner-up to Roger Clark's Escort Twin Cam.

Returning to contest the Tour de France in 1969, a fuel-injection car was entered for John Handley/Paul Easter (No 56) and a split-Weber carburettor car for Paddy Hopkirk/Tony Nash (No 57). Handley crashed but Hopkirk won the class.

Rallycross

The first regular televised rallycross events occurred during the 1969 season and the Abingdon team entered this new sport with some enthusiasm. Knowing of Lord Stokes's love of good publicity and saving the budget, I reckoned that rallycross offered the prospect of the best return for money with regular audiences of some million viewers.

After a few early trials and tribulations, our regular rallycross team of John Rhodes and John Handley became very competitive with fuel-injection Minis. We also signed up two of the leading privateers to run works cars – Brian Chatfield and Jeff Williamson. With the admirable support of these clubmen, the rallycross Minis provided Abingdon with most of our 1969 'wins' – albeit all four of our drivers were well and truly thrashed in the Championship by the unbeatable clubman, Hugh Wheldon.

Rallycross, however, was not only good for publicity and very good fun, it also provided the team with a useful free-for-all development programme which gave us the opportunity to try out all sorts of ideas that could have been of use for future rally programmes.

Rallying '69

The season's rallying programme was a mere shadow of the team's former activities and for our lone team of Paddy Hopkirk and Tony Nash it brought an endless run of 'seconds'.

On his 'home' event, the Circuit of Ireland, Paddy was runner-up to Roger Clark's 180 bhp Escort Twin Cam. Paddy drove one of the lightest Minis (GRX 311D) ever produced at Abingdon with all-aluminium panels and a totally seamless body. The car was meant to run with a fuel injection engine but at the last moment this was changed to a conventional head with the split Webers. This was the first time that Paddy had used a limited-slip differential and with 12-inch wheels and low profile tyres the car was a bit of a handful, and Paddy switched to 10-inch wheels for many of the stages and wished that there had been more pre-event testing. The car suffered with misfiring and had to have the carburettors changed; Paddy also damaged the front suspension on one stage and suffered failing oil pressure.

Tour revival

With the team's racing experience and rallying background, we felt that the Mini would go well in the revived Tour de France run in September. The event featured races at the Nurburgring, Spa, Rheims, Rouen, Le Mans, Magny Cours, Auvergne, Albi, and Nogaro, plus some 10 hill climbs. We entered two 1,275s – a carburettor car for Paddy Hopkirk and Tony Nash (OBL 45F) and a fuel-injection one for John Handley and Paul Easter (URX 560G). A third Group I car (URX 550G) was entered for Brian Culcheth and Johnstone Syer.

The new partnership of Handley and Easter worked well until the very last test when John went off the road when lying in a creditable sixth place overall. Paddy moved up to take over the 1,300 cc class win against considerable opposition. In the equally well-contested Group I category, Brian Culcheth (despite big end failure which nearly shook the car to pieces) had a battle royal with Julien Vernaeve's privately entered Mini, Brian finally coming off second best to the Belgian, mumbling something about some Group I cars being more standard than others! In all, the Tour was one of our more successful ventures, bringing back memories of the classic Hopkirk performance with the Mini in the 1963 event.

Mexico or bust

Another Marathon, this time the World Cup Rally from London to Mexico, completely overshadowed all other activities at Abingdon during the latter half of 1969 and early 1970. All efforts were now centred on the development and testing of the team of Triumph 2.5s and Maxis, although one Mini Clubman was entered for the *BBC Grandstand* sports programme for John Handley and Paul Easter (XJB 308F).

Along with the main team of Triumph 2.5s for the 1969 World Cup Rally to Mexico was this Mini Clubman for John Handley and Paul Easter. The brief for the Mini was to grab the headlines by 'leading to Lisbon' or bust, on the basis that it probably would not survive the trans-South American leg. This Mini, jinxed from the start, had no intention of ever getting to South America and blew up on the San Remo stage in Italy.

The plan was that the Mini would be the trail-blazer for the British Leyland team and John's instructions were 'to lead at Lisbon or bust', on the basis that it was doubtful whether the car would last all the way to Mexico. John put in a tremendous amount of testing and, with Paul Easter, tackled recce after recce in Europe. But that Mini entry seemed to be jinxed! Snow prevented the team from carrying out a complete recce and just about everything went wrong with the car before it reached the start line. On the event, elusive fuel starvation on the Yugoslavian stage caused problems, then the engine started to use gallons of oil and finally a piston blew to pieces on the San Remo stage in Italy.

For John Handley that was the last of a long line of unhappy drives with the team and I never ceased to admire the way in which this charming driver accepted the Mini's failures with such good humour. John had been driving Minis in competition longer than anyone, for he bought one of the very first 850s. Although best known for his Mini racing exploits, in his earlier days he did a lot of rallying, including three Montes, three Alpines, three Tulips, and the Tour de Corse. Later John served as the eternal 'number two' to John Rhodes and it was a classic partnership. While Rhodes usually set the pace, Handley's less forceful driving style made him the ideal man to follow through. That is not to say that it was always Rhodes who set the pace, and Handley, on a good day, and particularly in the wet, often proved unbeatable.

The World Cup Rally was the last event with the team for John Handley, a Mini enthusiast from the earliest days of the 850 who had partnered John Rhodes for racing and rallycross programmes.

Scottish finale

To try and restore faith in the Mini, Paddy Hopkirk took the World Cup Rally Mini Clubman (XJB 308H) off to the Scottish Rally in June, which was to be the works Mini's last UK appearance. Once Paddy had decided that he favoured 10-inch rather than 12-inch wheels, he and Tony Nash enjoyed a splendid Rally, just failing to catch the eventual winner, Brian Culcheth in a Triumph 2.5. Paddy was in tremendous form in what turned out to be his last drive for the team. Without begrudging the popular and talented Culcheth his first international rally victory, it would have been appropriate for Paddy to have finished with a 'win' to crown his glorious Mini rallying career.

Marathon Clubman

Included in the racing programme for the year was the lone Group VI Mini Clubman entry (SOH 878H) in the 1970 84 Hours Marathon de la Route at the Nürburgring. The car was an ultra-lightweight Clubman driven by John Handley, Alec Poole, and Geoff Mabbs to back up the main Abingdon entry – the Rover 3500. Both cars led the field by an incredible margin for some 12 hours before the Mini went out with a blown head gasket and the Rover was withdrawn with a bad prop-shaft vibration. The showing of the Rover against all the works Porsches was quite sensational and the European motoring press in particular reported in glowing terms how British Leyland had demonstrated the potential of a new competition car to replace the ageing Mini.

But nobody in the Abingdon team cared very much, for on the eve of the event they had been told that this trip was to be the swan song for the Competitions Department.

Final sorties

Two fuel-injection Mini Clubman cars had been prepared for the Spanish Sherry Rally to be run at the end of the year but these entries had to be hastily withdrawn, much to the annoyance of the enthusiastic local dealer.

Finally, BMC Australia had contracted Abingdon to provide two cars for Andrew Cowan and Brian Culcheth to drive in the Southern Cross and the Rally of the Hills in October and November. These agreements were honoured and these were the last two works Minis to be prepared. Andrew Cowan was to drive a completely new car (YMO 881H) while Culcheth drove a rebuilt RJB 327F.

When the cars arrived in Australia they were entered for a shakedown in an autocross near

Last works drive for Paddy Hopkirk was on the 1969 Scottish Rally, when he drove the ex-World Cup Rally Clubman to second place behind team-mate Brian Culcheth in the Triumph 2.5.

Sydney. Andrew played himself in on this, his first Mini drive, while Brian Culcheth, over-keen to impress the locals, made a rare mistake and rolled the car in front of all the BMC Directors. In fairness both cars experienced deflating tyre problems and, before the start of the two rallies, tubes were fitted to the tubeless tyres.

Brian Culcheth recalls the Southern Cross Rally:

> The roads were fabulous to drive on but I remember hitting some bumps so hard that I thought that my teeth were coming out. At the end of the first leg after a day and a night of tough rallying, I had a four minute lead over the local Holden opposition with Andrew in fourth place.
>
> Halfway through the night of the second leg my engine started overheating and we started to lose water but could not trace where from. We started to lose time and the lead due to constantly stopping to fill up with water. The mechanics finally traced the problem to a leak from the auxiliary radiator which had been damaged when the engine had moved on one of the bumps and dented the inlet pipe. The roll on the Sydney autocross had probably weakened the engine mountings.
>
> Soon after this, and just before the final control of the second leg, the head gasket went. I dragged the car to the end of the leg in fifth place with Andrew third behind the Holdens. We decided to take the car out of parc ferme (for which there was a three hour penalty) and fit a new head gasket. We re-started in 36th place, gave it maximum 'welly' but on the second stage of the final leg came across Andrew, who had crashed into a bank and broken a drive shaft. As we had no hope of finishing well placed, I offered Andrew our drive shaft but to our dismay for some inexplicable reason there was something different with the flanges or the couplings and they could not be exchanged. Both cars were therefore out of the event.

Moving on to the Rally of Hills:

> This Rally had a couple of unusual features. Firstly, there was an opening qualifying special

With the imminent closure of the Competitions Department on their minds, a despondent service point scene for the man who was to drive the last of the works Minis in Australia, Brian Culcheth (sitting on the boot), his regular co-driver Johnstone Syer and the author wondering where to look for a new job!

stage run in a valley with cars going down one side and up the other and this attracted a lot of spectators as you could see the cars for most of the stage. I was fastest again, beating the fancied Holdens with Andrew fourth.

The second feature was that the Rally ran in a figure-of-eight layout starting in the middle. Cars started in the order of their qualifying stage times but the entry was then split into two with one half of the field going north and the other south while the rest halt was back in the middle. Andrew and I exchanged notes halfway but this did not help very much because we had both been going in different directions!

I was fastest on every stage except one and on this we wrong slotted and lost eight minutes. There was a lot of suspicion and protests about the junction where we went wrong as some competitors said the arrow was missing and some said not. The real frustration about the whole thing was that had we gone down the 'wrong' road for another mile or so we would have rejoined the stage. Some people knew this and had carried on. The works Renault Gordini's took the event, I was fourth and Andrew crashed out.

I would have been so proud to have given the Mini its last international win!

While the Australian events were being run, British Leyland confirmed the official closure of the Competitions Department in October 1970. While the Special Tuning Department was to stay, everyone in the Competitions shop was made redundant although some were able to take production line jobs within the MG factory. The contracts for the remaining drivers and co-drivers in the team were not renewed. There was a fairly substantial sale of cars and parts. One policy instruction that epitomized the new management's attitude to Competitions was that all of the Department's records, the treasured build sheets for all the cars going back to the 1950s and the photo library were to be destroyed. One of my last jobs before I left Abingdon was to ensure that this instruction was ignored and that this material was saved!

Thus almost overnight, the most successful works Competitions Department of all time was disbanded. Amazingly, no-one from the senior management of British Leyland made any statement or took the trouble to speak to anyone within the Department about the closure. Indeed, it is understood that Lord Stokes himself never actually visited the Abingdon factory once when he was British Leyland Chairman. Much the same attitude was adopted when, 10 years later, the MG factory itself was closed down.

Of the many reasons given for the closure of the Competitions Department, clearly the saving of finance was the most logical, bearing in mind the serious financial situation of the Company at the time. Excluding the cost of taking part in the Marathons, which were financed from separate publicity budgets, the annual expenditure on Competitions at the time was around £200,000. Little consideration was given to the growing profits from the associated Special Tuning Department, which prepared cars for private owners and dealers and sold parts that were developed, tested, publicized, and homologated by Competitions. Their annual profit was approaching £100,000 and if their programme of expansion, improved publicity, and marketing had been carried through there was little doubt that very soon the two Departments could and should have been run as a self-financing operation.

Special Tuning did carry on and, mainly through the persistence of Brian Culcheth – who had an on-going PR contract with Leyland – a Team Castrol Triumph venture was resurrected to be followed by a limited rallying programme with the Triumph Dolomite, Marina, Allegro, TR7, and finally the TR7 V8. With the final closure of the Abingdon factory at the end of 1980, such competition activity that remained was then centred on Cowley almost exactly 25 years after the creation of the original BMC Competitions team at Abingdon.

It is more than sad that of all the assets which British Leyland inherited from BMC, Abingdon's competition team was one unit that did its job better than most and still had the resources and certainly the motivation to fly the flag and challenge the European opposition.

Without doubt the little red and white Minis had earnt the British motor industry a prestigious record of world-wide achievement that was the envy of every other manufacturer.

Mini Racing

When the Competitions Department was formed at Abingdon in 1954 its brief was to go racing as well as rallying. But for the early accidents involving MGs and Austin-Healeys in the tragic Le Mans and Tourist Trophy Races of 1955, that policy might well have continued. However, with the consequent bad publicity of BMC cars being linked with these tragedies, it was agreed that Abingdon should concentrate only on rallying. The racing activities were therefore contracted to private teams, which operated on BMC's behalf with financial support from Abingdon, but entered under their own name. Although this book is primarily concerned with the Abingdon-prepared rally Minis, the story of the cars raced by the Abingdon-supported teams forms a significant part of the Mini competition story.

A very early association was formed with the Cooper Car Company which, since, 1962, received varying degrees of financial and material sponsorship from Abingdon to represent BMC in saloon car races. That first year could not have been more successful, with John Love winning the British Saloon Car Championship with support from John Whitmore. The talented young Christabel Carlisle, in a Don Moore prepared car, often added not only a little glamour to the scene but often gave the menfolk a run for their money.

In 1963 the Cooper team were represented by John Whitmore, Tim Meyer, and, in several races, Paddy Hopkirk. Although the Championship fell to Jack Sear's giant Ford Galaxie, the performance of the Cooper cars was one of the most spectacular features of the British Saloon car scene. In Europe, Dutchman Rob Slotemaker won the 1,300 cc class of the European Championship in a Downton Engineering entered car.

The Cooper Car Company received financial support from BMC to race the Mini from 1962, when John Love (seen here chasing John Whitmore) won the British Saloon Car Championship.

John Whitmore with the 1963 Cooper team car being harassed by the fearless Christabel Carlisle.

Towards the end of that season a new Mini team made its mark – Team Broadspeed, run by Ralph Broad out of a small garage in Birmingham. The team was to regularly challenge Coopers with drivers John Handley and John Fitzpatrick.

Another new team appeared in 1964, run by Ken Tyrrell, who recalls his early Mini exploits:

> We ran two works-supported Minis in the European Saloon Car Championship in 1964, the year Jackie Stewart joined us in Formula 3. Then we had a further season in the following year in the British Championship.
>
> The cars were built by Cooper with the power units coming from Morris Engines. We raced them with Warwick Banks, John Rhodes, and Julien Vernaeve.
>
> Banks won the European title for us but it was touch and go and the gamesmanship in that 1964 season was quite fun. Our class was invariably poorly supported. At Mont Ventoux, one of three hillclimbs in the Championship, fewer than five cars turned up for the class so we were ineligible for points. You had to score in two or three hillclimbs so for the other rounds we had to take extra cars to make up the numbers. I even drove one myself.

While Christabel Carlisle rudely assaults Peter Harper's Sunbeam Rapier, Paddy Hopkirk scuttles out of danger!

Ken Tyrrell ran the works Mini team to contest the European Touring Car Championship in 1964, having previously run a car in the 1962 Brands Hatch Six Hours for John Whitmore and Bill Blydenstein.

In the Austrian hillclimb Banks was beaten by a local DKW and it was pointed out to me afterwards that he did not have the interior carpet that the rules required. It shames me to think about it now but I protested against this local privateer. But for that we would not have won the European Championship. I got a telling off from Stuart Turner – 'We never protest,' he said.

When we raced around the streets in Budapest we also took extra cars to make up the numbers but, with everyone in contention for the Championship regularly winning their class and scoring maximum points, it became apparent that the distance between each class winner and the rest of the cars in its class would become crucial.

As you had to cover 90 per cent of the distance to be classified as a finisher, we arranged for Warwick to win and for our other cars to hold back to only 91 per cent of the distance. We bewildered the officials by stopping in the pits and washing the cars. We had the spectacle of a terrible Wartburg beating one of the works Mini-Coopers.

The last event of the year was a four-hour race with refuelling at Monza on the old banked circuit. All the usual contenders looked like winning their class but Alan Mann, who ran the works Lotus Cortinas in the class above us, pulled a lovely trick to try and nail us. He entered an Anglia in our class and ear-marked one of the Cortinas to tow it for the entire race. The Anglia murdered us and Warwick was running second. But with two laps to go the Anglia ran out of fuel because the team had miscalculated its consumption by running so fast – and we won the European Championship.

Moving on to 1964, Coopers pinched John Fitzpatrick from Broadspeed and retained Paddy Hopkirk – their job was to contest the British Championship, where Fitzpatrick won the 1,300 cc class. Broadspeed had a roving commission, and with drivers Ralph Broad and John Handley this team campaigned in both home and overseas events.

For 1965 there was a further re-shuffling of drivers and a re-allocation of responsibilities to be shared by Coopers and Broadspeed, although the latter team had considerably less support, only receiving a small budget for parts from Eddie Maher at Morris Engines Branch.

Coopers signed John Rhodes (1,300 cc class) and Warwick Banks (1,000 cc class) for the British Championship. John Fitzpatrick went back to Broadspeed for a 1,000 cc drive, partnering John Handley in a 1,275 for European events. John Terry acted as a third team member on occasions. Warwick Banks finished overall runner-up in the British Championship (and 1,000 cc class winner) with John Rhodes in third place (and 1,300 cc class winner). The season was memorable for some splendid racing against the Superspeed Anglias of Mike Young and Chris Craft.

Broadspeed found the European challenge rather hard going and through lack of finance

One of Cooper's race cars was borrowed by the Abingdon team to take to Sebring in 1965 for Paddy Hopkirk and Warwick Banks to drive in the Three Hour Sedan Race. The car was handicapped by a faulty fuel system.

were unable to contest all of the Championship rounds. Nevertheless, on the few home events when the Broadspeed cars raced against the Cooper team, it was clear that Ralph Broad certainly had the advantage, causing some embarrassment.

The Abingdon team had regularly supported the Sebring 12 Hour Sports Car Race with entries for MGs along with the Austin-Healeys entered by the Donald Healey Motor Company at Warwick. For 1965 it was decided to also have a go at the Three Hour Saloon Car Race which took place the day before the World Sports Car Championship qualifier. Minis claimed three class wins, Warwick Banks and Paddy Hopkirk driving a Cooper works car leading the class and lying seventh overall when they lost time due to a blockage in the fuel lines between the twin petrol tanks. This meant that only one tank could be used, so they lost more time refuelling during the race. While a local privateer driving an ex-Broadspeed team car took the 1,300 cc class, Banks and Hopkirk finished seventh overall and runners-up in the class.

After the success of the Broadspeed cars there was some bad feeling when it was announced that for 1966 only Coopers would gain BMC support. Ralph Broad very quickly switched to Ford, leaving John Rhodes and John Handley to team up for Coopers. It was at this time that the Cooper cars were powered by Downton prepared engines rather than those provided by BMC's Engines Branch. John Rhodes had a creditable season and the year was also memorable for the performances of the Don Moore 1,000 cc car in Europe, driven by Paddy Hopkirk.

The Cooper team remained the same for 1967 with John Rhodes and John Handley contesting only the British events, both now running fuel-injection engines. The Superspeed Anglias of Mike Young and Chris Craft usually had the legs of the Minis but the Cooper team remained competitive thanks to reliability. The final round decided the Championship, with the honours going to the John Fitzpatrick 1,900 cc Anglia from John Rhodes.

Some significant intervention through the season had come from Steve Neal in a car prepared by Arden, Harry Ratcliffe in the British Vita entry, and from Gordon Spice, who impressed with the forceful driving of his own car.

John Rhodes

One name, however, that always stands out above all others in Mini racing is that of John Rhodes, whose arrogant style behind the wheel was in complete contrast to his charming and unassuming character.

John started racing seriously in 1960 with a new Formula Junior Cooper-BMC and, after many successes, became the leading driver with the Midland Racing Partnership. With this team he won 15 races including the Formula Junior Championship of Ireland. John had also shown himself to be a good long-distance sports car driver, having won the Guards 1,000 mile sports car race at Brands Hatch in an MGB with John Fitzpatrick in 1965. He had also driven sports cars at Sebring, Le Mans, and the Targa Florio.

Success never spoilt this popular driver, who remained a great enthusiast for all levels of motor sport, however humble the rewards. Certainly he will always be remembered as someone who drove Minis in a style that gave pleasure to everyone who saw him, while at the same time regularly proving that he was usually just that little bit quicker than anyone else.

Two teams received support from Abingdon for the 1968 season, which was to be the last in which BMC provided financial backing. Coopers, who again ran in the British Championship with 1,275s for John Rhodes and Steve Neal, and the British Vita team, managed by Brian Gillibrand, who ran 1,000 cc cars in the European series for John Handley and Alec Poole. Despite a season-long search for more power, which not even the combined brains of BMC's Eddie Maher, British Vita's Harry Ratcliffe, and Harry Weslake could resolve, the British Vita team won through on reliability if not on speed. John Handley won the 1,000 cc category and was also proclaimed the unofficial European Champion by gaining more points than other drivers. Coopers, on the other hand, had a hard season at home but John Rhodes collected the 1,300 cc class win. The season was remembered for the performance of Gordon Spice in the 1,300 cc Equipe Arden car.

The 1968 season had seen a closer liaison between Abingdon and their associated racing teams in terms of the exchange of technical know-how and the inter-play of drivers. Under British Leyland rule, however, the 1969 programme was to bring the termination of all support to these teams.

Finally, while the Abingdon-prepared cars were driven by Rhodes and Handley, for 1969 Coopers continued with the Cooper-Britax-Downton team, with Gordon Spice and Steve Neal. While the four Minis and Escorts had a pitched battle in the 1,300 cc class of the British Saloon Car Championship, the title was carried off by a private team, Equipe Arden, with Alec Poole driving the amazing 155 bhp 1-litre Mini-Cooper.

The works and works-supported racing Minis may not have achieved the award-winning outright victories of their rallying sisters but certainly their often giant-killing and always spectacular antics on the track remain exciting memories of saloon car racing in the 1960s.

The ever-forceful John Rhodes dominated the 1,300 cc class in the British Saloon Car Championship from 1965 to 1968.

Mini Mechanics

Those who are interested in the technical aspects of the works Minis will hopefully appreciate having all this information together in one chapter rather than dotted about in the story of the competition achievements. The most significant aspects of the preparation of the works 850, 997, 1,071 and 1,275 models are therefore reviewed in this chapter.

It should be emphasized that this technical information and the build sheets reproduced in the following pages were selected as typical examples of the works cars as they were prepared at Abingdon for the events of the period to be eligible for the Appendix J regulations applicable for each event. Since those days, there have been many changes in the regulations and a lot of new thinking on many aspects of tuning. This is, therefore, an historical report on Mini competition specifications as applied to the works cars of the period, not an up-to-date tuning guide for present-day owners. Particular reference is made to modifications that were first carried out by the Competitions Department which led to later modifications on the production model.

850 Mini-Minor

The early 850s were very little modified from the standard specification and, like the other rally cars of the day, preparation consisted mainly of the careful selection and assembly of standard components. There were very few special parts available at the time and the cars had, in any case, to be very close to standard production specification when running in the touring car category.

There was little development in the early days apart from experiments to put right known weaknesses or faults that continually occurred on events. As the 850 could really only hope to compete for class awards, and its superior handling alone often made it reasonably competitive against the class opposition of the day, there was no need for a dramatic increase in performance, although the drivers, of course, were always seeking more power. Mechanical reliability was the priority, coupled with suspension durability for rough road events.

The early power units were hand-built at Abingdon with transmissions being provided ready-built from Longbridge. There was no test bed available and no rolling road to check performance. Indeed, testing the cars was pretty elementary by modern standards, recalls Cliff Humphries, who was Abingdon's chief engine technician: 'We took the cars up the road alongside the local golf course by the factory, and gave them full stick along the flat, starting opposite an AA box. If they pulled 5,000 rpm in top by the end of the straight, that was good enough. If they pulled any more it was probably a faulty rev counter!'

The first 850s used Weslake modified cylinder heads, mainly because Longbridge had a long-standing engine development contract with that company and any work done by Abingdon could be conveniently charged on that budget. Towards the end of the first year of competition with the Mini, an evaluation exercise was carried out on various cylinder heads which subsequently led to the use of Don Moore modified heads for all future works 850s.

Speedwell valves of improved material but standard dimensions were used and the com-

The build sheet for TMO 559 is reproduced in this chapter as representative of the early works 850 Mini-Minors.

pression ratio was increased to 9:1. Carburretor tuning was quite basic, but on the later Don Moore heads a special inlet manifold was used, the carburretor flange being cut off at the manifold and turned upside down to improve the flow.

The standard camshaft was retained on early cars but later Derek Frost of Engines Branch produced the 630 profile, the same cam form as the 148 camshaft later used on the Mini-Cooper 'S'. The standard crankshaft and flywheel assembly were used but carefully balanced. Because the standard single crankcase breather used to discharge a lot of oil, this was replaced by twin breathers.

Clutch oil seals caused many problems on the early 850 and 997 cars and modified oil seals with steel casings and retaining plates did a lot to solve these troubles. Solid steel timing chain sprockets were later introduced along with idler gears made from a solid forging. Early gearbox casings were in magnesium and, when these were replaced by aluminium ones on the production car, Abingdon acquired most of the magnesium stock and these were always used on the rally cars.

The suspension on the 850 suffered mainly from shock-absorber failures and breakages of the shock-absorber mounting brackets. Competition specifications did much to improve the life of the units and the modified front brackets, designed and developed at Abingdon, were later incorporated in the production car. The same applied to the replacement of the earlier bushes in the rear suspension swing arm with needle roller bearings.

The following build sheet is for one of the early works 850s (TMO 559) built for the 1959 RAC Rally and driven by 'Tish' Ozanne. Power output would have been around 42 bhp.

Check compression ratio 9 to 1
Fit Weslake gas-flowed cylinder head
Petrol test valves
Check oil way not breaking through cylinder head
Fit Speedwell valves
Fit Speedwell valve springs
Fit air cleaner element
Fit E3 needles
Fit Sprite dashpot and needles
Fit 0.070 in. dampers
Cut off and solder carburettor butterfly screws
Set tappets 0.015 in. hot
Strip and overhaul carburettor
Fit 74 degs thermostat

Fit radiator blind
Fit balanced crankshaft and flywheel assembly
Fit standard camshaft
Fit Vandervell bearing, white metal (mains) lead indium (big ends)
Line up connecting rods
Fit Reynolds timing chain
Fit new oil filter element
Match manifolds to ports
Check pistons and rings
Fit N3 fixed top plugs
Fit HA12 coil
Fit dual crankcase breathers
Fit 10 lb radiator cap and wire on

Check dynamo fixing and fit flat washers to bolts
Check starter motor
Overhaul distributor (type D3A/H4-LT-18047)
Check battery and charge
Fix washer to dipstick and paint white
Fit guide tube to dipstick hole
Check for oil leaks
Fit magnesium sump casings
Fit modified bottom end
Fit selected differential assembly
Fit oil seal retaining plate to flywheel
Fit standard fan
Fit hard engine mounting rubbers
Fit modified engine-steady ferrule
Check engine number plate
Fit standard primary gear
Check oil pressure to 55 lb maximum
Check clutch adjustments to 0.060 in.
Modify accelerator pedal for heel-and-toe operation
Blank off the off-side half of the front grille
Cut front grille down the centre
Fit special clutch oil seal
Check drive shafts and grease
Fit strengthener plate to the differential housing
  for exhaust bracket
Seal all holes in the clutch housing
Remove nylon pad and spring from gear lever
  linkage
Overhaul complete front suspension
Overhaul complete rear suspension
Fit new shock absorbers all round
Fit latest type top rubbers to rear shock absorbers
Fit competition exhaust system
Check all exhaust hangers
Modify rear exhaust hanger
Modify front exhaust hanger
Grease all round
Remove over riders
Increase ride height front and rear with 0.100 in.
  washer
Modify front shock absorber bracket
Fit latest type front suspension tie rods
Check and overhaul complete steering
Modify steering wheel nut
Track front wheels (toe out $\frac{1}{16}$ in)
Track rear wheels (toe out $\frac{1}{8}$ in)
Check camber and castor angles
Overhaul front and rear brakes, thoroughly clean
  wheel cylinders
Fill brake system with heavy duty fluid
Fit AM4 linings and bed in
Fit 250 lb limiting valve
Cover brake pipes where necessary
Modify handbrake to fly-off operation
Waterproof front and rear brake back plates
Remove petrol tank and flush out
Blank off breather pipe and vent cap
Protect fuel gauge tank attachment wires

Fit latest type petrol pump and clean filter
Fit Zenith filter
Fit quick-release petrol cap
Check laminated windscreen fitted
Fit GB sign to rear
Fit stick-on registration letters
Fit Tudor windscreen washer
Fit Elopress
Fit small fire extinguisher
Fit Scotchlite tape to rear bumpers and door shuts
Fit map stowages division to near-side door
  pockets
Fit grab handle above near-side door
Fit Union Jacks on each side of the car
Check doors for draughts and waterproof
Water test car and seal as necessary
Make provision for fitting rally plates
Fit perspex side and rear windows
Fit bonnet safety strap
Modify bonnet release
Fit protection for door lock catch
Blank off side vent in heater
Fit clips to heater duct pipes
Modify heater air duct vents
Fit padding to door pockets and pillars
Fit passenger's Barnacle mirror
Blank off all holes in bulkhead
Fit wind operated horns
Fit passenger horn button
Fit rubber mats to front of car with fasteners
Modify sliding window catches
Fit wooden battery cover
Fit under-wing sealing plates
Fit Ecurie Safety First transfers
Check recommended heater switch fitted
Fit speedometer with trip and magnified apertures
Fit illuminated clocks
Fit Weston revolution counter and illuminate
Fit oil and water pressure and water temperature
  gauge and illuminate
Supply three ignition keys
Supply two boot lid keys
Check instruments and controls
Fit latest type Butler navigation lamp
Check speedometer for accuracy
Fit two-pin plug on near-side parcel shelf
Fit two-pin plug on near-side of the handbrake
Fit driver's demister bar
Fit 700 LHD headlamp units
Fit 494 reversing lamp
Fit rheostat switch for driver's instruments
Fit rheostat switch for Smith's clocks
Focus lamps
Fit single-speed wiper motor
Renew wiper blades
Fit headlamp flick switch
Fit plastic covers to headlamps
Fit covers for fog lamps

Fit Duraband tyres and valve caps
Fit stowage for tyre gauge and brake adjusting
  spanner
Stow modified jack
Stow wheel-brace
Change clutch springs to latest type
Check sealing for carburettors
Check sealing for cylinder head
Fit paddings to both door locks
Check driver's and passenger's seat
Check seat belts
Check sun visors

Check stop clocks
Stow spare headlamp bulbs
Fit two fog lamps
Stow two spare wheels
Fit sump guard
Fit latest type shock absorber rubbers
Use castellated nuts and split pins on ball joints
Check sub frames for working loose
Fit air cooling to front brakes
Fit modified rear pivot shafts
Clean car inside and out
Wash and polish, repaint as necessary

997 Mini-Cooper

In comparison to the 850, the first Mini-Cooper gave such a vast improvement in performance that there was little need for much engine modification from the standard specification. The rally cars produced around 70 bhp, they proved a lot more reliable than the 850s, and the same suspension modifications that were proved on the 850 could be applied to the new model. Some experiments were carried out using the 731 in place of the 948 camshaft and, with a rev limit of 7,000 rpm, the 948 was preferred as it gave better low-speed torque.

Starting with the 997 Mini-Cooper, Abingdon began to carry out its own engine development programme with Cliff Humphries working in close co-operation with Eddie Maher, chief of the Engines Branch at Coventry.

A more detailed build sheet for the works cars was instituted at this time, as is shown by the following sheet for the car (977 ARX) built for Rauno Aaltonen to drive on the 1963 Monte Carlo Rally.

Cylinder block

Bore size	Standard	Clutch	Standard, bonded and riveted facings
Fume pipes	Standard	Release bearings	Standard
Camshaft	Standard	Camshaft bearings	Standard
Crankshaft	Standard, balanced with Deva bush	Crankshaft bearings	Standard
Flywheel	Standard, balanced	Connecting rods	Standard, lined up

Specification of the works 970 Mini-Cooper is given with the build sheet for 977 ARX.

Pistons	Standard
Oil pump	Standard Hobourn
Oil pump drive	Standard, latest type
Camshaft gear	Steel
Crankshaft gear	Steel
Timing chain	Reynolds
Core plugs	Standard
Dip stick and washer	Standard
Oil filter element	Standard
Distributor	Model 40819
Ignition setting	5 degs BTC
Engine rubbers	Standard
Engine number plate	Check with log book
Idler gear	Solid
Primary gear	Deva bushed
Oil pressure	Check
Sump and protection	RAF type guard
Sump plug	Standard
Oil cooler	None

Cylinder head

Type	Standard, do not polish
Compression ratio	Check 9 to 1
Combustion space	31.1 cc
Exhaust valves	Standard
Inlet valves	Standard
Top collar	AEA 402
Bottom caps	AEA 403
Valve spring inner	AEA 401
Valve spring outer	AEA 311
Thermostat	74 degs
Exhaust manifold	Match to ports, do not polish
Inlet manifold	Match to ports, do not polish
Plugs	N3
Rocker assembly	Standard

Transmission

Gear ratios	Standard
Gear material	Special EN36B (second gear), rest standard
Type of transmission	Special straight cut
Selector bars and forks	Standard
Gear lever	Fit anti-rattle
Drive shafts	Standard
Differential ratio	4.1 to 1
Clutch adjustment	Standard

Carburettor

Type	Twin 1½ in. SU
Modified	No
Needles	MME
Dash pot springs	Red
Dampers	Standard
Air cleaners	None
Choke cables	MGB type
Heat shields	None
Heat collecting box	Yes
Induction	Standard
Linkage	Peg and fork type
Accelerator cable	Special nylon insert type
Float level	Fit extensions
Vibration	None

Chassis

Front struts	Standard with packing washers
Rear struts	Standard van type with 0.100 in. washer
Anti-roll bar	None
Wishbones	Standard
Bump rubbers	Standard
Front shock absorbers	Special Armstrong
Rear shock absorbers	Special Armstrong turned down to clear body
Torsion bar	None
Chassis strengthening	None
Chassis modifications	Fit bump rubbers for rear swing arm
Engine mounting brackets	Standard
Shock absorber mounting	Special brackets at front
Bumpers	Remove overriders
Jacking points	Standard
Height of car	Raise to maximum
Front hubs	Overhaul
Rear hubs	Overhaul
Stub axles	Overhaul
Towing eyes	Special U bolts fitted to rear subframe
Radius arms	Standard
Tie rods	Standard

Cooling System

Fan	Standard 16 blade
Radiator	Standard
Water pump	Standard
Hoses	Check
Fanbelt	Fit stretched and spare
Radiator blind	Fit Moray type
Blanking	Fit muffs
Anti Freeze	Castrol
Radiator cap	Standard
Header tank	None
Temperature gauge	Fit capillary type
Radiator drain plug	Check

Electrics

Dynamo	C40 with cast iron plates

Starter	Standard race tested
Coil	HA12 race tested
Regulator box	RB310 race tested
Battery and fixing	Standard, reverse battery and lengthen cable
Dynamo pulley	Standard
Waterproofing	Silicone grease
Wiper motor	Single speed race tested with special wheel boxes
Wiper motor switch	Standard
Wiper blades and arms	Renew
Headlamps	Special
Headlamp bulbs	White vertical dip
Fog lamps	Pair 700 lamps
Fog lamp switch	One for each lamp
Fog lamp bulbs	White transverse
Long range lamps	One 576 fitted central
Long range switch	Yes
Long range bulb	White axial
Reverse lamp	576 fitted to boot lid
Reverse lamp switch	Special with indicator incorporated
Reverse lamp bulb	Standard white
Tail lamps	Standard
Stop lamps	Standard
Flasher lamps	Standard
Flasher switch	Standard
Two-pin plugs	Fit one to dash panel
Navigator's lamp	Flexible Butler type
Demister bar	One on driver's side
Lamp covers	Fit to all front lamps
Horns	Twin Mixo Minors
Horn buttons	Standard for driver, foot operated for passenger
Panel lights	Switch rheostat type
Panel light rev counter	Standard internal
Panel light speedometer	Standard
Panel light clocks	External
Ammeter	None
Headlamp flick switch	Yes
Brake light switch	None
Tail light switch	None
Screen washer	Electric Tudor
Battery protection	Check terminal rubbers

Steering

Column	Standard
Steering wheel	Wood rim
Steering wheel nut	Check
Rack and pinion	Standard
Steering arms	Standard
Track arms	Standard
Track wheels	$\frac{1}{16}$ in. toe out
Camber and castor	Check
Lubricate	All points
Lock nuts	Fit castellated nuts and split pins
Steering ratio	Standard
Adjustment	Check
Line up steering wheel	Yes

Exhaust

System	Competition type
Silence	Special
Hanging brackets	Standard
Front support bracket	Standard

Petrol system

Tank	Fit twin tanks
Tank fixing	Standard
Fuel gauge	Standard
Bumps	Standard with protection
Pipes	Standard
Tank fillers	Quick release
Tank protection	Wood strips for studded tyres
Pipe protection	Cover with metal channels
Leaks	Check
Petrol filters	Check
Tank breather	Check vents in the caps and increase holes

Body

Driver's seat	Microcell
Driver's seat belts	Britax lap strap and diagonal
Passenger's seat	Microcell recliner
Passenger's seat belts	Britax full harness
Windscreen	Laminated
Windscreen washers	Tudor
Sun visors	Standard
Perspex windows	Fit full set
Snow deflector	None
Perspex heat shield	Fit inside windscreen
Rear window wiper	None
Demist	Fit panel to rear window
Heater	Standard
Front and rear wings	Standard
Doors	Standard, check for draughts
Bonnet	Lightened
Bonnet fixings	Fit straps
Safety catches	None
Crash bars	None
Window fixings	Standard
Carpets	Fit full front carpet and secure
Trim	Remove as necessary
Map stowage	Divide passenger's door pocket
Parcel shelf	Standard
Paddings	Fit to doors and locks

Facia	Make and fit special	Safety gauges	Fit water temperature and oil pressure
Switch positions	Arrange as instructed by driver	Ignition key	Check number and fit spare
Registration numbers	Fablon stick on	Boot key	Check number and fit spare
GB plate	Fablon on rear		
Competition numbers	Paint on		
Elopress	Fit bracket		
Fire extinguisher	Fit bracket		
Driving mirror	Standard		
Passenger's mirror	Barnacle		
Petrol can stowage	None		
Kit stowage	As instructed by driver		
Spare wheel stowage	Extra clamp for two spares		
Scotchlite tape	Rear bumper and door shuts		
Grab handles	Fit above passenger's door		
Safety Fast emblem	Yes		
Union Jacks	Yes		
Rally Plates	Prepare for fitting		

Tyres and wheels

Tyres	Four SP Dunlops in car
Tubes	Yes
Spare wheels	Two SP with spikes in boot
Valve caps	Check
Balance	Yes

Brakes

Master cylinder	Standard
Master cylinder mountings	Standard
Wheel cylinders	Standard
Front calipers	Standard
Front pads	DS11
Rear shoes	VG95
Bed brakes and fade	Yes and fade spare set
Pipes	Run inside car and protect where necessary
Fluid	Heavy duty Lockheed
Limiting valve	Standard
Air cooling	None
Servo	None
Waterproofing	Check back plates

Controls

Accelerator pedal	Modify for heel and toe
Accelerator pedal brackets	Modify
Accelerator cable	Standard
Brake pedal	Standard
Pedal box	Standard
Clutch pedal	Standard
Handbrake lever	Modify to fly-off type
Handbrake cables	Check quadrant and grease

Kit

Jack	Modified
Plug carrier	None
Spare coil	None
Wheelbrace	Two modified
Tyre gauge	Clip in cockpit
Route card holder	Yes
Chains	Yes
Oil stowage	Yes

Instruments

Speedometer	Special KPH calibrated
Trip instrument	Fit magnifier
Cables	Standard
Clocks	Twin Heuer
Rev counter	Smiths electrical

1,071 Mini-Cooper 'S'

The first Mini-Cooper 'S' gave as big an advantage over the 997 Cooper as that model did over the 850. The 1,071 proved that with only basic conventional tuning, lightening, balancing, and careful assembly, it could win outright the rallies of the day.

The works cars produced around 92 bhp but, with a smooth power curve, the standard transmission assemblies were still capable of standing up to hard rally work. The suspension too gave little trouble. The only major modification with this model was the replacement of the standard wheel hub bearings with Timkin roller bearings. These later came into use on the standard production car, as did modified steering arms.

This is the build sheet of the famous 1,071 Mini (33 EJB) which Paddy Hopkirk drove to victory on the 1964 Monte Carlo Rally.

Cylinder block

Bore size	Standard	Crankshaft	Standard balanced
Fume pipes	Fit two	Flywheel	Special balanced
Camshaft	Standard	Clutch	Special diaphragm type
		Release bearing	Standard

Twin-carburettor power unit of the 1,071 Mini-Cooper 'S'.

Camshaft bearings	Standard	Engine rubbers	Standard
Crankshaft bearings	Standard	Engine plate	Check with log book
Connecting rods	Standard	Idler gear	Standard
Pistons	Standard bore, flat top	Primary gear	Standard
Oil pump	Standard	Oil pressure	Check (80 lb)
Oil pump drive	Standard	Sump and protection	RAF type sump guard
Camshaft gear	Standard	Sump plug	Standard
Crankshaft gear	Standard	Oil cooler	MGB type with special flex pipes wire locked
Timing chain	Standard		
Core plugs	Fit retainers		
Dip stick and washer	Blue dip stick end		
Oil filter element	Standard		
Distributor	Race tested		
Ignition setting	7 degs BTDC		

Cylinder head

Type	Standard cleaned only
Compression ratio	Maximum given with pistons 10.5 to 1
Combustion space	Check (21.3 cc)

Paddy Hopkirk's Tour de France and 1964 Monte Carlo-winning car (33 EJB) is chosen for a typical works 1,071 specification reprinted here.

Exhaust valves	Standard
Inlet valves	Standard
Top caps	Standard marked W
Bottom caps	AEA 654
Valve spring inner	AEA 652
Valve spring outer	AEA 524
Thermostat	Fit wax type
Sealing points	Fit bracket as instructed
Exhaust manifold	Standard
Inlet manifold	Standard
Plugs	Champion N4
Rocker assembly	Standard

Transmission

Gear ratios	Standard
Gear material	Standard
Type of transmission	Spur cut gears
Selector bars and forks	Tighten
Gear lever	Check for rattle and easy movement
Drive shafts	Standard
Differential ratio	4.1 to 1
Clutch adjustment	Standard

Carburettors

Type	Twin 1½ in. SU
Modified	Fit float chamber extensions
Needles	MME
Dashpot springs	Red
Dampers	0.070 in.
Air cleaners	None, fit trumpets
Choke cables	Standard
Heat shields	None
Heat collecting box	Yes
Induction	Standard
Linkage	Fork and peg
Accelerator cable	Nylon insert, special check on alignment
Float level	Check with extensions
Vibration	Special check

Chassis

Front cones	Standard
Rear cones	Standard
Front struts	Standard
Rear struts	Standard
Anti-roll bars	None
Wishbones	Standard
Bump rubbers	Fit extra to rear
Front shock absorbers	Special competition
Rear shock absorbers	Special competition, turn down the tops
Chassis modification	None

Engine mounting brackets	Standard
Shock absorber mounting	Fit special brackets to the front
Bumpers	Standard
Jacking points	Standard
Height of car	Standard
Front hubs	Standard, overhaul
Rear hubs	Standard, overhaul
Stub axles	Standard
Towing eyes	Front and rear
Overriders	Standard
Radius arms	Standard
Tie rods	Split pin nuts

Cooling System

Type of fan	Four bladed
Type of radiator	16 gills per inch
Water pump	Standard
Hoses	Standard
Fanbelt	Special and fit spare to engine
Radiator blind	None
Blanking	Blank off half off-side and fit muffs
Anti freeze	Yes
Radiator cap	13 lb/in^2
Header tank	Standard
Temperature gauge	Standard
Radiator drain plug	Wire lock
Flush system	Yes

Electrics

Dynamo	C40-22746 28 amp with bearings
Starter	Standard race tested
Coil	HA12
Regulator box	To suit dynamo
Battery and fixing	Standard battery turned round with larger terminal covers and insulate
Dynamo pulley	AEA 535 large
Waterproofing	Maximum
Wiper motor	Twin speed maximum wipe, not wired through ignition
Wiper motor switch	Twin speed
Wiper blades and arms	Standard
Headlamps	Special fitted with iodine bulbs
Headlamp bulbs	Iodine with dip to two 576 fog lamps
Fog lamps	Two 700 latest type
Fog lamp switch	One for each lamp
Fog lamp bulbs	White
Long range lamps	One 576 fitted central
Long range switch	Three position wired with main beam
Long range bulb	White axial
Reverse lamp	One 576 fitted to boot lid

Reverse lamp	
switch	Special with indicator
Reverse lamp bulb	White transverse
Tail lamps	Standard
Stop lamps	Standard
Flasher lamps	Standard
Flasher switch	Standard
Two-pin plug	One fitted to facia
Navigator's lamp	Flexible Butlers type
Demister bars	None
Lamp covers	All front lamps
Horns	Twin Mixo Minors
Horn buttons	Standard for driver, foot button for passenger
Panel lights	Standard
Light for rev counter	Standard
Panel light for speedometer	Standard
Panel light for odometer	Special
Panel light for clocks	External
Ammeter	None
Headlamp flick switch	Yes
Brake light switch	None
Tail light switch	None
Screen washer	Tudor electrical
Headlamp washers	Tudor electrical
Starter switch	Fit push button control
Roof lamp	Fit one with 700 iodine bulb

Steering

Column	Standard and check bottom clamp bolt
Steering wheel	Wood rim
Steering wheel nut	Tighten and check
Rack and pinion	Standard
Steering arms	Standard
Track arms	Split pin nuts
Track wheels	1/8 in. toe out
Camber and castor	Check
Lock nuts	Fit castellated nuts and split pins
Steering ratio	Standard
Adjustment	Check
Line up steering wheel	Yes

Exhaust

Type of system	Special competition latest type
Type of silencer	Special competition latest type
Hanging brackets	Special
Support bracket at front	Special

Petrol system

Tank	Fit twin tanks
Tank fixing	Standard
Fuel gauge	Standard
Pumps	Fit twin pumps with protection
Pipes	Cover where necessary
Tank fillers	Quick release
Tank protection	Yes, both tanks
Pipe protection	Yes
Heat protection	None
Petrol filters	Check and clean
Tank breather	Check hole in caps

Body

Driver's seat	Microcell
Passenger's seat	Microcell recliner
Seat belts	To be specified by crew
Windscreen	Laminated heated Triplex
Windscreen washer	Tudor with de-icing fluid
Sun visors	Standard
Perspex windows	Yes, side and rear
Snow deflector	None
Perspex heater shield	Yes, inside windscreen
Rear window wiper	None
Demist	Modify ducts as instructed
Heater	Latest type
Front wings	Standard, modify for lamps
Rear wings	Standard
Doors	Standard, check for draughts
Panels	Standard
Bonnet	Standard
Bonnet fixings	Fit safety strap
Safety catches	None
Crash bar	None
Window fixings	Standard
Carpets	Fit full front
Trim	Remove as necessary
Map stowage	Divide near-side door pocket
Parcel shelf	None
Padding	Fit to doors and locks
Facia	Special
Switch positions	Arrange as instructed
Registration numbers	Fablon stick on
GB plate	Fablon stick on
Competition numbers	Painted
Elopress	Fit one
Fire extinguisher	Fit one
Driving mirror	Standard for driver, Barnacle for passenger
Petrol can stowage	None
Spare wheel stowage	For two spiked tyres
Scotchlite tape	Rear bumper and door shuts

Paddy Hopkirk regularly returned to his native Ireland where, partnered by Terry Harryman, he won the Circuit of Ireland in 1965 and 1967 and was runner-up in 1969.

The combination of Timo Makinen's stunning driving and Paul Easter's pace notes, and of the Mini's total suitability for the conditions and its amazing competitiveness in Group I 'showroom' specification, all came to nothing on the 1966 Monte Carlo Rally when the works Minis were disqualified from their 1–2–3 finish.

The Abingdon Competitions Department workshops in 1967, with Timo Makinen's Acropolis Rally car (No 99) awaiting a rebuild, JMO 969D, with the roof rack, being used as a recce car. On the far side of the shop cars are being prepared for the forthcoming Geneva Rally.

Timo Makinen blasts away from the start of the Ballon test on the 1967 Tulip Rally on his way to winning the touring car category.

Paddy Hopkirk and Ron Crellin await the start of a stage on the 1967 Acropolis Rally, which they went on to win and avenge their protested first place the previous year.

Traditional servicing technique for the works Minis to facilitate quick and easy access for a drive shaft change. Tony Fall and Mike Wood went on to win the 1967 Geneva Rally.

Scrutineering for the 1968 Tulip Rally. Julien Vernaeve (No 74) won the touring category, while Timo Makinen (No 73) made what was probably the only serious driving error of his Mini rallying career and crashed.

Arriving at Monte Carlo at the end of the concentration run on the 1967 event, eventual winners Rauno Aaltonen and Henry Liddon. This was the year when the cars were restricted to the use of only eight tyres and the works Minis used roof racks for the run-in sections.

Timo Makinen and Paul Easter after a troubled 1968 run with mechanical troubles press on to finish the last Monte Carlo Rally contested by the works Minis.

Described by Mike Wood (who took the picture) as the most famous victory drive of them all – en route to the prize-giving on the 1968 Monte Carlo Rally, Rauno Aaltonen and Tony Fall follow the two leading Porsches.

Finishing the Common Run, Timo Makinen and Paul Easter head for the sunshine of Monte Carlo in 1967.

Cold and wet service halt for Rauno Aaltonen and Tony Fall on the 1968 Italian Flowers Rally – and a miserable result, with both cars failing to finish.

Last works Mini drive for Paddy Hopkirk was on the 1970 Scottish Rally, when he used the ex-World Cup Rally Clubman to finish second overall and win the class.

Paddy Hopkirk and EBL 56C (owned by Guy Smith) came out of retirement to take a class win on the 1989 Pirelli Classic Marathon, Paddy having won the event the previous year in a works Mini replica. Timo Makinen has also competed regularly in retrospective events, winning the 1,000 Lakes Historic Rally in 1990 and the Autoglass Historic RAC in 1991 driving Minis prepared by Tom Seal.

The three Monte Carlo Rally-winning Minis from 1964, 1965 and 1967 on display at the British Motor Industry Heritage Trust Centre at Gaydon in Warwickshire. Also in the line-up are the Rover Minis which made up a commemorative 30th anniversary entry in the 1994 Monte Carlo Rally, in which Paddy Hopkirk (pictured above) and Timo Makinen took part.

Line-up of ex-works Minis at the annual Abingdon Works Show run by the local centre of the MG Car Club and organized by former competitions department mechanic, Brian Moylan.

Grab handle	Above passenger's door
Safety fast emblem	Yes
Union Jacks	Yes
Rally plates	Prepare for fitting

Controls

Accelerator pedal	Modify for heel-and-toe
Accelerator pedal brackets	Modify
Accelerator cable	Nylon insert type
Accelerator linkage	Fork and peg
Brake pedal	Standard
Pedal box	Standard
Clutch pedal	Standard
Handbrake lever	Modify to fly-off

Instruments

Speedometer	KPH special
Trip instrument	Halda with magnifier
Cables	Halda specials and check reduction box screw
Clocks	Pair Heuer
Rev counter	Smiths electric
Safety gauge	Yes, water and oil
Ignition key	Check number and mount spare
Boot key	Check number and mount spare

Tyres and wheels

Type of tyre	To be decided after recce
Tubes	Yes
Spare wheels	Two spikes

| Valve caps | Yes |
| Balance | Yes |

Brakes

Master cylinder	Standard
Master cylinder mountings	Standard
Rear wheel cylinders	Standard
Front wheel cylinders	Standard
Front calipers	Standard
Front pads	DS11
Rear shoes	VG95
Bed brakes and fade	Yes, with spare set pads
Pipes	Cover as necessary, run main inside body
Fluid	Disc brake heavy duty
Limiting valve	Standard
Servo	Move to inside the car on passenger's side
Waterproofing	Yes

Kit

Jack	MGB modified type
Wheel brace	Pair stowed
Tyre gauge	Yes, clip on facia
Route card holder	Yes
Crash helmet stowage	Yes
Chains	Yes
Oil stowage	Yes

1,275 Mini-Cooper 'S'

With the introduction of the 1,275 Mini-Cooper 'S' a lot more engine and transmission development work was carried out at Abingdon. The Department now had the use of the engine test beds of the MG Development Department and a rolling road was also available. Considerable liaison work started with Daniel Richmond at Downton Engineering and with John Cooper and 'Ginger' Devlin at the Cooper Car Company. Eddie Maher and Derek Frost at Engines Branch maintained a close watch on all that went on. On the transmission side there was considerable co-operation from Harry Gardner at Longbridge and Jimmy Cockrell at Tractors and Transmission Branch.

The competition development of the 1,275 is best documented by reference to each major component in turn.

The early 1,275 cars ran with standard cylinder heads, mildly polished and gas flowed by the Abingdon mechanics. Later, heads were purchased from Downton Engineering and these were used on all Group II cars, basically without any further development, throughout the full period of the 1,275 in competitions. The larger valve heads produced by Janspeed Engineering were tried on later Group VI cars, and for rallycross, but these were found to offer only minimal advantages. As a direct result of experience in competitions (racing rather than rallying in this case) cylinder blocks with strengthened centre main bearings were later introduced – also a stronger flange between the crankcase and the gearbox.

The 148 camshaft was used on early cars, then the 648 became most popular for Group II.

Variations of the 1,275 works power units. Group VI with the single Weber carburettor (above), Group II using the Abingdon-designed split-Weber carburettors in place of the earlier twin SUs (right), and the eight-port head fuel-injection engine (below).

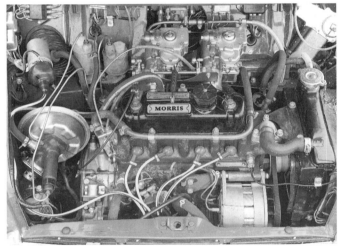

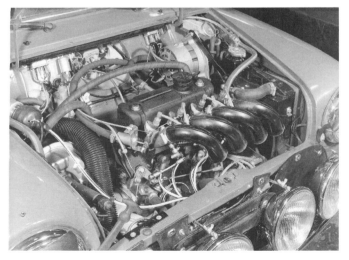

The 510 camshaft, designed principally for the 1966 Monte Carlo Rally (Group I), gave smoother torque and a slight increase in valve crash. This camshaft, which became the standard 'S' type camshaft, was favoured by some drivers, particularly on forestry stages, for it gave much improved low-down flexibility which saved wear and tear on transmissions in the lower speed range.

Standard inlet manifolds were used for Group II with twin H4 half-inch SU carburretors which gave about 90 bhp. A further 7 bhp, improved torque, and improved acceleration was later gained by use of the special twin split Webers, tried for the first time with some drama on the 1968 Monte Carlo Rally.

The rocker gear on early 1,275s was used in its standard form, but later lightened gear was used which incorporated eccentric rocker bushes to increase the lift. This was found to be as effective as a camshaft change.

Overheating problems with the 1,275 were generally caused by piston failures. Early cars, fitted with standard pistons, gave troubles with the piston ring lands cracking and the gudgeon pins tightening up. This was partially cured by increasing the gudgeon pin clearance and by reducing the number of compression rings from three to two, thus increasing the width of the land. Piston ovality was also increased so that the gudgeon pin was less likely to come into contact with the cylinder wall. Later, forged pistons were used which had the advantage of staying in one piece if they did crack. Fred Cockcroft of Hepworth & Grandage contributed a lot to solving the Mini's piston troubles. To further assist with the overheating problems, an increased capacity impeller was fitted to the water pump and this item was subsequently put into production on the standard car.

The standard nitrided crankshaft gave little trouble and the 1,275 must have had one of the strongest crankshafts of any production engine at the time. The standard connecting rods, crack-tested and balanced, also proved quite adequate, as did steel flywheels – even when they were excessively lightened.

On the transmission side, the diaphragm-spring clutch with an increased rating was used with the standard centre plate and lining bonded and riveted. Standard material crack-tested drive shafts gave little trouble but the early rubber couplings were replaced by the Hardy Spicer steel coupling from the 1966 Monte Carlo Rally onwards. This modification was also adopted on the standard car. Early cars ran with standard gearboxes but later close-ratio spur-cut gears in special material were introduced.

The cone rubber suspension of the early cars was modified only with the use of competition shock absorbers. With the introduction of hydrolastic suspension, higher front and rear units were used. Later front shock absorbers were homologated in Group II along with

Quickly removable radiator grille and hinged spot lamp brackets to improve engine access on a 1964 team car.

Build sheet for the 1,275 is for the car driven by Tony Fall on the 1968 Monte Carlo Rally.

adjustable front tie rods. For circuit racing a rear anti-roll bar was favoured on the hydro-lastic cars but not on the cone rubber suspension cars. Aeon bump rubbers were also fitted at the rear.

Other items which were introduced onto the production car or homologated in Group II included the wider 4-inch wheels, an oil cooler, twin fuel tanks, limited-slip differential, an improved gearbox mounting kit, perspex windows, and lightweight panels.

The following is the build sheet for the 1,275 (ORX 707F) driven by Tony Fall on the 1968 Monte Carlo Rally.

Cylinder block

Block	Latest strengthened type	Timing chain	Standard
Bore size	Plus 0.020 in.	Core plugs	Peen around the edges
Modifications	Machine the face to 0.010 in. off the piston crown	Dip stick and washer	Blue the dip stick and check the length
Fume pipes	One standard with long hose. Blank off the clack valve and cut holes in the hose	Oil filter element	Standard
		Distributor	40979B with latest condenser and rotor arm grease point pivot
Camshaft	AEA 648		
Crankshaft	Balanced, double drilled and blanked off	Ignition setting	Test on rolling road and report
		Engine rubbers	Latest standard rubbers
Flywheel	Steel, extra lightened and balanced	Engine number plate	Check with log book
Clutch	Diaphragm (orange) balanced	Idler gear	Standard helical, EN355 material
Release bearing	Standard, repack with HMP grease	Primary gear	Special, Vandervell steel back bush, helical in EN355 material
Bearings cam	Standard		
Bearings crank	Special Vandervell	Oil pressure	Check and report
Connecting rods	Standard, line up and balance. Machine a groove in the rod stretch bolts (0.003 in.)	Sump and protection	Standard guard
		Sump plug	Standard
Pistons	Forged (plus 0.020 in.) ovalized with 450 pad rings	Oil cooler	ARO 9809 with special flex pipes, check for fouling Modify oil cooler mounting and the front steady bracket to clear the alternator
Oil pump	Standard concentric, strip and clean rough casting		
Oil pump drive	Standard		
Camshaft gear	Machine to line up and tighten	Engine steady bracket	Modify the bush at the bulkhead end. Fit a spacer and a bolt for easy removal
Crankshaft gear	Standard, machine to line up and tighten		

Cylinder head

Type	Downton
Modified	Check for six brass plugs
Compression ratio	12.6 to 1
Amount removed	Downton specification
Combustion space	16.4 cc
Exhaust valves	Standard
Inlet valves	Standard
Top caps	Marked W
Bottom caps	AEA 403
Valve spring inner	AEA 652, check pressure
Valve spring outer	AEA 524, check pressure
Thermostat	Standard. Do not blank off bypass
Sealing points	None
Exhaust manifold	Downton
Inlet manifold	Downton
Plugs	Champion N60Y
Rocker assembly	Fit latest type. Remove 0.055 in. from the pillars. Fit modified shaft, drill and countersink plain pillar for oilway. Line up rocker arm with valve stem

Transmission

Gear ratios	Close ratio
Gear material	Special crack tested
Type of transmission	Spur cut gears
Sump plug	Standard
Selector bars and forks	Check and tighten
Filler cap modifications	Check and drill holes in the slot of the filler cap and one ⅜-in. hole in the middle
Gear lever	Standard, check ease of change
Drive shafts	Special latest modified type from Hardy Spicer with needle roller bearings
Differential ratio	4.2 to 1
Clutch adjustment	Standard
Oil pick up pipe	Fit modified type
Remote control mounting	Fit Mitchell type rubbers

Carburettors

Type	Twin split Webers
Air cleaners	Fit stub pipes, less breathers
Choke cables	Standard
Heat shields	Fit asbestos to bulkhead under the bonnet
Heat collecting box	Make and fit
Induction	Downton
Linkage	Fork and peg, line up
Accelerator cable	Special Smiths nylon insert
Vibration	Wire lock banjo bolts to the float chamber bolts

Chassis

Displacer units	Double blue rear, single blue front. Fit double locating bracket at front
Rear struts	Standard, orange (30 lb) helper spring and split pin the bottom pin
Anti-roll bar	None
Wishbones	Standard, fit standard rubbers latest type
Bump rubbers	Aeon
Engine mounting brackets	Standard
Bumpers	Standard
Jacking points	Quick lift brackets, front and rear
Ride height	Standard, approximately 13 in. from wheel centre to wheel arch
Front hubs	Standard, checked and packed with FCB grease
Rear hubs	Special Timkin with FCB grease
Stub axles	Standard
Towing eyes	Two at front
Overriders	None
Radius arms	Standard
Tie rods	Split pin nuts and fit new rubbers. Fit skid shields
Fog lamp brackets	Fit quick release type
Mud flaps	Front and rear

Cooling System

Radiator	Type DEV 3023 and bolt bottom end solid
Type of fan	Fit four bladed with machined ends
Radiator capacity	16 gills per inch with ¼ in. fixing screws
Water pump	Standard small pulley
Hoses	Standard
Fan belt	Goodyear special 1304 H and fit spare
Radiator blind	Fit muff to the grille
Blanking	None
Anti freeze	Yes
Radiator cap	13 lb wire on
Header tank	Standard with expansion tank
Temperature gauge	Special Smiths capillary tube
Radiator drain plug	Wire lock

Electrics

Alternator	Modify earth wire
Starter	Standard RT 25110 wired with solenoid and push button

Coil	HA12 with water proofing
Regulator box	For alternator 4 TR 37423A
Battery and fixing	Special type fitted with terminals away from the petrol tank
Alternator pulley	AEA 535
Waterproofing	Silicone grease, rubber covers on coil and distributor with alloy plate in front
Front auxiliary lamps	Fit five-way connectors for quick removal
Wiper motor	Two speed
Wiper motor switch	Two speed to driver's and navigator's panel
Wiper blades and arms	Standard with deep-throated wheel boxes
Headlamps	European E4 (white)
Headlamp bulbs	Vertical dip 80–60
Fog lamps	Two 700 latest type fitted with iodine bulbs
Fog lamp switch	One for each light mounted adjacent
Fog lamp bulbs	Iodine
Long range lamps	Fit two centre with headlamp units
Long range switch	One for each light mounted adjacent
Long range bulb	Iodine
Reverse lamp	576 with 21 watt bulb
Reverse lamp switch	Mechanical fitting to gearbox
Tail lamps	Standard
Stop lamps	Standard
Flasher lamps	Standard position incorporated with side lamp
Flasher switch	Standard
Two-pin plugs	One in navigator's glove pocket
Navigator's lamp	Butlers flex type in the glove pocket
Demister bars	None
Lamp covers	All front lamps
Horns	Maserati
Horn buttons	Standard for driver, foot operated for navigator
Panel lights	Standard
Panel light for clocks	Four external
Ammeter	None
Headlamp flick switch	Standard
Battery	Make and fit cover and supply bolt on protection
Battery cable	Fit large type terminal covers to insulate and run inside the car
Screen washer	Tudor electric. Fit switch to driver's and navigator's panel. Fit special Tudor chrome jets (0.040 in.)

Headlamp washers	Specials
Cigar lighter	Standard, on driver's side

Steering

Type of column	Standard, check bottom clamp bolt and tighten
Steering wheel	Leather covered with thumb pads and matt black spokes
Steering wheel nut	Tighten
Rack and pinion	Special, latest type. Fit modified U bolt to location on the side of the rack
Steering arms	Standard, latest type, strip and clean lap faces
Track arms	Standard, split pin nuts and check taper fit
Camber and castor	Check
Lock nuts	Fit castellated nuts and split pin both ends of the rods
Steering ratio	Standard
Steering adjustment	Check and line up steering wheel
Track wheels	⅛ in. toe out
Ball pins	Fit special, BTA 445

Exhaust

System	Fit skid under the silencer and turn the end up
Silencer	Competition
Hanging brackets	Drill special rubbers and fit bolt
Front support bracket	Special and fit steel exhaust clips in place of Jubilee clips and weld on

Petrol system

Tank	Fit twin and wire up rear connection
Tank fixing	Standard
Fuel gauge	Standard with bi-metal strip
Pumps	Fit twin pumps under the rear seat but wire one only
Pipes	Run inside car
Tank fillers	Standard, wire on
Tank protection	Asbestos shield. Mould in sharp edges with Isopon
Pipe protection	Inside cars where necessary
Petrol filters	Standard, clean
Tank breather	Fit standard pipes and check outlets are clear

Body

Driver's seat	Special, fibreglass
Driver's harness	Special Irvin lap and diagonal snap in fixing
Passenger's harness	Special Irvin full harness
Passenger's seat	Special recliner, fit straps for harness

Windscreen	Laminated Triplex electric
Windscreen washer	Tudor electric, fit two nozzles to driver's side
Sun visor	Standard, latest type
Demist	Fit rear Clearview as high as possible
Heater	Standard
Front wings	Standard with wheel spats, pop rivet finisher
Rear wings	Standard with wheel spats, pop rivet finisher
Doors	Standard with plastic finisher inside
Panels	All standard
Bonnet fixings	Standard, fit safety straps
Crash bar	Fit Aley type
Carpets	Insulated with asbestos blanket under front
Trim	Standard
Map stowage	Divide nearside door pocket
Parcel shelf	None
Door draughts	Check, crews are complaining of this
Water test	Check and rectify
Paddings	Fit to door pockets, locks and pillars
Facia	Special made by Competitions, matt black all chrome
Switch positions	Arrange as instructed
Intercom	Fit to crash bar
Remote control	Make up and fit emergency strap
Registration plates	Stick on front, number plate rear
GB plate	Fablon
Competition numbers	Paint matt black on white patch
Elopress	Fit one
Fire extinguisher	Fit one
Driving mirror	Latest Mini type with large arm and dip
Passenger's mirror	Barnacle type
Petrol can stowage	None
Kit stowage	Check with crew
Scotchlite tape	Rear bumper and door shuts
Grab handle	Fit one above passenger's door
Rally plates	Prepare for fixing
Crew names	Latest stick on type

Controls

Accelerator pedal	Modify for heel-and-toe
Accelerator pedal brackets	Standard
Accelerator cable	Nylon insert Smiths type
Accelerator linkage	Fork and peg
Brake pedal	Standard
Pedal box	Standard
Clutch pedal	Standard
Handbrake lever	Modify for fly-off type
Handbrake cables	Grease well, use PBC on quadrant and pivots

Instruments

Speedometer	KPH with trip
Trip instrument	Halda Twinmaster with windows removed and taped
Cables	Halda special
Clocks	Twin Heuer
Rev counter	Smiths electric
Safety gauge	Yes
Ignition key	Fit spare

Tyres and wheels

Tyres	As instructed after tyre tests
Tubes	Yes
Spare wheels	Roof rack with four, two in boot
Valve caps	Yes
Balance	Yes
Wheels	Minilite

Brakes

Master cylinder	Standard 'S' type
Master cylinder mountings	Standard
Rear wheel cylinder	Special checked with threaded boss
Front calipers	Standard with heat pads
Front pads	DS11
Rear shoes	VG95/1
Bed brakes and fade	As many sets as possible
Pipes	Run inside car
Fluid	Lockheed disc
Limiting valve	Fit 450 lb/in^2
Servo	Standard
Waterproofing	Maximum
Protection	Re-run the rear brake pipes behind the brake cables and make up a shield and fit special front flex pipes

Kit

Jack	Quick action, stow upright behind driver's seat
Wheel brace	Two, spinner type
Bulbs	One box
Tyre gauge	One, clip on door
Route card holder	Yes
Helmet stowage	Yes
Oil stowage	One can
Pencil holder	On passenger's side

Homologation

To complete this record of Mini specifications, reproduced below is the complete homologation form for the 1,275 Mini-Cooper 'S'. This was the definitive technical specification of the car as submitted through the RAC (as the UK governing body of the sport) to the FIA in Paris (who governed all aspects of international competition). The form specifies all of the major technical details of the standard production car and then lists all of the approved options for competitions. The original technical details would have been checked by the RAC against samples of cars taken from the production line and they would have checked minimum production quantities where applicable for the approval of optional equipment.

Mini-Cooper 'S' Homologation Form
Form of recognition in accordance with Appendix J to the International Sporting Code of the Federation Internationale de l'Automobile for the Mini-Cooper 'S'.

FIA Recognition No. 5028
Group 1 Series Production Touring

Manufacturer: British Motor Corporation
Model: Austin/Morris Mini-Cooper 'S'
Cylinder capacity: 1275 cm³, 77.9 in³
Serial No. of chassis/body: K/A2S4 and C/A2S7
Manufacturer: British Motor Corporation
Serial No. of engine: F-SA-Y
Manufacturer: British Motor Corporation
Recognition is valid from 1st January 1966. The manufacturing of the model described in this recognition form started on 7th December 1964 and the minimum production of 5,000 identical cars, in accordance with the specifications of this form, was reached on 3rd December 1965.

Capacities and dimensions
Wheelbase: 2036.0 mm, 80.15 in
Front track: ±, 6.35 mm (0.25 in) 1222.4 mm, 48.125 in
Rear track: ±, 6.35 mm (0.25 in) 1176.0 mm, 46.31 in
Overall length of the car: 305.5 cm, 120.25 in
Overall width of the car: 141.0 cm, 55.5 in
Overall height of the car: 135.0 cm, 53.0 in
Capacity of fuel tank (reserve included):
  Group 1 25.0 ltrs, 5.5 gall, Imp
  Group 2 50.0 ltrs, 11.0 gall, Imp
Seating capacity: four
Weight. Total weight of car with normal equipment, water, oil, and spare wheel but without fuel or repair tools: 651.0 kg, 1435.0 lb

Chassis and Coachwork
Chassis/body construction: unitary construction
Unitary construction, material(s): all steel
Separate construction, material(s) of chassis: all steel
Material(s) of coachwork: all steel
Number of doors: 2. Material(s): all steel

Material(s) of bonnet: steel
Material(s) of boot lid: steel
Material(s) of rear-window: safety glass
Material(s) of windscreen: toughened or laminated glass
Material(s) of front-door windows: safety glass
Material(s) of rear-door windows: safety glass
Sliding system of door windows: horizontal channels
Material(s) of rear-quarter light: safety glass

Accessories and upholstery
Interior heating: yes
Air conditioning: no
Ventilation: yes
Front seats, type of seat and upholstery: leathercloth
Weight of front seat(s), complete with supports and rails, out of car: 7.27 kg, 16.0 lb each
Rear seats, type of seat and upholstery: leathercloth
Front bumper, material(s): steel. Weight 2.15 kg, 4.75 lb
Rear bumper, material(s): steel. Weight 2.15 kg, 4.75 lb

Wheels
Type: pressed steel
Weight (per wheel, without tyre): 3.52 kg, 7.75 lb
Method of attachment: four studs
Rim diameter: 254.0 mm, 10.0 in.
Rim width: 88.9 mm, 3.5 in

Steering
Type: rack and pinion
Servo-assistance: no
Number of turns of steering wheel from lock to lock: 2.33

Suspension
Front suspension type: independent
Type of spring: hydrolastic displacer unit
Stabilizer (if fitted): none
Number of shock absorbers: 2
Type: incorporated in displacer unit
Rear suspension type: independent
Type of spring: hydrolastic displacer unit
Stabilizer (if fitted): none

Number of shock absorbers: 2
Type: incorporated in displacer unit

Brakes
Method of operation: hydraulic
Servo-assistance (if fitted), type: diaphragm servo
Number of hydraulic master cylinders: 1
Number of cylinders per wheel: 2 front, 1 rear
Bore of wheel cylinders: front 44.45 mm, 1.75 in
                         rear 15.875 mm, 0.625 in

Drum brakes
Inside diameter: 177.8 mm, 7.0 in
Length of brake linings: 171.5 mm, 6.75 in
Width of brake linings: 31.75 mm, 1.25 in
Number of shoes per brake: 2
Total area per brake: 10887.0 mm^2, 16.8 in^2

Disc brakes
Outside diameter: 190.5 mm, 7.5 in
Thickness of disc: 9.52 mm, 0.375 in
Length of brake linings: approx 69.85 mm, 2.75 in
Width of brake linings: approx 42.85 mm, 1.68 in
Number of pads per brake: 2
Total area per brake: 5575.0 mm^2, 8.64 in^2

Engine
Cycle: 4 stroke
Number of cylinders: 4
Cylinder arrangement: in line
Bore: 70.63 mm, 2.78 in
Stroke: 21–33 mm, 3.2 in
Capacity per cylinder: 318.7 cm^3, 19.4 in^3
Total cylinder capacity: 1275 cm^3, 77.9 in^3
Material(s)of cylinder block: cast iron
Material(s) of sleeves (if fitted): cast iron
Cylinder head, material(s): cast iron
Number fitted: 1
Number of inlet ports: 2
Number of exhaust ports: 3
Compression ratio: 9.75 to 1
Volume of one combustion chamber: 21.4 cm^3,
  1.306 in^3
Piston, material: aluminium alloy
Number of rings: 4
Distance from gudgeon pin centre line to highest
  point of piston crown: 37.91/38.03 mm, 1.492/
  1.497 in
Crankshaft: stamped
Type of crankshaft: integral
Number of crankshaft main bearings: 3
Material of bearing cap: sg iron
System of lubrication: oil in sump
Capacity, lubricant: 5.11 ltrs, 9 pts
Oil cooler: yes
Method of engine cooling: pressurized water
Capacity of cooling system: 2.981 ltrs, 5.25 pts
Cooling fan (if fitted) diameter: 26.51 cm, 10.44 in

Number of blades of cooling fan: 16

Bearings
Crankshaft main, type: thin wall, dia 50.82 mm,
  2.00 in
Connecting rod big end, type: thin wall, dia
  41.29 mm, 1.69 in

Weights
Flywheel (clean): 7.36 kg, 16.25 lb
Flywheel with clutch (all turning parts): 11.89 kg,
  26.25 lb
Crankshaft: 11.43 kg, 25.25 lb
Connecting rod: 0.68 kg, 1.50 lb
Piston with rings and pin: 0.354 kg, 0.78 lb

Four stroke engines
Number of camshafts: 1
Location: cylinder block
Type of camshaft drive: duplex chain
Type of valve operation: ohv pushrod and rocker

Inlet
Material(s) of inlet manifold: aluminium alloy
Diameter of valves: 35.59/35.71 mm, 1.401/1.406 in
Max. valve lift: 7.62 mm, 0.300 in
Number of valve springs: 2 per valve
Type of spring: coil
Number of valves per cylinder: 1
Tappet clearance for checking timing (cold):
  0.53 mm, 0.021 in
Valves open at (with tolerance for tappet clear-
  ance indicated): 10° BTDC
Valves close at (with tolerance for tappet clear-
  ance indicated): 50° ATDC
Air filter type: replaceable paper element

Exhaust
Material(s) of exhaust manifold: steel pressing
Diameter of valves: 30.86/30.96 mm, 1.214/1.219 in
Max. valve lift: 8.10 mm, 0.318 in
Number of valve springs: 2 per valve
Type of spring: coil
Number of valves per cylinder: 1
Tappet clearance for checking timing (cold):
  0.53 mm, 0.021 in
Valves open at (with tolerance for tappet clear-
  ance indicated): 51° BBDC
Valves close at (with tolerance for tappet clear-
  ance indicated): 21° ABDC

Carburation
Number of carburettors fitted: 2
Type: variable choke
Make: SU
Model: HS2
Number of mixture passages per carburettor: 1
Flange hole diameter of exit port(s) of carburettor:
  31.75 mm

Minimum diameter of venturi/minimum diameter
with piston at maximum height (example: SU)
23.01 mm, 0.906 in

Engine accessories
Fuel pump: electrical
No. fitted: 1
Type of ignition system: HT coil
No. of distributors: 1
No. of ignition coils: 1
No. of spark plugs per cylinder: 1
Generator type: dynamo/alternator – number
fitted: 1
Method of drive: wedge belt
Voltage of generator: 12 volts
Battery, number: 1
Location: luggage compartment
Voltage of battery: 12 volts

Engine and car performances
(as declared by manufacturer in catalogue)
Max. engine output: 75 (type of horsepower: BHP)
at 5.800 rev/min
Max. torque: 80 at 3,000 rev/min
Max. speed of the car: 152.9 km/h, 95.0 mile/h

Camshaft dimensions
Inlet cam
Centre of camshaft to tip of lobe: 20.37 mm,
0.802 in
Centre of camshaft to radius of bearing: 13.97 mm,
0.550 in
Diameter of bearing: 26.17 mm, 1.109 in
Exhaust cam
Centre of camshaft to tip of lobe: 20.55 mm,
0.809 in
Centre of camshaft to radius of bearing: 13.79 mm,
0.543 in
Diameter of bearing: 27.69 mm, 1.09 in

Clutch
Type of clutch: diaphragm spring
No. of plates: 1
Diameter of clutch plates: 18.1 cm, 7.125 in
Diameter of linings, inside: 13.34 cm, 5.25 in
                       outside: 18.1 cm, 7.125 in
Method of operating clutch: hydraulic

Gearbox
Manual type, make: BMC
No. of gearbox ratios forward: 4
Synchronized forward ratios: 3
Location of gear-shift: remote control central
floor lever

Gear ratios
1st gear ratio: 3.2   no. of teeth: 26/30 x 32/13
2nd gear ratio: 1.916 no. of teeth: 26/20 x 28/19

3rd gear ratio: 1.357 no. of teeth: 26/20 x 24/23
4th gear ratio: 1.0:1
Reverse ratio: 3.2   no. of teeth: 26/20 x 18/32
                            x 32/18

Gear ratios (alternative)
1st gear ratio: 2.57   no. of teeth: 23/22 x 32/13
2nd gear ratio: 1.72   no. of teeth: 23/22 x 28/17
3rd gear ratio: 1.25   no. of teeth: 23/22 x 24/20
4th gear ratio: 1.0:1
Reverse ratio: 2.57   no. of teeth: 23/22 x 18/13
                            x 32/18

Final drive
Type of final drive: helical spur gear
Type of differential: bevel pinion
Final drive ratio: 3.44:1
Number of teeth: 62/18

Amendments
The vehicle described in this form has been subject to the following amendments:

Final drive ratio: 4.133:1
Number of teeth: 15/62
Alternative heavy duty export suspension. Hydro-
lastic displacer unit part numbers C-21A 1819
and 1821
Front track: 49.125 in, 1247.8 mm
Rear track: 47.31 in, 1201.4 mm
Fuel tank: 60 litres, 13.21 galls
Road wheel: weight 4.65 kg, 10.23 lb
Rim width: 114.3 mm, 4.5 in
Flywheel (steel): 5.03 kg, 11.06 lb
Exhaust manifold: C-AEG 365
Limited slip differential: C-AJJ 3303
Final drive ratio: 3.765:1, 3.938:1, 4.26:1, 4.788:1,
4.35:1
Number of teeth: 17/64, 16/63, 16/64, 14/67, 15/65
Sump guard: C-AJJ 3320 (21A 1675, 22A 437)
Inlet cam: diameter of bearing 28.17 mm
Fuel tank capacity: 50 litres, 11.0 gall, Imp (Group 1)
Magnesium alloy wheel: part number 21A 1968
(Group 2)
Weight: 2.31 kg, 5.094 lb
Fixing: four studs and nuts
Diameter: 254.0 mm, 10.0 in
Width: 114.3 mm, 4.5 in
Peg drive conversion kit: C-AJJ 3338 (Group 2)
to be used in conjunction with magnesium alloy
wheel part number 21A 1968
Track dimensions with this conversion are: front
49.75 in, 1264.0 mm; rear 47.93 in, 1217.4 mm
(±, 0.25 in, 6.35 mm)
Wing extension kit: C-AJJ 3353
Magnesium alloy wheel: part number 21A 2132
(Group 2)
Weight: 2.84 kg, 6.25 lb

Fixing: four studs and nuts

Diameter: 254.0 mm, 10.0 in

Width: 139.7 mm, 5.5 in

Track front: 1285.24 mm, 50.62 in (± 6.35 mm, 0.25 in)

Track rear: 1240.30 mm, 48.85 in (±6.35 mm, 0.25 in)

Inlet manifold: (material) aluminium alloy (evolution)

Wing extension kit: part number C-AJJ 3316 (Group 2)

Supplementary front shock absorber kit: part number C-AJJ 3362 (Group 2)

Front suspension adjustable tie rod: part number 21A 1092 (Group 2)

Rear suspension heavy duty bump rubber kit: part number C-AJJ 3313 (Group 2)

Crankshaft locking plate: part number C-AHT 146 (Group 2)

Steering column rake adjusting bracket: part number AHT-164 (Group 2)

Heavy duty gearbox mounting kit: part number C-AJJ 3366 (Group 2)

Modified rocker shaft: part number AEG 399 at engine number 9F-SA-Y 48058 (evolution)

Perspex window set for rear-window, front-window and rear-quarter windows: part number C-AJJ 3363 (Group 2)

Suspension arms lower wishbone set: part number C-AJJ 3364 (Group 2)

Thermostat blanking insert: part number 11G 176 (Group 2)

Four-speed synchromesh gearbox introduced at engine number 9F-XE-Y (evolution Group 1)

Steel road wheel (Group 2)

Weight: 477 kg, 10.5 lb

Fixing: four studs and nuts

Diameter: 304.8 mm, 12.0 in

Width: 114.4 mm, 4.5 in

Front track: 1268.5 mm, 49.94 in

Rear track: 1225.0 mm, 48.19 in

Aluminium alloy doors: part number C-AJJ 3379 (Group 2)

Aluminium bonnet and boot lid: part number C-AJJ 3380

Magnesium alloy road wheels: part numbers C-AHT 248 and 249 (Group 2)

Weight: 4.08 kg, 9.0 lb

Fixing: four studs and nuts

Diameter: 304.8 mm, 12.0 in

Widths: 117.8 mm, 7.0 in and 152.4 mm, 6.0 in

Front track: 1284.0 mm, 50.56 in and 1291.0 mm, 50.81 in

Rear track: 1250.9 mm, 49.25 in

Plastic cooling fan 11 blades: part number 12G 1305 (evolution)

Diameter: 26.51 cm, 10.44 in

Eight-port cylinder head: part number C-AEG 612 (Group 2)

Material: cast iron

Number of inlet ports: four

Number of exhaust ports: four

Inlet valve diameter: 35.6 mm, 1.40 in

Exhaust valve diameter: 29.3 mm, 1.15 in

Cylinder head: part number 12G 938 introduced at engine number 9F-XE-Y 54437 (evolution)

Diameter of exhaust valve: 29.21 mm, 1.15 in

Rubber cone spring suspension (Group 2)

Number of shock absorbers: two

Type: hydraulic telescopic

Type of spring: rubber cone

Aluminium alloy eight-port cylinder head: part number C-AHT 346 (Group 2)

Number of inlet ports: four

Number of exhaust ports: four

Inlet valve diameter: 35.6 mm, 1.40 in

Exhaust valve diameter: 29.3 mm, 1.15 in

Mini tyres

Tyre design is an aspect of motor sport which few people appreciate, yet it plays a vital role in the search for ultimate performance. Certainly the works Minis could not have achieved their rallying or racing successes without the co-operation of Dunlop, who had provided tyres for the Abingdon team since it was formed in 1954. Such was the significance of Dunlop's association with Abingdon, and with the Mini in particular – typical of the behind-the-scenes efforts of trade companies – that many projects involving new equipment were given the same priority by Dunlop as their Formula 1 activities.

Abingdon will always be grateful to Dunlop's former chief racing tyre designer, Iain Mills, who, at a time when he was desperately involved with Formula 1 work, never failed to help us with fresh thoughts on Mini tyre problems. The team will also always owe a big debt to the Dunlop rally managers, Jeremy Ferguson and his predecessors, David Hiam and Oliver Speight, for the enthusiastic way in which they always made sure that the team had the right tyres in the right place at the right time.

It was *Motor's* famous cartoonist, Russell Brockbank, who very early on illustrated the basic handicap of the Mini. He portrayed a Mini rocketing past a Jaguar on the motorway, the Jaguar driver remarking to his passenger: 'If the good Lord had meant cars that size to do 100 mph he'd have given them larger wheels.' Indeed, it was the fitting of larger wheels or, more to the point, larger tyres that could get more rubber on to the road, that was so often the Achilles heel of the Mini in competitions.

Rally tyres

For the first three years of rallying, the works Minis presented no tyre problems. The 850s ran on normal Durabands on 3½-inch steel wheels and, for the snow and ice on the Monte Carlo Rally, the popular bolt-through tungsten carbide studs were used. The 997 Mini-Coopers also ran on standard Durabands and, later on, Weathermasters, without any dramas.

When Rauno Aaltonen and Timo Makinen joined the team in 1963 more serious thought was given to rally tyres, and particularly to studded tyres for the Monte Carlo Rally. The Finns introduced all sorts of strange things from their home country, including the vicious 'chisels' and 'spikes' which had been developed from local ice racing experience and which were remoulded onto standard covers. At this time came the idea to have SP3 tyres and the cross-ply CW44 fitted with push-in studs.

The 1964 Alpine Rally saw the first use by the works Minis of racing tyres for rallies, the 5.00 L10R6 proving exceptionally good in wet or dry conditions on road tarmac. Later the R6 and R7 were used with equal success on the smoother dirt roads, where drivers found that the sharper shoulder of the racing tyres 'knifed' into the loose to give better cornering grip than the conventional rounded shoulder of the road tyre. The R6, and later the R7, stood up remarkably well on rough roads and its racing pattern gave adequate traction in all but the most muddy conditions.

Tyre options for the Mini were increasing steadily by the 1965 Monte, and that year's Abingdon team used R6 racers, SP3, the new SP44, and various Scandinavian 'spikes' and 'chisels'. A special version of the SP44 was introduced for the following Monte. This had an extra block in the centre of the tread to increase the stud platform and to allow an increase in the studding by up to 400/500 studs.

Inevitably, when talking about rally tyres for the Minis one talks only of the Monte, because this was the event on which major developments in rally tyres occurred. On all the other events the works Minis used either the latest racing tyres available or the SP44.

Although the Monte organizers' move in 1967, to restrict to eight the number of tyres used for the final tests, was actually aimed at reducing costs for all competitors, many felt that the rules were set to handicap the Minis. In practice the restrictions proved no such handicap and they did little to cut down the costs to works teams, because it was still the number of tyre types available for the crews to choose from that mattered. Thus the BMC/Dunlop plan for the 1967 event included no fewer than 572 tyres for the five works Minis.

The following year there were 731 tyres available for the four works cars, the selection including no fewer than 12 different options. Novelties included the use of wet and dry compounds for all of the SP44s, which also had extra rubber depth to stabilize the bottom flange of the studs. The selection of the wet or dry compounds was not only determined by the 'sticky' qualities of the tyre tread on the road, but it also affected the wear rate of the stud and its holding capacity in the tyre when running upon partly dry roads. This was also the first appearance of the new Dunlop snow tyre, an improved version of the Scandinavian Hakkapelita.

Finally, 1968 was the year of graded stud protrusion. This idea was another innovation introduced by the Finns, and although Dunlop technicians agreed with the theory, there were doubts regarding any practical advantages – but if the idea gave the drivers extra confidence and a psychological boost, the effort was worthwhile! Certainly it caused the biggest confusion and complication of the BMC Monte tyre plan!

The concept was that the stud protrusion was graded across the tyre, the shallowest pro-

For the 1968 Monte Carlo Rally the works Minis had available a total of 731 tyres and 12 optional tread patterns and stud formations! From left to right: CR70 racing tyre, Green Spot R7L10 racing tyre, plain SP44 dry compound, plain SP44 wet compound, SP44 half-studded with graded stud protrusion dry compound, SP44 half-studded with graded stud protrusion wet compound, SP44 three-quarter stud with graded stud protrusion, SP44 with full graded stud protrusion, SP44 fully studded, fully studded snow pattern, 'knobbly' snow tyre, and 'chisel' snow tyre.

trusion being upon the outside of the tyre with the longest protrusion on the inside. This improved the handling of the car in the corners on ice or snow. The straight-line driving grip was provided by the protrusion on the inside shoulder while, in cornering, the pressure on the outside shoulder forced the studs through the rubber. It also meant that the shallowest studs lasted longer when running upon dry roads. The studs were also placed into the tread blocks in a special pattern, one into the leading block and two into the trailing block. This helped to reduce the wear and the tendency for the studs to come out when running upon dry roads.

The ever-increasing number of tyres required for the Monte Carlo Rally and the need for the cars to carry additional spares prompted the use of the lighter and much more durable Minilite wheels.

Conventional spare wheel stowage was two in the boot, with protective plates on the twin fuel tanks against damage by studded tyres.

The grading of the studs and their position in the tread blocks meant that the tyres were now 'directional' and it was essential that they were put on the correct side of the car. A colour marking code was therefore devised, blue and red to denote wet and dry compounds and green and yellow for the off-side and near-side of the car.

Racing tyres

There were five basic generations of racing tyres during the period when the works Minis were contesting the British and European Saloon Car Championships. With each generation there were many minor improvements effected by changes of tread pattern, casing, compound, or tread width.

Each generation denoted a shift in then-current thinking regarding racing tyre design. The first two generations were directed by Vic Barlow and Terry Hampton, and then by Jack Leonard. From the third generation onwards, Iain Mills was in charge.

The only requirement of the first generation Mini racing tyre was that it should offer rather better handling characteristics than the road tyre. Dunlop therefore took their road pattern mould, the D2/103, and put a nylon low-angle casing on it with the racing D7 tread compound. The dimensions of this first racing tyre were the same as the old road tyre. It did the job well by simply changing the handling of the Mini, from characteristic insensitive steering and understeering, to fairly instant response, considerably harsher but more balanced handling.

This first generation tyre worked well until the works racing Minis began to develop power in the range of 80–85 bhp, when it became clear that more rubber was wanted on the road. Thus in 1964 the first proper Mini racing tyre appeared. This paralleled early developments

The unique, aggressive but effective driving style of John Rhodes really influenced the later race tyre development for works Minis.

in the Formula 1 field – the adoption of slightly wider tyres with a lower aspect ratio, bigger tread width, a more square shape on wider rims, and lower pressures.

The first of the four developments in the second generation tyre was the well-known R6 (CR48) pattern with the green spot compound. This proved pretty adequate until midway through the 1965 season when Mini engines gained a further 10 bhp. Dunlop met this by introducing their Mark I CR65 pattern, the same that was coming into use for Formula 1. It was expected that the CR48 would be used for dry conditions only, with the CR65 being used in the wet. But then both Mini and Formula 1 drivers presented problems when they found that the CR65 gave considerable advantages in the dry as well as in the wet. Very quickly, a Mark II pattern had to be evolved by reducing the number of ribs across the tyre which, for the Mini, meant a reduction of one complete rib. It was at this stage that the white spot compound was introduced, the first of the all-synthetic more sophisticated compounds that were soon to become the norm.

This led in turn to more problems with pattern stability, and these were the days when John Rhodes in the Cooper Car Company Mini could achieve little more than seven or eight laps on a set of tyres when driving at 'ten tenths' in the style for which he was famous. A change of pattern to CR70 solved that problem for about one year and this, and the CR65 Mark II, proved to be very good when used in green (dry) and white (wet) spot compounds.

By now the Mini's handling problems required the adoption of different equipment at front and rear. To achieve the required balance, CR65 was used at the rear with CR70 at the front. Although there was little difference in tread widths, the combination of patterns gave the front end the desired higher stability than the rear.

With the Cooper team cars producing yet more power for the 1966 season, there were further troubles. There was still a lack of adhesion because the tyre was too small, and now it was overheating and losing its stability. This was particularly noticeable when racing upon an oily track, which was usually the case when the saloon car event was the last race of the day. Quite often the Minis were able to record competitive times in practice, when the track was in good condition, only to find themselves running up to 10 seconds per lap slower in the race. Furthermore, the lap times in the race inevitably got slower and slower as tyre temperatures went up into the 95–100°C mark, when the whole tyre pattern and the compound lost its stability.

Rallycross

When in 1969 the Abingdon team started to use the Mini in rallycross events, a new tyre problem was presented to Dunlop. The Minis were losing out to the rear-wheel drive cars, and particularly the rear-engined rear-wheel drive cars, like the Imp. The start, usually on muddy tarmac, was always very important to enable the drivers to get into the first corner ahead of the opposition and thus avoid the flying mud. Chunky tyres which coped well with the mud were far from satisfactory on the tarmac start, particularly with the weight transfer on the Mini.

The solution was to make a tyre that gave ultimate grip on tarmac while providing acceptable grip on the loose. A 12-inch tyre was used with a very soft compound which gave lots of grip when the tyre was cold. A special tread pattern was designed that helped squeeze the mud out of the tread. The CR89 pattern was put upon an SP44 type of shoulder with a high stability centre, the centre tread functioning on normal drive grip while the SP44 shoulders coped with the muddy cornering.

In their 15 year association with the Abingdon team, Dunlop were involved in some 18 major design projects for race and rally tyres for the works Minis. In the course of time 12 of these became production tyres that were sold to the public.

Behind the Wheel

When you watch the leading rally drivers in action, either on a rally special stage or on television, you will undoubtedly find yourself impressed by their speed but perhaps puzzled by their technique. The Scandinavians were responsible for introducing the 'sideways' style of driving into Europe, first with the redoubtable Erik Carlsson in his Saab and later, to devastating effect, with Rauno Aaltonen and Timo Makinen in their works Minis.

The technique was evolved in the days when Saabs were the most popular rally car in Scandinavia. With front-wheel drive and a free-wheel device, the Saab drivers developed the art of left-foot braking in their endeavours to achieve faster, safer cornering on dirt or snow-covered roads. The 'sideways' style was both impressive and effective in the Saab, and even more so when applied to a car with the handling and performance of the Mini.

Rauno Aaltonen explains the theory:

> In about 1962 I heard a rumour that the big boys, like Erik Carlsson, were using left-foot braking but it seemed impossible to get any details. I could find nobody who could explain it to me and Erik himself said he was not using it! So I had to learn it myself.
>
> Some people always throw the car sideways before the corner. It helps to reduce the speed quickly at the last moment and, of course, it looks very impressive for the spectators! But when

The ultimate perfectionist, Rauno Aaltonen, has some unusual theories about left-foot braking, both for front and rear-wheel drive.

Paddy Hopkirk demonstrates the Mini's ultimate handling capabilities at a press day. Passenger Alan Brinton is either unimpressed or speechless!

you are driving fast over an unknown road, nine corners out of 10 look slower than they really are. So my technique quite simply is to go into every corner a little faster than the speed which appears to be the maximum for each one.

This means that in practice nine corners go just right but on the tenth one I find that I am going too fast. By the time I have realized this it is much too late to throw the car sideways – there is no more time for that. I am going off the road – straight off with the front end.

Now I keep the steering wheel position just the same, and I keep the accelerator still hard down, but very quickly I hit the brake pedal hard with my left foot – I don't keep it down, I just hit it. This causes the rear wheels to lock while the front wheels keep driving. Locked wheels have very little grip, so the tail begins to slide out, the car turns on its axis, and you can continue through the corner, on the road instead of using the ditch.

Paddy Hopkirk on left-foot braking:

I never did master left-foot braking. I could demonstrate it to a journalist or someone, but I never used it on rallies. I knew the theory but I think I was too old to learn. It's very hard on the car too; most of the people who left-foot braked broke motor cars. Putting the power on and the brakes on at the same time is very hard on the differential and the transmission. I think the whole thing with left-foot braking was that, once you could do it, you could go into a corner unknown that much faster and get away with it if it suddenly tightened up.

Although not a left-foot braking exponent, Paddy nevertheless gave a good explanation of the theory in an interview after the 1964 Monte.

Whereas front-wheel drive is generally accepted as safer than rear-wheel drive for the ordinary motorist, most enthusiast drivers of the old generation probably favour rear-wheel drive to get them out of a sticky position. But, after the early successes of front-wheel drive cars in rallies, and the demonstration of the Scandinavians' driving technique, many more keen drivers now favour front-wheel drive.

It is not generally appreciated that the more power the front-wheel drive car has the better the technique works. But, of course, this only holds true when the car is in the hands of an expert who knows exactly how to utilize the power in the right manner. It is also important that the technique is practised in a car which is inherently well balanced on corners.

Serious understeer demonstrated by Rauno Aaltonen at the Zandvoort race circuit on the Tulip Rally.

Two facts make the front-wheel drive car a better proposition for the expert in emergencies. You can play the brakes against the accelerator for combined braking and steering, which is the basis of left-foot braking. Furthermore, you need not lose control of the car even if the tail swings out far beyond a point where most rear-wheel drive cars would be irretrievably lost.

These principles may be more easily understood if we consider some examples and weigh them against what could be done, or rather not be done, in a rear-wheel drive car in the same situations.

If the angle of the car against the direction of travel gets bigger during a slide than an angle which represents the maximum steering lock, then the rear-wheel drive car cannot easily be prevented from spinning. With the powerful front-wheel drive car you can make the front end move faster than the rear end and thus straighten up the car.

On gravel you get more braking from wheels that move sideways than from forward-moving wheels because you get more retardation from the build-up of gravel against the side of the wheel. This was one of the reasons why racing tyres were later used on the works rally Minis to such good

The art of left-foot braking demonstrated by Harry Kallstrom, who gets the tail well out on the 1966 RAC Rally.

effect, because the sharp shoulder of the racing tyre provided better sideways grip under these conditions than the more rounded shoulder of the rough road tread pattern.

In the case of a car being brought into a corner far too fast, hard braking would normally make the car run out of road but with front-wheel drive it is possible to steer the car out of danger. The technique is to floor the accelerator and the brake as hard as possible without quite locking the front wheels. With full throttle you will, in this way, postpone the point of locking the driving wheels while, at the same time, locking the rear wheels. Simultaneously, you flick the steering wheel slightly towards the outside of the corner to make the tail slide outwards.

The car will now slide sideways with locked rear wheels, while the front wheels are pulling against the brakes as you continue to play the brakes against the accelerator. To keep the car on the road you now turn the front wheels into the corner, still letting them pull at full power against the brakes and with the rear wheels locked. The car is still drifting sideways so that the front wheels will scrub against the road surface and help retard the car in the sideways direction. If you have done the job properly, the car will now be well positioned for being gently straightened up on its way out of the corner and, still with the power on, but with the brakes now released.

Left-foot braking technique was not popular with the mechanics and those who had to design stronger gearboxes, transmissions, and brake systems to cope with it! Clearly, continuous left-foot braking caused enormous strain on the transmission and tortured the brakes, which would regularly catch fire at service points after a particularly tough stage. Left-foot braking also meant that with the left foot constantly hovering over the brake pedal, the experts like Timo and Rauno used clutchless gearchanges – again not so kind on the gearbox.

Rauno had some interesting theories about left-foot braking with rear-wheel drive. Just before the corner he would press the brake pedal to get the car to drift slightly; he was very much against cars which oversteer and liked neutral handling characteristics. By putting full power on before the corner you have the car drifting with the tail out a little. Supposing that you now find that you have estimated the speed incorrectly, the tail will slide out more, you correct by steering into the skid but soon you will come to the full lock position and the car will start to spin. This is when you can use left-foot braking. Keeping the power to the rear wheels with the right foot on the accelerator, you hit the brake pedal hard with the left foot. The front wheels lock and slide so that the front of the car comes back to the right direction for the corner. This, in fact, is the exact reverse of the effect achieved with the front-wheel drive car.

The other advantages of using left-foot braking with rear-wheel drive comes when you are drifting, with equal grip on all four wheels, and the inside wheel starts to lift. If you have no limited-slip differential, this wheel will immediately start to spin, and then you will lose all the driving power to the other rear wheel. By stamping the left foot on the brake you can stop the inside wheel from spinning and apply more torque to the outside wheel.

Another advantage claimed by Rauno for both front- and rear-wheel drive cars is that with the sudden application of the brakes at the right moment when cornering, you can cause a 'twist' in the suspension which locks the joints and makes them stiffer. This makes the car more stable, there is less roll, and it does not bounce about and sway so much.

Timo paid a visit to Abingdon after the 1963 Monte Carlo Rally, in which he had driven an Austin-Healey 3000 to a class win with Christabel Carlisle, and gave *Safety Fast* editor Wilson McComb a memorable ride around the snow-covered Abingdon roads in a Group III Mini-Cooper.

Unfortunately the Berkshire County Council had been altogether too efficient in clearing the roads, so we were unable to find some ideally slippery conditions; the best we could do was to tackle a few country lanes where the snow was about a foot thick and deeply rutted. In most places, in fact, we would have said that the surface was impassable – especially for a small-wheeled car of comparatively little ground clearance such as a Mini-Cooper.

Timo's methods were determined, thrusting, and efficient. He charged through the rutted snow

Using all the available road, the fastest Mini rally driver Timo Makinen on the 1968 Monte Carlo Rally.

at a startling 40 mph, one foot on the accelerator and the other hovering over the brake pedal. Similarly, his left hand rested on the gear lever. With his right hand he gripped the steering wheel at the top of the rim, making fantastically rapid corrections to left and right as the ruts threw the Mini-Cooper from side to side.

On a couple of occasions when the tail slid so far round that we were almost sideways-on to the road, he made a lightning change from third to second and gunned the Mini back into position. It was also interesting to note that where the snow was not so thick, he refused to run in the wheel tracks of other cars but off-set the Mini to one side or the other so that both front wheels were running in thin snow.

I questioned Timo at some length in an attempt to analyse his technique, though considerably handicapped by the fact that I speak no Finnish and he has very little English. However, as far as we could make out, his basic method is the highly developed control of what is usually a four-wheel drift. On the approach to a loose-surfaced or snow-covered bend, he will deliberately break adhesion quite early and set up the car for the bend, which is then taken in a full-blooded drift under superlative control by throttle and steering.

There is nothing unconventional about this – it is the method used by any racing driver in a reasonably high-powered car. But a racing driver does it on a closed circuit of known surface characteristics which he has lapped many times in practice and knows intimately. Timo does it on snow and on open roads which are generally unknown to him, playing it strictly by ear. A sudden reduction in adhesion when he hits an icy patch, or a change in yaw angle as an unexpected ridge of snow throws the car off-course, is taken in his stride.

One very interesting refinement, very popular amongst the top-flight Finnish and Scandinavian drivers, is simultaneously braking and accelerating – and by that we do not mean heel and toe; this is done without using the clutch. The right foot is used on the accelerator in the normal way, but simultaneously the brake is operated with the left foot, one balancing against the other. The effect is to reduce the understeering tendency of a front-wheel drive car when cornered under power, and thus allow it to round the bend on a tighter radius.

Mind you, it is not easy to make a precise analysis of cornering technique when you are being deafened and pounded to jelly in a plunging, slithering, rally car, approaching a blind bend on a snow-covered road at about twice the speed which seems adequate and reasonable for the conditions!

Race driving

Some rally drivers have put up some spectacular performances on race tracks by applying their left-foot braking technique to circuit racing. But none were able to match either

The tyre-smoking antics of John Rhodes delighted spectators and there was reasonably serious discussion with Dunlop technicians at one time as to whether it would be possible to have a set of tyres which smoked in red, white and blue colours!

the spectacle or the speed of the man who was the fastest Mini racer for many years – John Rhodes. Many experts criticized John's tyre-burning style as excessively dramatic, but the fact remains that, given cars of equal performance, John was usually just that little bit quicker than anyone else.

The Rhodes smoke-screen cornering technique owed nothing to left-foot braking. It was achieved by having the car set up with such balance at the entry to the corner, that it was possible to put the car into the angle of drift by simply lifting the foot off the accelerator and, at the same time, giving the steering wheel a slight flick towards the apex of the corner. This had the effect of applying slight braking to the front wheels, thus causing the tail to go 'light' and to break away. Braking for the corner was thus achieved by allowing the rear of the car to 'hang out' quite dramatically, and all of this could be done really deep into the corner, thus gaining an advantage on rear-wheel drive competitors. Then the car could be controlled by steering and by throttle work, keeping the front wheels ahead of the rear.

With the improved grip of the later 12-inch diameter tyres, it was necessary only to let the rear of the car 'hang out' a fraction and then the car would be driven through the corner in the conventional manner. The 12-inch tyres thus demanded more conventional braking than the 10-inch did.

Having tried to explain briefly the basics of these very advanced techniques, I must add that they require intense skill and years of practice, and should only be performed properly and safely in a car with adequate power and competition handling characteristics, which is fitted with the right tyres.

If you must try them for yourself, practise in the biggest field you can find and ideally use someone else's Mini!

Where Are They Now?

The prosperous years of the 1980s were seen by many as a good time to make investments for the future, or perhaps to spend one's money on either starting a new hobby or expanding existing interests. Among the many collectors' markets which flourished was the classic car scene, as people invested in all sorts of marques and models ranging from exotic Grand Prix machines to bubble cars.

Owning, restoring, and possibly competing with a classic car appealed to a whole new generation of enthusiasts, many of whom may previously have never driven anything other than the family runabout or the company car. At the same time many do-it-yourself enthusiasts, who were into rebuilding or restoring cars, some on the fringes of the motor trade, turned their interest to the classic car scene.

Thus it was not long before a whole new group of enthusiasts found themselves the proud owners of 'fun' cars of yesteryear. After restoring this or getting it rebuilt by someone else, they wanted something to do with the car other than have it sitting in the garage or taking it out for a run on high days and holidays. This led to a strong demand for more classic car events.

For the serious competitor events included national – and, later, international – racing and rallying championships for all classes and ages of cars. There were major classic events, starting with the 1982 RAC Golden Fifty Rally, and later came the annual historic event run in conjunction with the RAC Rally. At the same time many national rallies started to include categories for classic cars. These were events for the keener driver, who wanted to compete with a car prepared to period eligibility regulations against marques and models of a similar era.

Then came more adventurous events, like the Pirelli Classic Marathon, first run in 1988. This attracted considerable support from those who wanted to experience something of the challenge and flavour of the European classic rallies of the 1950s and 1960s. Later came the Monte Carlo Challenge, which was a 1990s re-run of the great winter classic. These events legally had to be run on a 'regularity' basis rather than over flat-out timed sections. Even so the organizing team, led by the imaginative and resourceful Philip Young, contrived to make them pretty tough. Certainly there was no shortage of entries.

For those who could afford it and wanted the ultimate adventure there were events such as the revived London to Sydney Marathon run in 1994 and the London to Mexico Rally in 1995 organized by Nick Brittan. These were not events for the faint-hearted, although the challenge appealed to a surprising number of classic car crews.

For many active race and rally drivers these events became a refreshing and less-commercial alternative to the ultra-competitive categories of other branches of the sport. This did not only apply to the older generation of drivers nearing the end of their active competition career. One of the largest growth areas of people applying for competition licences in recent years has been among newcomers to the sport and younger competitors in the classic and historic car categories.

But the largest support has been for events which come under the category of the 'touring assembly' and the weekend social type of event. This might be a leisurely non-competitive drive around the countryside, and perhaps a few sedate laps of a racing circuit or a blast up a classic hillclimb course in your own time. It appealed to those who wanted to mix with like-minded enthusiasts but did not want to risk their valuable cars in serious competition. Important for many owners was the fact that cars did not have to comply with all the modern safety regulations which, in many cases, could spoil a thoroughbred classic.

The annual Norwich Union RAC Classic Run is typical of this type of event. Some 1,500 cars from around the country converge on a rallying point. It is all very friendly. Any roadworthy car eligible by a specified minimum age should make it to the finish; there are no winners or losers – just the pride of taking part in what has become the largest event of its type in the world.

This new interest in the classic car movement fostered the remarkable growth of bigger and better classic car shows, autojumbles, and the proliferation of countless new classic car magazines. It has all been very good news for the one-make, classic and historic car clubs whose memberships and activities have flourished at a time when the traditional regional motor clubs have generally fallen upon harder times.

While many owners had the skill and enthusiasm to restore or rebuild the cars themselves, a whole new industry was born of companies specializing in classic and historic car work. The manufacture and marketing of parts for classic cars also flourished.

Ex-works appeal

It was not surprising that, while many people were happy to restore any good example of the car of their choice (and even the most humble and unlikely marques and models have their following), ex-works competition cars became sought after by the keener collectors. Any serious collector wants to aim for the rarer specimens and, of course, ex-works cars are more valuable and, with possible long-term investment in mind, more worthy of restoration. They are also technically more interesting than a standard production model.

Of all the ex-works competition cars, the Mini is without question the most popular. More works Minis were built than any other car used by a factory Competitions Department, and for the do-it-yourself enthusiast they are probably simpler and cheaper to rebuild than many other models. A lot of Mini parts, many of them authentic, are still available, and are probably marketed by more people than those of any other marque. The result has been unprecedented interest in ex-works Minis. Today virtually every ex-works car that has survived, in whatever form, has been traced and is in the hands of an enthusiastic owner.

Life after Abingdon

Most of the works Minis have enjoyed a chequered history since they left Abingdon. They were either sold to one of the team drivers or co-drivers or, as the official Competitions Department records show, were 'written off'.

If the car went to one of the team members, it was usually sold as seen and in whatever condition it finished its last event. Sometimes cars would be sold in lieu of payment of a fee or expenses for an event. This was a convenient, no-hassle way of getting rid of unwanted cars and at the same time saving something from the always stretched competitions budget. The team members were usually shrewd enough to realize that they could make something on the deal by selling the car immediately to a keen private owner! The ex-works prices charged for the cars ranged from £50 for what was probably a well-thrashed recce car to £300–£500 for a good runner. Occasionally cars would be tidied up before sale at a concessionary price to a deserving private owner but this was rare.

When a car was 'written off' by the works, the registration documents would have been returned to the licensing authorities and what was left of the body shell either sold as scrap or cut up and dumped. Items sold off from any department at MG had to be signed off as scrap by the head of the department simply to prevent the obvious sale of useable components. However, as far as the Competitions Department was concerned, certain items listed as scrap

The majority of the ex-works Minis were initially sold to works drivers, many of whom used them for competitions – like Peter Riley and Ann Wisdom, seen here on the 1964 Tulip Rally.

clearly may have had some value to the buyer! Certainly one or two written off body shells found their way to new owners and were later built up as complete cars and re-registered. These old shells usually went to deserving cases, such as factory employees who had been particularly helpful in supplying various in-house services to the Department.

As far as works engines were concerned, these were usually scrapped or dismantled as spares within the Department, or more likely passed on to deserving private owners and others who were closely associated with the Department and who used them to support their club rallying activities. Very seldom would engines have been sold off with scrapped body shells for these well-worn units were generally beyond re-building and would not have been suitable for use anyway by someone building up a road car.

Returning to the typical post-Abingdon life of a works Mini that was sold as a runner, most of them quickly found their way into the hands of the leading private owners of the day for use in national and sometimes international events. These cars were, therefore, immediately back into the rough and tumble of rallying. Today's ex-works Mini enthusiasts may not approve of the fact that most of the cars were rallied until they were either crashed, severely damaged, or simply worn out. But one has to appreciate that this is what the owners bought them for at the time; it is what they were built for and why they were sold to selected private owners. Nobody gave much, if any, thought to preserving them as future valuable collectors' items.

The majority of ex-works Minis, therefore, have at one time or another had to be rebuilt with one if not more new body shells. In most cases the original body shell has been replaced with one of the same vintage but sometimes, unfortunately, less discerning owners have simply used any available Mini shell.

Authenticity

Trying to authenticate what is original and what is not is, in many cases, virtually impossible. One has to admit that such is the technology and skill available today – coupled in rare cases with the unscrupulous determination of an owner – that anyone who wishes to create a faked item can probably do so, confounding the scrutiny of even the most astute expert or ex-works mechanic.

With ex-works Minis the problem of checking authenticity has been made more difficult, and sometimes impossible, by the various dubious practices that went on within the Competitions Department. These included re-shelling cars, swapping bodies from one car to another, and changing registration numbers – all done at the time to make the optimum use of resources.

Tracing a works Mini's original history can be thrown into total confusion. Take the case of a road test that was carried out by one of the motorsport magazines after a rally. The magazine wanted to test-drive the winning car, but this was in such a bad state that the registration numbers were swapped with another team car that had retired early from the same event and was in perfect condition. This was probably achieved at the time by the simple transfer of the bonnets and boot lids carrying the number plates! Thereafter, it appears that the two cars retained their new identity and nobody was any the wiser until present owners of the cars started to compare notes and investigate what really happened. The determined and ingenious researches of ex-works Mini owners would qualify them as private investigators!

Most of the cars involved in Abingdon's busy rally programme carried the same registration number through quite a few events but in many cases the cars were re-bodied, possibly more than once during their works competition career. Some cars ran with different specifications (Group I, Group II, Group III, or Group VI) and may therefore have been fitted with standard and then lightweight body shells and, of course, more than one type of engine. Certainly, most cars would have had a new engine for each event. Bodies and engines may or may not have continued to carry the same identification number.

A typical example of this is the case history of GRX 5D. It started life as a Group I car for the 1966 Monte Carlo Rally and stayed in Group I form for the 1966 Flowers and Tulip Rallies. It was converted to Group II for the 1966 RAC Rally and the 1967 Circuit of Ireland. The car was then written off on the 1967 London Rally and re-shelled with a lightweight racing body for the 84 Hours Marathon at the Nürburgring in 1967, where it ran in 970 form. GRX 5D then had its third body shell fitted for a Group VI entry on the 1967 Tour de Corse. The ex-Marathon race car was used as one of the 1969 rallycross cars before it was sold to Bob Freeborough. Finally a Mark II version of GRX 5D was built for its last event, the 1968 Shell 4000 Rally in Canada. The original Group I body was first passed on to the Pressed Steel apprentices at Cowley and later purchased by rallycross exponent Trevor Smith before being bought by Welsh enthusiast Gethin Jones. The ex-Shell 4000 car passed to Victor Gauntlett (for a reputed £55,000) and then to the present owner Simon Howes in France.

GRX 5D, therefore, carried four body shells, ran Group I, Group II and Group VI during its career, had many different engines and totally different build specifications. Here, then,

To illustrate the problems of proving the authenticity of ex-works Minis today, these photos record the confusing and various forms in which GRX 5D appeared from 1964 to 1968. The car was built for the 1964 Monte in Group I form (left), it ran Group II for the 1967 Circuit of Ireland (opposite, top), it was re-built into a Group VI 970 'racer' for the 84 Hour Marathon in 1967 (opposite, middle), and then as a Group II car for the 1968 Canada Shell 4000 (opposite, bottom).

we have four 'cars', each of which have their own little piece of competition history. If, by chance, all four survived today, they would each be valuable collectors' cars and well worth restoration. They all carried the GRX 5D registration mark in their time but clearly only one of the present 'owners' holding the original registration documents would be entitled to the cherished number.

As some of the case histories later in this chapter show, a number of ex-works body shells originally 'written off' have more recently been discovered. The new owners have painstakingly traced the shell to a particular event and thus the appropriate registration number has been reclaimed from the authorities.

Ex-works Minis today really fall into four general categories. Firstly, there are the totally complete cars which have survived with the original body shell, engine, probably most of the original rally equipment still in place, the original works registration number, and a continuous recorded history of ownership. These are pretty rare; there are probably not more than a handful and, of course, they are the most valuable. The highest recorded price for such an ex-works Mini is reputed to be £72,500.

The second category are cars that have been built up from authenticated original body shells which have a continuous recorded history and carry the original registration number, but may not be complete, having suffered the ravages of time and, probably, a tough competition life since leaving Abingdon.

The third category are cars whose original body shell was beyond repair. They have been re-shelled (either by the present or a previous owner) but have been rebuilt using a significant number of original parts and continue to hold an original works registration number.

The fourth group are the replicas. These are not based on an original body shell and have been built up on a new or period shell using replacement or replicated parts. The owners of some of these cars have been successful in claiming the registration numbers of works cars that have in the course of time been written off or simply not traced. Purists may suggest that these owners have no right to claim original works registration numbers but there is a case to support the view that it is better that famous registration numbers at least end up on a well-built replica than a clapped-out boy-racer's Mini van! Technically the old numbers should not have been re-issued and the danger, of course, is that today's replica can very soon become tomorrow's prized collectors' original!

Whichever the category, I have nothing but admiration for those who set out to restore any car. These enthusiasts possess incredible patience to devote many years of their life to working on such a project. Their attention to detail and determination to authenticate every item is amazing, while the craftsmanship in many cases equals the skill of the original works

Robert Young has built one of the most professionally-presented works Mini replicas. While many of the components are original ex-works parts, some are faithfully replicated from originals.

mechanics. Hours are spent locating and studying photos and records, travelling to auto-jumbles in search of items, talking to former mechanics and crew members, seeking out original suppliers, and gathering details from other ex-works car owners.

This is usually done purely for the pleasure of owning and restoring a special piece of motorsport heritage. Unfortunately, however, the image of such genuine enthusiasts could be spoiled by one or two owners who are clearly only in it for financial gain. There is a proposal that a formal registration body be set up to issue authenticity certificates for all ex-works cars (not only Minis). This seems a good idea – but I would not envy the people taking on the job!

There follow a few case histories of some of the better restored or more interesting ex-works Minis, and some details regarding the people who have carried out the work.

Register founder

Dave Gilbert is your archetypal ex-works Mini enthusiast, who lives in a charming Somerset cottage attached to a miniature replica of the Abingdon Competitions Department! He currently owns three ex-works cars, two of which are beautifully restored to their former glory, while the third awaits attention. Dave also has a fourth Mini, a unique home-built replica of one of the 1969 Cooper-Britax-Downton race cars, with which he competes in local events. His garage is an Aladdin's cave of Mini engines, spares, and memorabilia. In a nearby workshop he runs a specialist car preparation and restoration business (recently restoring one of the last of the works Minis, YMO 886J, prepared for the aborted 1970 Sherry Rally).

Dave's interest in Minis, and particularly the exploits of the works cars from Abingdon, prompted him to sow the seeds of a Register for ex-works cars, and today his records, photographs and correspondence with ex-works Mini owners around the world is quite astounding.

It was in 1983 that the licensing authorities brought into effect a new policy stating that any car not registered with them by the end of the year would lose the right to that registration number. This was one reason behind Dave's Register, because clearly there were a number of cars around not registered at the time which could have lost their claim to their original cherished numbers.

Dave's Register was later invited to join the Mini-Cooper Register but more recently Basil Wales (formerly manager of the Special Tuning Department) has taken over the responsibilities of the Club's ex-works Register. Basil can be contacted through the Mini-Cooper Register and he holds authoritative files on all the cars traced to date.

The first of Dave's three cars is GRX 310D. This car (or more correctly this registration

Paddy Hopkirk's famous 1,071 car (8 EMO) is now restored by ex-works Mini archivist Dave Gilbert, who also owns GRX 310D and is about to restore one of the 'disqualified' Monte Carlo Rally cars, GRX 555D.

CRX 88B has been rejuvenated by Chris Spennewyn, who uses the car for historic events. Chris has been responsible for the restoration of a number of ex-works Mini body shells.

number!) took part in more events than any other works Mini, 12 in all starting with the Swedish Rally in 1966. Its rally history runs through the 1966 season to the RAC Rally; then it was not seen again in competition until the 1967 Alpine, followed by another gap until the 1968 Acropolis. During these gaps GRX 310D was extensively used as a recce car.

The car was certainly re-shelled during this period, probably after the 1966 RAC Rally and before the 1967 Alpine. The 'new' shell was most likely LBL 606D, Tony Fall's car from the 1967 Monte Carlo Rally. Dave's detective work to find out which shell was used for the rebuild was solved when, during the restoration of GRX 310D, a spare key fob with an LBL 606D tag fell out of a gap behind the parcel shelf! All of the 1967 Monte team cars were involved in a promotional tour of BMC dealers after the event and GRX 310D bears the scars of the fluorescent light fittings that were fitted on the headlining rails. The main wiring loom had also been modified, probably to accommodate the mains feed for the display lighting.

Going back to the car's original history, Tony Fall used GRX 310D on the 1967 Alpine Rally but hit a wall with the front wing. After the 1968 Acropolis the GRX 310D registration was used on a new race shell prepared for the 1969 season, when it was driven regularly by John Rhodes.

The original 'Acropolis' rally car was sold to Bill Price, the Competitions Department assistant manager, in 1972. The car had a Mark I shell (small rear window) fitted with Mark II grille and rear lights and was bought complete with all original and then-current works rally fittings. The original 1,275 engine had seized and a standard 998 unit, from one of the Mini Clubman cars prepared for the aborted 1970 Sherry Rally, was fitted when sold.

Bill Price then advertised the car for sale in September 1973. Dave was interested but could not afford it at the time and the car was sold to Bill's next door neighbour. Dave traced the new owner and eventually bought the car from him later in 1973 and started on a full restoration to Acropolis Rally specification.

Apart from extensive damage to the front floor and some rusting, the shell was generally in fair condition, though bearing some scars at the rear which have been retained for posterity. The chances of obtaining an original works 1,275 engine were remote so Dave set about building a replica works unit from a build sheet. Parts were obtained from the local Special Tuning agent, and a great deal of help came from Neville Challis and Cliff Humphries; Bob Freeborough came up with a number of ex-works parts, while John Smith from Lucas solved a few wiring problems. A local autocross competitor, who was breaking his Mini for spares, advertised some ex-works carburettors and they turned out to be the rare but genuine split-Webers, which have been fitted.

The car was finished in the summer of 1979, just in time for the Mini 20th Birthday Celebrations at Donington Park. First time on the road the car won the concours, judged by Paddy Hopkirk and John Cooper.

Paddy later called to try and use the car for the 1982 RAC Golden Fifty Rally but he was subsequently able to borrow the 1965 Monte Carlo Rally winning car (AJB 44B) from British Heritage, this car being fitted with a Richard Longman tuned Metro engine for the event (which it still has). Dave decided to do the event himself in GRX 310D. He finished fourth overall, being beaten by only 1/100th of a second by Paddy over 10 laps of the Silverstone Grand Prix circuit – and beating Paddy up the Prescott hillclimb.

Dave's second ex-works Mini, GRX 555D, was originally sold after the 1966 Polish Rally to the MG Managing Director, Les Lambourne. But the car immediately passed to the former Dunlop Rally Manager, David Hiam, who passed it on to one of his garage mechanics. Dave made a chance contact with him through an advertisement in 1973.

> I wanted some gears for the Halda twinmaster on GRX 310D and there was an advert for parts in *Motoring News*. I called the number, the guy asked what car it was for and I told him a Mini with a 4.2 differential. He said that the gears in it would be fine because they had come from an ex-works Mini. I naturally enquired where the Mini was and learnt that he had sold it to his brother in law.

Dave tracked down the owner, a carpenter living near Leicester, who was using the car as a run-about, stacked with tools, bits of timber and ankle-deep in sawdust. The owner agreed to swap it for a Mini van (which Dave duly provided) – and the car now awaits restoration.

Dave's third car is 8 EMO, originally the rare 1,071 'S' built for Paddy Hopkirk for the 1963 RAC Rally. This was sold to Mike Wood and then passed to Geoff Halliwell before finding its way to North Wales and finally to the Chester area, where it was campaigned by a northern rally enthusiast, Tom Fletcher.

> When I acquired the car from Fletcher the shell was very rusty and on inspection it was clear that it did not even have the original bodyshell. While this was disappointing, at least all the original parts had been transferred to the new shell and the car had a continuous history with the original Abingdon documentation.
>
> I was then lucky to spot an advert in *Classic & Sportscar* for a complete set of Mark I Mini body panels to make a complete shell. It turned out that these were being sold by Terry Mitchell, formerly of the MG Development Department, and I decided that these would be ideal as the basis of the rebuild of the car.

The engine in the car when found was a 1,071. But further checking with the works records proved that after its first event the car was converted to a 970 'S' with hydrolastic suspension for the 1965 Monte Carlo Rally, when it was driven by Raymond Baxter. Unfortunately, the car threw a rod on the way to the start in Minsk and Baxter was a non-starter. Later the car was fitted with a 1,275 engine and loaned to former BMC team captain, John Gott, to do the 1965 International Police Rally. Dave, therefore, decided that he should restore the car as it finally left Abingdon.

The restoration was completed just in time for the Mini's 30th Celebration at Silverstone in 1989.

Guy Smith's collection

Guy Smith, who works as a British Telecom cable planning engineer and comes from Walton-on-Thames, was brought up in a motoring family. His father was an Aston Martin man, but Guy has always been a Mini fanatic and currently owns three ex-works cars.

A pair of 1967 Tulip Rally cars (LRX 827E and 829E) are undergoing restoration by Guy Smith.

Guy started to build a works replica Mini and then went on the 1982 RAC Golden Fifty Rally where, among other ex-works Minis, he saw EBL 56C.

> I did not know much about works cars at the time so bought a copy of the first edition of *The Works Minis*, which fired up my enthusiasm. Then, towards the end of 1983, I saw EBL 56C advertised for sale, bought the car from the then-owner Graham Brown and started to research its history.

The car was originally built in March 1965 for the Alpine Rally (Paddy Hopkirk), then used on the 1,000 Lakes and RAC Rallies (Hopkirk again) and as a recce car on the 1966 Monte. Competitions then re-shelled the car for the 1966 Geneva Rally (Tony Fall) and the Czech Rally (Sobislav Zazada) when it ran in Group I form on both events. The car's last appearance with the works was for an entry for Rauno Aaltonen's sister, Majietta, on the 1966 RAC Rally when the entry was looked after by British Vita, one of the prominent works-assisted Mini racing teams of the day run by Brian Gillibrand.

After the RAC the car was purchased by British Vita in July 1967. They used it as a test-bed for 1,400 cc fuel-injection engine development and converted it to dry suspension. The car was entered for a number of rallycross events, sometimes driven by Paddy Hopkirk. In June 1968 the car was taken over by William Simpkin (son of the British Vita managing director) and then sold to Graham Brown in July 1969.

Brown was an enthusiastic Cheshire-based national rally competitor who over the years modified the car considerably to keep pace with the then-current competition evolution of the Mini.

> It was in this form that I bought the car in 1983 (less Brown's rally engine but with all the ex-works parts). I partly restored the car and got it running to works specification fairly quickly, and entered for the 1984 Coronation Rally. I then undertook a painstaking five-year restoration, Chris Spennewyn handling the body preparation while I gathered together a lot more ex-Competitions parts to add to the ex-Brown original EBL 56C items. At the same time, I researched the original specification from former Abingdon mechanics, the works build sheet for the car, and a library of photos.

The attention to detail of this restoration is typical of the truly dedicated work of those who build up cars to works specifications, even down to items such as the original seat belts with Paddy Hopkirk's name engraved on the buckles. The tool kit is complete with the works tool roll, spare parts (like Champion spark plugs and Lucas electrical items packed in their original boxes), one of the rare five-gallon rubber petrol bags, and even a set of spanners etched with 'Comps' donated by a former mechanic!

Three weeks after the car was finished, Paddy Hopkirk phoned and asked Guy whether he knew anyone with a works Mini which he could drive on the 1989 Pirelli Classic Marathon with co-driver Alec Poole. Guy recalls:

> The rebuilding of the car took me five years, and I have to say I was not at first too keen to loan them EBL 56C. Then I thought about it and reasoned that it would be a fitting conclusion to the project to see it driven by Paddy in a representative event.

Rover and Pirelli undertook and sponsored the preparation of the car, sending the engine to Richard Longman. They also removed a lot of original items from the car which would not have been needed on an event of this type. Unfortunately the one thing they failed to do was to fit a new set of CV joints on the drive shafts, which would have been standard practice for a works Mini of any vintage. These finally disintegrated on the climb of the Stelvio and, despite the efforts of Guy who was following the event, Paddy could only finish 13th overall, albeit winning his class.

Today the car has been restored to its original specification. It is a fine example of a rebuilt works car with a continuous record of ownership and certainly containing a very fair proportion of original works parts.

Tulip twins

The story of Guy's other two Minis, two former Tulip Rally team cars, is rather more complex.

LRX 829E was one of a series of four cars built in March 1967 (LRX 827E, 828E, 829E, and 830E). LRX 829E was prepared for the 1967 Tulip Rally (driven by Rauno Aaltonen) and then for the Geneva Rally (driven by Tony Fall). The car was then documented as having been sold to BMC Australia (along with LRX 828E) and it had been presumed that these two original cars were re-fettled and shipped down-under. It now transpires, however, that two new or alternative body shells were probably obtained and these, along with new power units, went to Australia while at least one of the original LRX shells was later sold off by Competitions as scrap. The registration documents would have been returned to the authorities as having been exported; the two 'new' cars in Australia would presumably have been registered with Australian plates.

This is how in 1988 a red and white Mini was observed parked outside a house close by the factory at Abingdon. It was seen by a passing local policeman, one Peter Laidler, who happened to be a prominent and enthusiastic member of the Mini-Cooper Register. Peter thought that it could be an ex-works car and approached the owner. It transpired that the car had been acquired by a former MG employee (Jack Privett from the paint shop) who bought it as scrap and had it rebuilt as a road car. The Mini was now fitted with an 850 engine, the original works engine having proved unsuitable for road use and, sadly, having later been stolen from a local garage where it was being stored.

Guy was brought in to look at the car and was able to confirm from various instantly visible clues that it was certainly an ex-works body shell. After some six months of persistent bargaining, Peter Laidler dropped out of the negotiations leaving Guy to finally persuade Jack Privett's widow to sell the car in mid-1988. Then its true authenticity had to be proved.

Guy was sure that this particular body shell had not been shipped to Australia, and certainly had not been scrapped.

> Proving the authenticity of LRX 829E was not too difficult. Firstly, the body numbers tied up with the Heritage Certificate. Then I found a photo of the rear of the car on the Tulip Rally with the boot lid open and noticed that there were some distinctive scratches on the back panel of the

boot where various items had marked the paint. These tied up with the marks in the boot of my car. We had a lot of photos of the car on the Tulip and every small item led to LRX 829E. One of the most telling was a photo of a mechanic carrying out temporary body repairs around the offside rear lamp which had been damaged in an accident. When we rubbed down the original paintwork we found the subsequent repair marks. Then we came across some new and at first confusing clues.

LRX 829E was entered for only two events, the 1967 Tulip and Geneva Rallies, and after two 'smooth' events it appeared to have been in good condition and the shell was used as a replacement body for another earlier car, GRX 311D, and run on the 1967 Alpine Rally, driven by Timo Makinen.

The car ran in Group II form for the Tulip and the Geneva but the car when I bought it had certain items on it which indicated that it had also been run as a Group VI car. It had red fablon on the rear parcel shelf, modified handbrake cables fitted on the cross member to achieve the regulation Group VI twin-braking system and, most significant, the bulkhead was modified to allow space for the fitting of a Weber carburettor. Prodding away around the offside front sidelight, we also found the hole for the rubber electrical connection plug fitted for the detachable auxiliary driving lamp bar on Group VI cars. There were also other tell-tale things like the pop rivet holes around the front flange of the bodywork where the chrome strip had been fitted (bumpers removed for Group VI).

Clearly, therefore, the car had run in Group VI and the only possible Group VI event in 1967 was the Alpine Rally. More research with photos traced this to be the car driven by Timo Makinen (GRX 311D). Clear examination of photos of GRX 311D on the Alpine also showed various dents in the front underside of the bodywork which matched up with my body shell. Finally, a copy of the original build sheet for the Alpine car was traced and at the top of the sheet was written LRX 829E with the Alpine competition number 103.

Guy was at the time of writing about to start a five-year full restoration of LRX 829E, which will have a period specification Group II engine and as many original ex-works parts and items as he can provide from his impressive store.

The story of how Guy found what he believes to be the sister car, LRX 827E, is one of remarkable coincidence.

I drove up to Abingdon to collect LRX 829E from the lady, parked outside her house and there, just across the road, was another red and white Mini. I just could not believe it. When you see a Mini in works colours anywhere near Abingdon you have to go and have a closer look. The closer I got to the car the more I was convinced that this was another ex-works car. Just by looking inside you could see the tell-tale signs – knee pads on the front door pockets, works steering wheel, twin tanks, rally plate holes on the bonnet which had been filled.

I honestly could not believe my eyes. Anyway, as the objective of the trip was to collect LRX 829E, I made a note of where the second car was parked and set off home. The following weekend I returned to Abingdon, the car of course was not there and I was sure that I had missed my chance. However, I knocked on the door of the house where it had been parked and discovered that the car now belonged to the daughter of a previous MG employee. He had bought it from Competitions in April 1968 and produced the receipt.

Unfortunately for Guy the father now intended to restore the car himself and initially did not want to sell it. It is typical of Guy's patience and persistence that it was over four years later that he finally became the owner of his third works Mini! He then set about trying to trace its history.

I could not expect to be as lucky with this car as I had been with LRX 829E. I am convinced from photographs that this shell was prepared for the 1967 Tulip Rally as LRX 827E and it undoubtedly did several events subsequent to that in 1967. However, I have not yet found the right pictures to prove it further than the Tulip.

So, amazingly, after 20 years it would appear that the two sister rally cars had been found together, parked in the same road in Abingdon! The current restoration would see the car reappear in Group VI form complete with lightweight panels and Weber carburettor.

Rally replica

One of the finest examples of a works Mini replica has been built up by Robert Young, a chartered surveyor from Tenterden in Kent. Robert is the archivist of the Mini-Cooper Register. He has been a keen rally competitor since the mid-1960s, mainly as a co-driver. He won the *Rallysport* Championship in 1980 and has competed on the RAC Rally, the Welsh Rally, and several overseas events.

> I have always been very keen on Minis, bought my first Cooper 'S' 25 years ago and have still got it, having used it for all sorts of competitions and written it off twice. When I did it a third time I decided that the time had come to put all the pieces in a box and when the time was right rebuild it as a works replica.

Robert is completely honest that his replica (BFX 404B) has not got a works number plate, a works body shell, or a works engine. However, the engine is to full works specification in every detail, as is the rest of the car. As a replica it is unquestionably one of the best. The car is well-used and often commissioned by Rover to be transformed into a showroom exhibit for special promotions.

Five years of trying to find original parts, or people who were prepared to manufacture parts, led Robert to head up something of a cottage industry in the specialized business of either replicating unavailable parts or locating the original 1960s supplier and seeing whether they are prepared to produce a limited quantity.

A good example is the four-position heavy duty dashboard switch used on the works cars to control the Triplex heated windscreens. After searching for an original, Robert found that they were made by a company named TOK. But on tracking them down he discovered that the original design was no longer being produced. Despite the fact that the company had been taken over, Robert persuaded them to set up a limited production run using the original drawings; this they did, and a supply of these unique items has now been made available.

Finding original seats is extremely difficult because few of them have survived. The driver's moulded light-weight fibreglass seats were often not sold with the cars. Being personally tailored to the driver, they were retained for subsequent rally cars until they eventually broke or wore out and were thrown away. The same fate befell the passenger's hand-built reclining seats. Robert has therefore found a manufacturer who is replicating the original designs perfectly, even down to finding exactly the right coloured and textured trim materials.

The special works instrument panels have been faithfully copied from originals that have survived. Finding period switches and instruments involves trawling through autojumbles. Robert has produced such items as radiator muffs, tool bags, and door pocket knee pads – all to original specification. Even the original Irvin seat belts have been remade. Among the most difficult items to locate are period Halda distance recorders and the pair of Heuer time clocks, which obviously cannot be replicated.

The correct electrical items are also difficult to find. For the amateur, wiring up the car is perhaps the most time-consuming aspect of such a project. Robert and his brother David took 120 hours to complete the wiring loom for his replica, and he was very pleased when John Smith, the former resident Lucas technician at Abingdon, complimented them on a fabulous job!

Robert is now tackling another project – to restore what remains of a 1964 ex-works body shell, BJB 77B. This car was damaged on its last event when driven by Timo Makinen and

Paul Easter on the 1964 Tour de France. With a badly bent rear radius arm, the Mini crabbed its way back to England but it was stopped by the police in Dover and the crew charged with driving an unroadworthy vehicle. The offending radius arm was subsequently changed and used in evidence when the case came up. It is reported that the court proceedings ended with a caution. The judge turned out to be a Mini rallying enthusiast!

Robert recounts the post-Abingdon history of the car:

> The original BJB 77B bodyshell was 'written off' by the works but was passed on to a member of the Competitions staff. Peter Laidler, the previously mentioned Abingdon policeman, stumbled across the remains in a back garden when he was called out late at night to investigate a disturbance.
>
> I acquired the shell and the remains in late 1990 with a view to building the car back up to the specification it was when it competed in the 1964 Tour de France. However, at this time Tom Seal was embarking upon building a car for Timo Makinen and Paul Easter to compete in the 1991 Historic RAC Rally. As they were the last to use BJB 77B it seemed only fitting for them to use it again. Seal prepared a car to current FIA historic regulations for the ex-works crew, who went on to win the event in fine style.

Robert was recently planning a rebuild of the car to its 1964 works specification. BJB 77B is unusual in many ways, being a 970 'S', one of only three built without closed-circuit breathing, all assigned to Abingdon for the Tour de France. The lighting is also unusual, having two fog lights fixed directly to the front over-rider to act as dip beams.

Purists may well scoff at the fact that BJB 77B has been restored from the sad remains of the original car. Robert responds:

> The remains I had of BJB 77B were an awful lot more than some people have started with when restoring ex-works cars. At least the history and the documentation of this car cannot be questioned, and is certainly continuous. It is surely more appropriate that BJB 77B appears exactly as it competed in 1964 than fade away for ever, just for someone else to claim this historic registration number and put it on any old Mini.

Top shop

One of the top bodyshops for Mini restorations is run by Chris Spennewyn in Hitchin, Hertfordshire. Ex-works Mini enthusiast Chris has followed Minis in rallying for many years.

David Thomas from the Isle of Mull owns the last of the works Minis, the Clubman which ran in the 1970 84 Hour Marathon.

One of the most original ex-works Minis to have survived is Timo Makinen's 1967 1,000 Lakes-winning car, now owned by Gerry Braithwaite. As the photo shows, the car still has an ill-fitting bonnet as a result of the incident when the bonnet flew up in mid-stage.

Chris spent five years rebuilding CRX 88B in original lightweight Group III form, taking a great deal of time to track down works parts from various sources. The car currently has an ex-works fuel-injection engine built for the aborted 1970 Sherry Rally. Chris regularly uses the car for competition events.

Chris's recent project was the restoration of EJB 55C, a 1965 car used by Rauno Aaltonen to win the Geneva and Czech Rallies and then damaged by Harry Kallstrom on the 1965 RAC Rally. The original rolling shell, however, was bought by one Tex Robertson, who came to Abingdon to buy a car and was offered EJB 55C (less engine). He sprayed it blue and white and rallied it as a 998 car. It then passed to Edward Richards of Kingston Bagpuize, near Abingdon, and when he died his estate was going to throw it away. It was rescued by Geoff Myers and, after a somewhat roundabout route, ended up with Chris.

The car was found with a lot of original bits. It was in Group III form, with wheel arch extensions, heatshield, internal hydrolastic pipes and fuel lines, oil cooler panel modified, holes in the roof for the intercom box, blanked off hole for the roof light, original seat belts, and the tell-tale jacking point marks on the bumper.

Safari replica

John Lafferty from Cambridge has set himself one of the most challenging restoration projects, creating a replica of the only works Mini ever to tackle the Safari Rally – HJB 656D.

Driven by Rauno Aaltonen and Henry Liddon in 1967, the car bristled with special Safari equipment and gadgets when it left Abingdon and was modified further after pre-start testing by Rauno in Nairobi. Unfortunately the car suffered a number of problems on the event and was finally forced out when dust clogged the carburettor filters.

After the event the car was sold to the local BMC importer, Benbros Motors in Nairobi, and was then returned to England. Its more recent history is somewhat vague. John bought a car from the St Ives Mini and Metro Market in Cambridgeshire some five years ago and is determined to create a true Safari replica. Although he has detailed photographic records of the car when it left Abingdon, he is currently trying to research contemporary reports and photos of the car on the event to get the final specification absolutely correct.

John comments:

> There are now so many Group I, II and some Group III ex-works Minis around, that this Safari car will at least be something different – even if it will look like a Christmas tree and was originally described as the 'Mini with the Mostest'!

Luck of the Irish...

A surprising number of ex-works Minis found their way to Ireland. Among them was JBL 494D, originally sold to the successful Irish rally star Adrian Boyd after the 1966 RAC Rally. He used it as a private entry on the 1967, '68 and '69 Circuit of Ireland Rallies plus the 1969 Scottish in much modified form. It was handed down to various members of the Boyd family and used on a variety of events – autocross, autotests, rallying, and even stock car racing. The car then passed to Willie McGarrigle, J. Crossey and, in 1987, to the present owner, Derek Entwistle from Blackburn. With his son Stephen, an enthusiastic ex-works Mini archivist, Derek has carried out a full restoration to the car's original 1966 RAC Rally specification.

...and the Welsh

The very well-researched and fully documented rolling shell of JBL 172D has found a good home in Wales, owned by John Lloyd from Cardiff. John is very much involved in the historic rally car scene both as a competitor and a rally official. This car, one of the least successful works Minis (it retired on every event for which it was entered) was one of many sold to former co-driver Mike Wood. Although its final event with the works was in Group VI form for the 1967 Tour de Corse, the car was sold off with various Group II mechanical parts. After some 14 subsequent owners, all of whom John has been able to locate, he bought the car in 1982 from Gethin Jones, who had used some of the parts to prepare GRX 5D for the 1982 RAC Golden Fifty Rally. John is currently gathering parts to complete a full Group VI restoration.

The 'OBL' collection

Norman Grimshaw from Manchester does nothing by halves and he currently owns three ex-works Minis (amongst his collection of eight Minis and a pair of ex-works big Healeys). Norman was a former mechanic with the British Vita Mini Racing Team in the 1970s and went on to join the mainstream British Vita Company.

His collection includes OBL 46F, which after the 1969 season was rebuilt by the works as a Clubman recce car for the 1970 World Cup Rally to Mexico. Later sold to Phil Cooper, it was acquired by Norman in 1992. Norman's second OBL is 47F, which was the Special Tuning Department demonstrator originally acquired by Willie McGarrigle in Ireland in 1991. Norman's rebuild is nearly complete. Finally, OBL 48F was one of the cars prepared for the cancelled RAC Rally of 1967, purchased from Gerry Braithwaite in 1982.

In addition to his Mini restoration work, Norman also finds time to race a Richard Longman prepared Mini in international pre-'65 historic car racing.

Italian job

Among the ex-works Minis that have found good homes overseas is ORX 7F, currently owned by Paul Lips of Milan. After the 1968 Monte Carlo Rally the car was used on various recces and then transferred to the Special Tuning Department as a demonstrator. It was then sold to W. Andrews & Co in Belfast in 1970. They used it for two years as a display car and for some local rallies, then sold it to James Cathcart, who rallied it extensively until 1983 when it passed to Willie McGarrigle, who sold it on to Paul Lips. He took three days to drive it from Northern Ireland to his garage in Italy, fearful that the very high final drive ratio would cause something to break! Paul was at the time of writing about to start a total restoration.

Mini Machine

Very few owners of cherished ex-works Mini registration numbers are quite as honest as John Kelly from Washington, Tyne and Wear. He is the current holder of the DJB 93B plate which appears on a much-rallied and successful Mini-Cooper 'S' replica run by the Mini Machine of Darlington. DJB 93B was originally written off by the works after a crash on the 1966 London Rally, then the number was resurrected by Jeff Wilson before passing to the present owners. John comments:

> This has never been a show car and has never been presented as an original works car. But at least it is probably the only original works registration number which is still battling it out on the historic rally front in Europe.

A tale of four Monte Minis

The post-Abingdon history of the four 'LBL' 1967 Monte Carlo Rally cars is somewhat confusing. Immediately after the Monte all four team cars went on a promotional tour of dealers at home and overseas and there are suspicions that perhaps there might have been more than one car carrying Rauno Aaltonen's winning LBL 6D plate at the same time! There is also a story that one of the four cars was rather badly damaged when a foreign journalist tried to drive it through some iron railings in the centre of London, an incident which may have required some hasty number plate swaps or even a temporary switch to another car!

LBL 6D (Rauno Aaltonen's winning car) was, of course, retained as a display car and is currently with the British Motor Heritage Centre at Gaydon in Warwickshire.

LBL 66D was the car driven by Timo Makinen which had its front end smashed by a falling rock. The car appeared immediately after the event at the Racing Car Show in London complete with a large fibreglass replica of the rock. This car was then sold to a colleague of Tony Fall and later passed to Martin Hunt, who used it for rallying. It was bought by the present owner, Ronnie Anderson from Northumberland, in 1973. He used it for stage rallying and unfortunately damaged it extensively with a roll in the notorious Keidler Forest in 1978. The car remains in a damaged state awaiting a rebuild.

A Mark II version of LBL 66D was used as the 1969 race car for John Rhodes. It later got badly damaged in a recce for the 1969 Tour de France and was probably written off by the works.

LBL 606D (driven by Tony Fall) was used for only one event after the 1967 Monte (for Paddy Hopkirk to drive on the 1968 TAP Rally). Then it was loaned to journalist Michael Frostick for the 1969 Monte in Group II form. The original body shell was most likely used to re-shell GRX 310D (see Dave Gilbert's story).

The fourth of the 1967 Monte cars, LBL 666D, is documented as having been sold to Germany; this was probably exported unregistered.

Minis from Mull

The Isle of Mull off the west coast of Scotland is the last place you would expect to find ex-works Minis, but garage owner David Thomas owns a contrasting pair of cars.

GRX 309D was last driven for the works by Graham Hill on the 1966 RAC Rally and has been resurrected in mainland Scotland. Although it is in poor shape, David is confident that a rebuild is possible. His other works car is the rare Mini Clubman, SOH 878H. This was the last works Mini to appear on a European event, the 84 Hour Marathon at the Nurburgring in 1970 on the eve of Competitions Department's closure. The car was bought after the event by John Handley (who drove it at the 'Ring with Alec Poole and Julien Vernaeve) before passing to Ron and Liz Crellin. Liz campaigned it successfully under the

AMOCO brand colours in a season of *Motoring News* events then, after four other owners, the re-shelled car was acquired by David, who has kept it in its unusual AMOCO livery.

Top price

What Gerry Braithwaite from Penrith owns is generally accepted to be one of the most original ex-works Minis, GRX 195D. Its originality and condition is reflected in the fact that it is reputed to have fetched £72,500 at auction – a figure which at the time when the car was built at Abingdon would probably have been sufficient to acquire the entire Competitions Department fleet of cars and spares!

Gerry's car remains almost exactly as it was when it finished its last event for the works, driven to victory in the 1967 1,000 Lakes Rally by Timo Makinen. This was the event on which the bonnet flew up, and the car still bears the scars of a slightly creased and ill-fitting bonnet!

Potter's pair

Long-time Mini competition driver David Potter, who farms near Canterbury in Kent, has two ex-works cars, CRX 90B and OBL 45F. He speaks of CRX 90B as very much part of his 'family' and swears that whatever anyone offers him for the car, it is not for sale. It was first acquired by Paul Easter after the 1965 Three Cities Rally and then vanished into the depths of club rallying. David's former rallying co-driver came across the rolling shell by chance in a barn in Bedford and, although the body was badly damaged after an incident with a gate post, it was repairable. Restored to 1965 Monte Carlo Rally specification (when it was driven by the Morleys), the car was entered by David for the 1982 RAC Golden Fifty Rally. He was delighted to finish runner-up to Paddy Hopkirk.

David's second works car, OBL 45F, was originally purchased as a road car by Abingdon's accountant, Norman Higgins. Through a succession of subsequent owners including Tom Seal, Mike Grearson, Philip Young, and Tom Warburton, the car was acquired by David with a full-race eight-port engine with Amal carburation. David, however, has an original eight-port injection engine from the Special Tuning Department and hopes to install this into the car to return it to authentic 1969 Tour de France specification.

First winner

Bernard Griffin from Burnley is the proud owner of the first works 1,275 Mini-Cooper 'S' to win a rally outright – Timo Makinen on the 1964 Tulip Rally. The car was subsequently fitted with a 970 engine for Pauline Mayman to drive on the Alpine Rally and the Tour de France. The car is one of the most complete ex-works Minis around which won the Concours Award at the 30th Mini Anniversary meeting at Silverstone in 1989.

When Bernard took the car over to show it to the late Pauline Mayman's family they not only handed over a collection of the original rally plates from events when she drove the car but also all of the trophies saying that it would be her wish that these stayed with the car.

This splendid gesture epitomizes all that is best amongst the current ex-works Mini scene where the cars, those who drove them, the mechanics who originally built them and the present owners, all contribute to the preservation of a unique part of Britain's motor sporting heritage.

The Works Mini Drivers

The following 'Mini' biographies feature all of those who drove the works Minis in international rallies and races, along with their individual achievements.

Majietta Aaltonen

Sister to Rauno, who persuaded Stuart Turner to loan her a car for the 1966 RAC Rally, her first overseas event – the prettiest Finn to drive a works Mini!

Works Mini drives
1966 RAC Rally (37th overall)

Rauno Aaltonen

Former Finnish Speedboat Champion, motor cycle and speedway racer. Started rallying aged 18 and had his first works drive partnering Eugen Bohringer in a Mercedes. First drive with BMC was on the 1962 Monte. The most successful works Mini driver, winning the European Championship in 1965.

Works Mini drives
1962 Monte Carlo Rally (Crashed)
1962 Alpine Rally (Retired)
1962 1,000 Lakes Rally (Retired)
1962 RAC Rally (5th overall, 1st in class)
1963 Monte Carlo Rally (3rd overall, 1st in class)
1963 Alpine Rally (1st in category, 1st in class)
1963 Tour de France (44th overall)
1964 Monte Carlo Rally (7th overall, 3rd in class)
1964 Acropolis Rally (Retired)
1964 Alpine Rally (4th overall, 1st in class)
1964 Tour de France (Retired)
1964 RAC Rally (Retired)
1965 Monte Carlo Rally (Retired)
1965 Swedish Rally (Retired)
1965 Geneva Rally (1st overall, 1st in class)
1965 Czech Rally (1st overall, 1st in class)
1965 Alpine Rally (14th in category)
1965 Polish Rally (1st overall, 1st in class)
1965 1,000 Lakes Rally (2nd overall, 2nd in class)
1965 Munich–Vienna–Budapest Rally (1st overall, 1st in class)
1965 RAC Rally (1st overall, 1st in class)
1966 Monte Carlo Rally (2nd overall – disqualified)
1966 Swedish Rally (Retired)
1966 Tulip Rally (1st overall, 1st in class)

1966 Acropolis Rally (Retired)
1966 Czech Rally (1st overall, 1st in class)
1966 Polish Rally (Retired)
1966 1,000 Lakes Rally (3rd overall, 2nd in class)
1966 Alpine Rally (3rd overall, 2nd in class)
1966 RAC Rally (4th overall, 2nd in class)
1967 Monte Carlo Rally (1st overall, 1st in class)
1967 Swedish Rally (3rd overall, 1st in class)
1967 Safari Rally (Retired)
1967 Tulip Rally (3rd overall, 2nd in category)
1967 Acropolis Rally (Retired)
1967 Danube Rally (Disqualified)
1967 Alpine Rally (Retired)
1967 Tour de Corse (Retired)
1968 Monte Carlo Rally (3rd overall, 1st in category)
1968 Flowers Rally (Retired)
1968 Acropolis Rally (5th overall, 1st in class)

Derek Astle

Successful north country privateer who finished 3rd overall in a Riley 1.5 on the 1959 RAC Rally. Member of MG Midget team on the 1961 RAC Rally. Went on to partner Peter Riley in a big Healey. Killed driving his ex-works big Healey on the 1963 Tulip Rally.

Works Mini drives
1961 Monte Carlo Rally (Retired)

Clive Baker

Best known for racing works Austin-Healey Sprites and big Healeys for Donald Healey Motor Company at Le Mans, Sebring, and Nurbürgring.

Works Mini drives
1967 84 Hour Marathon (Retired)

Raymond Baxter

BBC commentator adopted by the works Mini team for Monte Carlo Rallies (also finished the Monte in an MG 1100 in 1963). Later PR Director for BMC.

Works Mini drives
1964 Monte Carlo Rally (43rd overall, 2nd in class)
1965 Monte Carlo Rally (Retired)
1966 Monte Carlo Rally (Disqualified)

David Benzimra

Son of the BMC Importer in Nairobi who was offered a works drive on the 1967 Tulip Rally in return for support of the team on the Safari Rallies.

Works Mini drives
1967 Tulip Rally (Retired)

Marcus Chambers

The first BMC competitions manager, who was also the first driver of an 850 on an international event.

Works Mini drives
1959 Viking Rally (51st overall)

Tom Christie

Successful privateer who was one of the pioneer works 850 crews.

Works Mini drives
1960 Tulip Rally (36th overall, 3rd in class)
1960 RAC Rally (Retired)
1961 Monte Carlo Rally (Retired)

Andrew Cowan

Started rallying in 1959 with Sunbeam Rapier, and won his first international on the Scottish Rally in 1961. Drove for the works Rootes team for 10 years. Won the 1968 London to Sydney Marathon in a Hillman Hunter. Joined the British Leyland team for the 1970 London to Mexico Rally driving a Triumph 2.5. Drove works Mini on the 1970 Southern Cross Rally, having won the event the previous year.

Works Mini drives
1970 Southern Cross Rally (Retired)

Brian Culcheth

Started rallying with a Sprite and a Mini in 1959. Works co-driver for Standard-Triumph in 1963, and joined the BMC team in 1967 driving Austin 1800, and rallycross Triumph 1300. 2nd on 1970 London to Mexico Rally (Triumph 2.5). Drove the last of the works Minis on the 1970 Australian Southern Cross and Rally of the Hills. Later drove for Leyland Standard-Triumph with Triumph Dolomite, Morris Marina, and Triumph TR7.

Works Mini drives
1969 Tour de France (5th in category, 2nd in class)
1970 Southern Cross Rally (Retired)
1970 Rally of the Hills (4th overall)

Roger Enever

Son of MG designer Syd Enever. Had a successful racing career with semi-works backed MGB before joining the team for long distance races.

Works Mini drives
1967 84 Hour Marathon (Retired)
1969 Brands Hatch Six Hours (4th overall, 2nd in class)
1969 Nurbürgring Six Hours (Retired)
1969 Spa 24 Hours (Retired)

Tony Fall

Car salesman for Appleyards of Leeds, started club rallying in Yorkshire in 1964. Got his works Mini drive following the 1965 Alpine Rally when he won a Coupe des Alpes on his first overseas event. During his long stay with the team he provided strong back-up to the flying Finns and Paddy Hopkirk.

Works Mini drives
1965 Munich–Vienna–Budapest Rally (2nd in class)
1965 RAC Rally (15th overall, 3rd in class)
1966 Flowers Rally (Disqualified)
1966 Circuit of Ireland (1st overall, 1st in class)
1966 Austrian Alpine Rally (Retired)
1966 Scottish Rally (1st overall, 1st in class)
1966 Geneva Rally (2nd overall, 2nd in class)
1966 London Rally (Retired)
1966 German Rally (Retired)
1966 Polish Rally (1st overall, 1st in class)
1966 Welsh Rally (Retired)
1966 Alpine Rally (Retired)
1966 Munich–Vienna–Budapest Rally (Retired)
1966 RAC Rally (5th overall, 3rd in class)
1967 Monte Carlo Rally (10th overall)
1967 Flowers Rally (4th overall, 2nd in class)
1967 Scottish Rally (Retired)
1967 Geneva Rally (1st overall, 1st in class)
1967 London Rally (Retired)
1967 84 Hour Marathon (2nd overall, 1st in class)
1967 Alpine Rally (Retired)
1968 Monte Carlo Rally (4th overall, 2nd in category)
1968 Flowers Rally (Retired)

Peter Garnier

Former sports editor and later editor of *Autocar* and secretary of the Grand Prix Drivers' Association. Regular co-driver to Jack Sears during the early rallying evaluation of the big Healey.

Works Mini drives
1961 Monte Carlo Rally (Retired)

Tommy Gold

Former works Standard-Triumph driver from late 1950s, best known for his later Sebring Sprite successes.

Works Mini drives
1960 Alpine Rally (14th in category, 1st in class)

Geoff Halliwell

Club rallying enthusiast and general manager of Tillotsons & Sons who bought several works Minis via Mike Wood.

Works Mini drives
1965 Munich–Vienna–Budapest Rally (Crashed)

John Handley

One of the first to try the 850 Mini for rallying. Successful private Mini entrant in internationals, later regular team race driver for Coopers, Broadspeed, and British Vita, winning the 1968 European Saloon Car Championship. Partner to John Rhodes in the works 1969 race team.

Works Mini drives
1969 Brands Hatch (Crashed)
1969 Silverstone Daily Express (10th overall, 4th in class)
1969 Thruxton (9th overall, 4th in class)
1969 Silverstone Martini Trophy (7th overall, 3rd in class)
1969 Crystal Palace Annerley Trophy (3rd overall, 3rd in class)
1969 Hockenheim (5th in class)
1969 Brands Hatch 6 Hours (4th overall, 2nd in class)
1969 Mallory Park Guards Trophy (Retired)
1969 Nurbürgring Six Hours (Retired)
1969 Silverstone Grand Prix (10th overall, 6th in class)
1969 Spa 24 Hours (Retired)
1969 Oulton Park (15th overall)
1969 Tour de France (Crashed)
1969 Brands Hatch Guards Trophy (Retired)
1969 Salzbürgring (2nd overall, 2nd in class)
1970 World Cup Rally (Retired)
1970 Nurbürgring Six Hours (Retired)
1970 84 Hour Marathon (Retired)

Andrew Hedges

Regular racing partner to Paddy Hopkirk with MGs and Austin-Healeys at Le Mans, Sebring, and Targa Florio.

Works Mini drives
1967 84 Hour Marathon (2nd overall, 1st in class)

David Hiam

Successful 850 privateer (16 BOJ). Famous for just failing to be the first Mini driver to finish the Liège in 1961. Went on to rally ex-works MGB before becoming Dunlop rally manager.

Works Mini drives
1960 Circuit of Ireland (Retired)

Graham Hill

First raced an F3 Cooper in 1954. First GP win for Lotus in 1958. Drove for BRM and Lotus. He won the Indianapolis in 1966, and was World Champion in 1962 and 1968 for Lotus.

Works Mini drives
1966 RAC Rally (Retired)

Paddy Hopkirk

Started competition driving while at Trinity College Dublin in 1950s. Joined the BMC team in 1963 after successful careers with Standard-Triumph and Rootes. Soon switched from the big Healey to race and rally Minis. His 1964 Monte Carlo Rally victory was probably the most publicized rally victory of all time. Came out of retirement to win the 1990 Pirelli Classic Marathon and drive a Rover Mini on the 1994 Monte Carlo Rally.

Works Mini drives
1963 Monte Carlo Rally (6th overall, 2nd in class)
1963 Tulip Rally (2nd overall, 1st in class)

1963 Tour de France (3rd overall, 1st in class)
1963 RAC Rally (4th overall, 2nd in category)
1964 Monte Carlo Rally (1st overall, 1st in class)
1964 Acropolis Rally (Retired)
1964 Alpine Rally (Retired)
1964 Tour de France (Retired)
1964 RAC Rally (Retired)
1965 Monte Carlo Rally (26th overall, 1st in class)
1965 Swedish Rally (Retired)
1965 Circuit of Ireland (1st overall, 1st in class)
1965 Scottish Rally (Retired)
1965 Nordheim Westfalen Rally (6th overall, 1st in class)
1965 Alpine Rally (4th overall, 2nd in class)
1965 1,000 Lakes Rally (6th overall)
1965 RAC Rally (13th overall, 2nd in class)
1966 Monte Carlo Rally (3rd overall – disqualified)
1966 Flowers Rally (15th overall, 6th in category)
1966 Circuit of Ireland (Crashed)
1966 Austrian Alpine Rally (1st overall, 1st in class)
1966 Acropolis Rally (3rd overall, 1st in class)
1966 Geneva Rally (Retired)
1966 London Rally (Retired)
1966 German Rally (Retired)
1966 Alpine Rally (Retired)
1966 RAC Rally (Retired)
1967 Monte Carlo Rally (6th overall, 5th in class)
1967 Flowers Rally (2nd overall, 2nd in class)
1967 Circuit of Ireland (1st overall, 1st in class)
1967 Sebring Three Hours Race (1st in class)
1967 Acropolis Rally (1st overall, 1st in class)
1967 Alpine Rally (1st overall, 1st in class)
1967 Tour de Corse (Retired)
1968 Monte Carlo Rally (5th overall, 3rd in category)
1968 Circuit of Ireland (Retired)
1968 Canadian Shell 4000 Rally (Disqualified)
1968 Portuguese Rally (2nd overall, 1st in class)
1969 Circuit of Ireland (2nd overall, 1st in class)
1969 Brands Hatch Six Hours (7th overall, 3rd in class)
1969 Tour de France (14th overall, 1st in class)
1970 Scottish Rally (2nd overall, 1st in class)

Ken James

One of the early band of 850 drivers, equally at home as co-driver. Previously partnered BMC team captain John Gott in big Healeys. Went on to partner Rupert Jones.

Works Mini drives
1959 RAC Rally (Retired)
1960 Alpine Rally (Crashed)

Rupert Jones

The rallying vicar who after his early 850 Mini drives went on to partner several big Healey drivers on the Liège.

Works Mini drives
1962 Monte Carlo Rally (77th overall, 3rd in class)

Harry Kallstrom

Sweden's 1959 'T' Rally Champion, a regular driver for BMC Sweden. Followed disappointing results with the team in 1964/5 with near victory on the 1966 RAC Rally.

Works Mini drives
1964 RAC Rally (Retired)
1965 Monte Carlo Rally (Retired)
1965 Swedish Rally (Retired)
1965 RAC Rally (Retired)
1966 RAC Rally (2nd overall, 1st in class)

Simo Lampinen

Started rallying in Finland in 1961 after a remarkable recovery from polio. Finnish Rally Champion in 1963/4. Went on to drive for Saab, DAF, Leyland Standard-Triumph, and Lancia.

Works Mini drives
1966 RAC Rally (Crashed)
1967 Monte Carlo Rally (15th overall)

Jorma Lusenius

Was offered his works Mini drive after a notable performance with BMC Sweden on the 1965 1,000 Lakes Rally challenging Timo Makinen.

Works Mini drives
1965 RAC Rally (6th overall, 1st in class)
1966 1,000 Lakes Rally (6th overall, 3rd in class)

Geoff Mabbs

Graduated from club motor sport to drive for a number of works teams including Standard-Triumph, winning the 1961 Tulip Rally in a Herald. Co-drove the 1962 Monte with Aaltonen (on his first works drive). Later to work closely with the team on development of Austin, Triumph, and Rover.

Works Mini drives
1969 Nurbürgring Six Hours (Retired)
1969 Spa 24 Hours (Retired)

Denise McCluggage

American lady journalist who had partnered Christabel Carlisle in the works MGB at Sebring in 1963.

Works Mini drives
1963 Alpine Rally (Retired)

Timo Makinen

Started ice racing and rallying in Finland in 1960 with Volvo and Saab before driving Minis entered by local distributor. First BMC drive on the 1962 RAC Rally. Without question the fastest of the works Mini drivers if not the most successful. Also remembered for his stirring big Healey drives, particularly on the RAC Rally. Timo's 1965 Monte Carlo Rally win was probably the greatest single rally drive of all time.

Works Mini drives
1962 RAC Rally (7th overall, 1st in class)
1963 Tour de France (Retired)
1964 Monte Carlo Rally (4th overall, 2nd in class)
1964 Tulip Rally (1st overall, 1st in class)
1964 Alpine Rally (Retired)
1964 1,000 Lakes Rally (4th overall, 1st in class)
1964 Tour de France (Crashed)
1965 Monte Carlo Rally (1st overall, 1st in class)
1965 Swedish Rally (Retired)
1965 Tulip Rally (3rd in category, 1st in class)
1965 Acropolis Rally (Retired)
1965 Czech Rally (Retired)
1965 Alpine Rally (2nd in category, 1st in class)
1965 1,000 Lakes Rally (1st overall, 1st in class)
1966 Monte Carlo Rally (1st overall – disqualified)
1966 Swedish Rally (Retired)
1966 Tulip Rally (9th overall, 1st in class)
1966 Acropolis Rally (10th overall, 2nd in class)
1966 Czech Rally (3rd overall, 2nd in class)
1966 Polish Rally (2nd overall, 1st in class)
1966 1,000 Lakes Rally (1st overall, 1st in class)
1966 Alpine Rally (Retired)
1966 Munich–Vienna–Budapest Rally (1st overall, 1st in class)
1966 RAC Rally (Retired)
1967 Monte Carlo Rally (41st overall)
1967 Swedish Rally (Retired)
1967 Tulip Rally (2nd overall, 1st in category)
1967 Acropolis Rally (Retired)
1967 1,000 Lakes Rally (1st overall, 1st in class)
1967 Alpine Rally (Retired)
1968 Monte Carlo Rally (55th overall)
1968 Tulip Rally (41st overall)
1968 1,000 Lakes Rally (Retired)
1968 Acropolis Rally (Retired)

Pauline Mayman

Joined the BMC team to partner Pat Moss when Ann Wisdom retired, then became the team's lady driver when Pat Moss moved to Ford. Raced single-seaters, saloons, and sports cars before taking up rallying.

Works Mini drives
1963 Monte Carlo Rally (28th overall, 4th in class)
1963 Tulip Rally (21st overall, 4th in class)
1963 Triefels Rally (1st in class, Ladies)
1963 Alpine Rally (6th in category, 1st in class, Ladies)
1963 Tour de France (Retired)
1963 RAC Rally (30th overall)
1964 Monte Carlo Rally (Crashed)
1964 Alpine Rally (6th in category, 1st in class, Ladies)
1964 Tour de France (1st in class)
1965 Alpine Rally (13th in category, Ladies)

John Milne

Amongst the band of Scottish privateers well-known to Marcus Chambers from HRG days. Regular partner to compatriot Bill Shepherd. He had previously driven MGA. Later campaigned the third Jacobs MG Midget coupé in Scottish racing.

Works Mini drives
1960 Acropolis Rally (16th overall, 4th in class)

Nancy Mitchell

Joined the BMC team in 1956 to drive MG Magnette, MGA, Riley 1.5 and big Healey. Ladies European Rally Champion 1956/57.

Works Mini drives
1959 Portuguese Rally (54th overall)
1960 Monte Carlo Rally (Retired)

Don Morley

With twin brother Erle, started rallying in 1952. First BMC drive was with big Healey in 1959 following their win in private Jaguar on Tulip Rally. Claimed the Mini's first class win (Geneva 1960). Preferred sports cars and went on to achieve outstanding successes with MGA, MGB, and particularly the big Healey (consecutive Alpine Rally wins in 1961/62).

Works Mini drives
1960 Monte Carlo Rally (33rd overall)
1960 Geneva Rally (14th overall, 1st in class)
1961 Acropolis Rally (Crashed)
1965 Monte Carlo Rally (27th overall, 2nd in class)

Logan Morrison

Successful Scottish private owner who regularly supported the works with good class results. Also drove in the works big Healey team.

Works Mini drives
1962 RAC Rally (13th overall, 3rd in class)
1963 Monte Carlo Rally (44th overall, 1st in class)
1963 Scottish Rally (Crashed)
1963 RAC Rally (19th overall, 1st in class)

Pat Moss

Started rallying Morris Minor and Triumph TR in early 1950s. First works BMC drive was in 1955 with MG 'TF'. Went on to drive MGA, Magnette, Riley 1.5, A40, and big Healey. European Ladies Rally Champion in 1958 and 1962. Left BMC in 1963 to drive Ford. Unquestionably the fastest lady driver of her era (particularly in the big Healey) and probably of all time.

Works Mini drives
1961 Lyon Charbonnières Rally (Retired)
1962 Monte Carlo Rally (26th overall, 7th in class, Ladies)
1962 Tulip Rally (1st overall, 1st in class, Ladies)
1962 Baden–Baden Rally (1st overall, 1st in class, Ladies)
1962 Geneva Rally (3rd overall, 1st in class)

Carl Orrenius

Started rallying Saabs in 1956. Later enjoyed regular Mini drives with BMC Sweden entered cars.

Works Mini drives
1964 RAC Rally (Retired)

Pat 'Tish' Ozanne

Named Pat but known as 'Tish', she holds the honour of being the first and most active of the early works 850 drivers. Went on to drive Riley 1.5.

Works Mini drives
1959 RAC Rally (Retired)
1960 Monte Carlo Rally (Retired)
1960 Geneva Rally (27th overall, 2nd in class)
1960 Tulip Rally (72nd overall, 6th in class)
1960 Acropolis Rally (Retired)

Alec Pitts

Adventurous enthusiast who campaigned the early 850s both for the works and as a private entrant.

Works Mini drives
1959 RAC Rally (Retired)
1960 Monte Carlo Rally (73rd overall)
1960 Geneva Rally (Crashed)
1960 Alpine Rally (4th in class)

Alec Poole

Former MG apprentice who enjoyed a long career driving BMC cars as a private owner. Won the 1969 British Saloon Car Championship in an Arden 1-litre Mini. Partnered Paddy Hopkirk on the 1989 and 1990 Pirelli Classic Marathons with a Mini.

Works Mini drives
1967 84 Hour Marathon (Retired)
1970 Nurbürgring Six Hours (Retired)
1970 84 Hour Marathon (Retired)

John Rhodes

Spent his early career driving F3 Cooper single-seaters but is best remembered as the most successful and spectacular Mini racer for the Cooper and, later, Abingdon works teams, winning the 1,300 cc class in the British Saloon Car Championships from 1964 to 1968 and the European Championship class in 1968.

Works Mini drives
1967 Sebring Three Hours Race (1st in class)
1969 Brands Hatch (Crashed)
1969 Silverstone Daily Express (11th overall, 5th in class)
1969 Snetterton Guards Trophy (12th overall, 4th in class)
1969 Thruxton (22nd overall)

1969 Silverstone Martini Trophy (6th overall, 2nd in class)
1969 Crystal Palace Annerley Trophy (4th overall, 4th in class)
1969 Hockenheim (6th overall, 3rd in class)
1969 Brands Hatch Six Hours (7th overall, 3rd in class)
1969 Mallory Park (8th overall, 4th in class)
1969 Nurbürgring Six Hours (Retired)
1969 Silverstone Grand Prix (8th overall, 4th in class)
1969 Spa 24 Hours (Retired)
1969 Oulton Park (12th overall, 4th in class)
1969 Brands Hatch Guards Trophy (10th overall, 4th in class)
1969 Salzbürgring (1st overall, 1st in class)

Peter Riley

Started rallying and racing while at Cambridge University. Drove his Healey Silverstone on the 1950 Liège. Won his class on the 1959 Tulip Rally driving a Ford press car. First BMC drive was with the big Healey in 1959. Went on to drive 850s, MGA, and Austin A105. Married to Ann Wisdom.

Works Mini drives
1959 Portuguese Rally (64th overall)
1960 Monte Carlo Rally (23rd overall)
1961 Tulip Rally (12th overall, 1st in class)

David Seigle-Morris

Started rallying with Vic Elford with a South London motor club in the late 1950s. First BMC drive was in a Magnette in 1958. Went on to be one of the most consistently successful big Healey drivers.

Works Mini drives
1960 RAC Rally (6th overall, 2nd in class)
1961 Tulip Rally (23rd overall, 3rd in class)
1961 Acropolis Rally (Retired)
1961 Tulip Rally (Retired)

John Sprinzel

Highly successful and versatile racing and rallying privateer with Austin A30 and A35, Triumphs, Riley 1.5, MG Magnette, and his favourite Sprite. First drove with the BMC team in 1958 (A35). Went on to drive MGA, and for many other works teams.

Works Mini drives
1960 Tulip Rally (43rd overall, 2nd in class)
1963 Alpine Rally (Crashed)

Mike Sutcliffe

Previously competed in a works Riley 1.5 (1958). Regular partner driver/co-driver to Derek Astle.

Works Mini drives
1960 Acropolis Rally (31st overall, 5th in class)
1960 RAC Rally (8th overall, 4th in class)
1961 Acropolis Rally (Retired)

Jack Thompson

A South African who had one guest drive with the team.

Works Mini drives
1964 Monte Carlo Rally (Crashed)

Julien Vernaeve

Belgian Group I Mini exponent in races and rallying. Regularly supported the works team to win team prizes as privateer before first 1967 works drive.

Works Mini drives
1967 Geneva Rally (2nd overall, 2nd in class)
1967 84 Hour Marathon (2nd overall, 1st in class)
1968 Tulip Rally (3rd overall, 1st in category)
1970 84 Hour Marathon (Retired)

John Wadsworth

Invited to drive a works Mini on the 1964 Liège after winning a Coupe on the 1964 Alpine Rally as a private Mini entrant. The only driver to finish the Liège in a Mini.

Works Mini drives
1964 Liège (20th overall)

Tommy Wisdom

Doyen motoring correspondent and father of Ann Wisdom, he drove works race and rally cars for most British manufacturers.

Works Mini drives
1960 Monte Carlo Rally (55th overall)

Lars Ytterbring

Swedish star who joined the team for the 1967/8 season and regularly drove Special Tuning prepared cars.

Works Mini drives
1967 Scottish Rally (2nd overall)
1968 Circuit of Ireland (Retired)
1968 Scottish Rally (2nd overall, 1st in class)
1968 1,000 Lakes Rally (Retired)

Sobieslaw Zasada

Made his name driving the diminutive Steyr-Puch in his native Poland and then contested European Championship with Porsche, becoming Group II Champion in 1966, Group I Champion in 1967 and, with BMW, Champion in 1971.

Works Mini drives
1966 Czech Rally (4th overall, 1st in class)

The Works Mini Co-drivers

The following 'Mini' biographies and achievements are of the most successful of the co-drivers who crewed the works Minis in international rallies.

Tony Ambrose

A former Oxford student, the first of the professional co-drivers. Won the 1956 RAC Rally with Lyndon Sims in an Aston Martin. Partnered various drivers in the early 850s and was then regular co-driver to Rauno Aaltonen, winning the 1965 European Rally Championship. Also partnered Peter Riley and David Seigle-Morris in big Healeys.

Works Mini drives
1959 RAC Rally with A. Pitts (Retired)
1959 Portuguese Rally with P. Riley (64th overall)
1960 Monte Carlo Rally with A. Pitts (73rd overall)
1960 Geneva Rally with A. Pitts (Crashed)
1960 Circuit of Ireland with D. Hiam (Retired)
1960 Alpine Rally with A. Pitts (4th in class)
1961 Tulip Rally with P. Riley (12th overall, 1st in class)
1962 Tulip Rally with D. Seigle-Morris (Retired)
1962 1,000 Lakes Rally with R. Aaltonen (Retired)
1962 RAC Rally with R. Aaltonen (5th overall, 1st in class)
1963 Monte Carlo Rally with R. Aaltonen (3rd overall, 1st in class)
1963 Alpine Rally with R. Aaltonen (1st in category, 1st in class)
1963 Tour de France with R. Aaltonen (44th overall)
1964 Monte Carlo Rally with R. Aaltonen (7th overall, 3rd in class)
1964 Tulip Rally with T. Makinen (1st overall, 1st in class)
1964 Acropolis Rally with R. Aaltonen (Retired)
1964 Alpine Rally with R. Aaltonen (4th in category, 1st in class)
1964 Tour de France with R. Aaltonen (Retired)
1964 RAC Rally with R. Aaltonen (Retired)
1965 Monte Carlo Rally with R. Aaltonen (Retired)
1965 Swedish Rally with R. Aaltonen (Retired)
1965 Geneva Rally with R. Aaltonen (1st overall, 1st in class)
1965 Czech Rally with R. Aaltonen (1st overall, 1st in class)
1965 Alpine Rally with R. Aaltonen (14th in category)
1965 Polish Rally with R. Aaltonen (1st overall, 1st in class)
1965 Three Cities Rally with R. Aaltonen (1st overall, 1st in class)
1965 RAC Rally with R. Aaltonen (1st overall, 1st in class)
1966 Monte Carlo Rally with R. Aaltonen (Disqualified)
1966 RAC Rally with S. Lampinen (Crashed)

Ron Crellin

Former works co-driver for Standard-Triumph in the early 1960s. Joined the BMC team in 1965 to partner Tony Fall, and then was regular co-driver with Paddy Hopkirk. Reunited with Paddy to compete in the 1994 Monte Carlo Rally with a 30th Anniversary Mini entry.

Works Mini drives
1965 Three Cities Rally with A. Fall (2nd in class)
1965 RAC Rally with A. Fall (15th overall, 3rd in class)
1966 Flowers Rally with P. Hopkirk (15th overall, 6th in category)
1966 Austrian Alpine Rally with P. Hopkirk (1st overall, 1st in class)
1966 Acropolis Rally with P. Hopkirk (3rd overall, 1st in class)

1966 London Rally with P. Hopkirk (Retired)
1966 Alpine Rally with P. Hopkirk (Retired)
1966 RAC Rally with P. Hopkirk (Retired)
1967 Monte Carlo Rally with P. Hopkirk (6th overall, 5th in class)
1967 Flowers Rally with P. Hopkirk (2nd overall, 2nd in class)
1967 Acropolis Rally with P. Hopkirk (1st overall, 1st in class)
1967 Alpine Rally with P. Hopkirk (1st overall, 1st in class)
1967 Tour de Corse with P .Hopkirk (Retired)
1968 Monte Carlo Rally with P. Hopkirk (5th overall, 3rd in category)

Val Domleo

Joined the BMC team from Ford in 1963 to partner Pauline Mayman. Later married Don Morley.

Works Mini drives
(All with P. Mayman)
1963 Monte Carlo Rally (28th overall, 4th in class)
1963 Tulip Rally (21st overall, 4th in class)
1963 Triefels Rally (1st in class, Ladies)
1963 Alpine Rally (6th in category, 1st in class, Ladies)
1963 RAC Rally (30th overall)
1964 Monte Carlo Rally (Crashed)
1964 Alpine Rally (6th overall, 1st in class, Ladies)
1964 Tour de France (1st in class)
1965 Alpine Rally (13th in category, Ladies)

Paul Easter

A garage owner from Stony Stratford and a successful Mini private entrant. Got his first works drive as a result of a Mini class win on the 1963 Acropolis Rally. Formed a long-lasting co-driving career with Timo Makinen.

Works Mini drives
(All with T. Makinen)
1964 Tour de France (Crashed)
1965 Monte Carlo Rally (1st overall, 1st in class)
1965 Swedish Rally (Retired)
1965 Tulip Rally (3rd in category, 1st in class)
1965 Acropolis Rally (Retired)
1965 Czech Rally (Retired)
1965 Alpine Rally (2nd in category, 1st in class)
1966 Monte Carlo Rally (1st overall – disqualified)
1966 Swedish Rally (Retired)
1966 Tulip Rally (9th overall, 1st in class)
1966 Acropolis Rally (10th overall, 2nd in class)
1966 Czech Rally (3rd overall, 2nd in class)
1966 Polish Rally (2nd overall, 1st in class)
1966 Alpine Rally (Retired)
1966 Three Cities Rally (1st overall, 1st in class)
1966 RAC Rally (Retired)
1967 Monte Carlo Rally (41st overall)
1967 Swedish Rally (Retired)
1967 Tulip Rally (2nd overall, 1st in category)
1967 Acropolis Rally (Retired)
1967 Alpine Rally (Retired)

1968 Monte Carlo Rally (55th overall)
1968 Tulip Rally (41st overall)
1968 Acropolis Rally (Retired)
1969 Tour de France with J.Handley (Crashed)
1970 World Cup Rally with J.Handley (Retired)

Henry Liddon

A Bristolian who joined the team in 1963 to commence a long partnership with Paddy Hopkirk and later Rauno Aaltonen. Along with Tony Ambrose, he was one of the most active and successful of the BMC co-drivers.

Works Mini drives
1963 Tulip Rally with P. Hopkirk (2nd overall, 1st in class)
1963 Tour de France with P. Hopkirk (3rd overall, 1st in class)
1963 RAC Rally with P. Hopkirk (4th overall, 2nd in category)
1964 Monte Carlo Rally with P. Hopkirk (1st overall, 1st in class)
1964 Acropolis Rally with P. Hopkirk (Retired)
1964 Alpine Rally with P. Hopkirk (Retired)
1964 Tour de France with P. Hopkirk (Retired)
1964 RAC Rally with P. Hopkirk (Retired)
1965 Monte Carlo Rally with P. Hopkirk (26th overall, 1st in class)
1965 Swedish Rally with P. Hopkirk (Retired)
1965 Scottish Rally with P. Hopkirk (Retired)
1965 German Rally with P. Hopkirk (6th overall, 1st in class)
1965 Alpine Rally with P. Hopkirk (4th in category, 2nd in class)
1965 RAC Rally with P. Hopkirk (13th overall, 2nd in class)
1966 Monte Carlo Rally with P. Hopkirk (Disqualified)
1966 Swedish Rally with R. Aaltonen (Retired)
1966 Flowers Rally with A. Fall (Disqualified)
1966 Circuit of Ireland with A. Fall (1st overall, 1st in class)
1966 Tulip Rally with R. Aaltonen (1st overall, 1st in class)
1966 Acropolis Rally with R. Aaltonen (Retired)
1966 Czech Rally with R. Aaltonen (1st overall, 1st in class)
1966 German Rally with A. Fall (Retired)
1966 Polish Rally with R. Aaltonen (Retired)
1966 Alpine Rally with R. Aaltonen (3rd overall, 2nd in class)
1966 Three Cities Rally with A. Fall (Retired)
1966 RAC Rally with R. Aaltonen (4th overall, 2nd in class)
1967 Monte Carlo Rally with R. Aaltonen (1st overall, 1st in class)
1967 Swedish Rally with R. Aaltonen (3rd overall, 1st in class)
1967 Safari Rally with R. Aaltonen (Retired)
1967 Tulip Rally with R. Aaltonen (3rd overall, 2nd in category)
1967 Acropolis Rally with R. Aaltonen (Retired)
1967 Geneva Rally with J. Vernaeve (2nd overall, 2nd in class)
1967 Danube Rally with R. Aaltonen (Disqualified)
1967 Alpine Rally with R. Aaltonen (Retired)
1967 Tour de Corse with R. Aaltonen (Retired)
1968 Monte Carlo Rally with R. Aaltonen (3rd overall, 1st in category)
1968 Flowers Rally with R. Aaltonen (Retired)
1968 Acropolis Rally with R. Aaltonen (5th overall, 1st in class)

Tony Nash

Started rallying in the West Country in 1955. Former works Standard-Triumph co-driver with 'Tiny' Lewis (Herald) in the late 1950s. Had his first drive with the BMC team on the 1962 Liège with Peter Riley and was later to return as regular co-driver to Paddy Hopkirk.

Works Mini drives
(All with P. Hopkirk)
1966 German Rally (Retired)
1968 Portuguese Rally (2nd overall, 1st in class)
1969 Circuit of Ireland (2nd overall, 1st in class)
1969 Tour de France (14th overall, 1st in class)
1970 Scottish Rally (2nd overall, 1st in class)

Ann Wisdom

Daughter of Tommy Wisdom. Long-term co-driver to Pat Moss, starting in 1956 with MGs, Austin A40, Morris Minor, and big Healeys. Joint Ladies European Rally Champions in 1958. Married Peter Riley.

Works Mini drives
1961 Lyon Charbonnières Rally with P. Moss (Retired)
1961 Acropolis Rally with D. Morley (Crashed)
1962 Monte Carlo Rally with P. Moss (26th overall, 7th in class, Ladies)
1962 Tulip Rally with P. Moss (1st overall, 1st in class, Ladies)

Mike Wood

Started rallying in 1953 as a driver and navigator in club events, winning numerous national awards. Joined the works Standard-Triumph team in 1958. First drove for the BMC team in 1963, partnering Timo Makinen and Logan Morrison in big Healeys. Went on to form a successful partnership with Tony Fall.

Works Mini drives
1964 Liège with J. Wadsworth (20th overall)
1965 Three Cities Rally with G. Halliwell (Crashed)
1965 RAC Rally with J. Lusenius (6th overall, 1st in class)
1966 Austrian Alpine Rally with A. Fall (Retired)
1966 Scottish Rally with A. Fall (1st overall, 1st in class)
1966 Geneva Rally with A. Fall (2nd overall, 2nd in class)
1966 London Rally with A. Fall (Retired)
1966 Welsh Rally with A. Fall (Retired)
1966 Alpine Rally with A. Fall (Retired)
1966 RAC Rally with A. Fall (5th overall, 3rd in class)
1967 Monte Carlo Rally with S. Lampinen (15th overall)
1967 Flowers Rally with A. Fall (4th overall, 4th in class)
1967 Scottish Rally with A. Fall (Retired)
1967 Geneva Rally with A. Fall (1st overall, 1st in class)
1967 Alpine Rally with A. Fall (Retired)
1967 London Rally with A. Fall (Retired)
1968 Monte Carlo Rally with A. Fall (4th overall, 2nd in category)
1968 Flowers Rally with A. Fall (Retired)
1968 Tulip Rally with J. Vernaeve (3rd overall, 1st in category)

Works Mini Entries

The following is a list of all the works Mini entries in international rallies and races.

Date	Event	Driver/Co-driver	Model	Reg No	Comp No	Result
1959 September	Viking Rally	M.Chambers/P.Wilson	850	YOP 663		51st overall
November	RAC Rally	P.Ozanne/N.Gilmour A.Pitts/A.Ambrose K.James/I.Hall	850 850 850	TMO 559 TMO 560 TMO 561	129 135 126	Retired Retired Retired
December	Portuguese Rally	N.Mitchell/P.Allison P.Riley/A.Ambrose	850 850	TJB 199 618 AOG	57	54th overall 64th overall
1960 January	Monte Carlo Rally	P.Riley/R.Jones D.Morley/E.Morley T.Wisdom/J.Hay A.Pitts/A.Ambrose N.Mitchell/P.Allison P.Ozanne/N.Gilmour	850 850 850 850 850 850	618 AOG TMO 561 619 AOG TMO 560 617 AOG TMO 559	110 263 299 284 18 307	23rd overall 33rd overall 55th overall 73rd overall Retired Retired

Month	Rally	Crew	cc	Reg.	No.	Result
April	Geneva Rally	D.Morley/E.Morley	850	618 AOG	44	14th overall, 1st in class
		P.Ozanne/P.Allison	850	617 AOG	47	27th overall, 2nd in class
		A.Pitts/A.Ambrose	850	619 AOG	45	Crashed
April	Circuit of Ireland	D.Hiam/A.Ambrose	850	TMO 559		Retired
May	Tulip Rally	T.Christie/N.Paterson	850	TMO 560	161	36th overall, 3rd in class
		J.Sprinzel/M.Hughes	850	TJB 199	99	43rd overall, 2nd in class
		P.Ozanne/P.Allison	850	TMO 561	159	72nd overall, 6th in class
May	Acropolis Rally	J.Milne/W.Bradley	850	619 AOG	124	16th overall, 4th in class
		M.Sutcliffe/D.Astle	850	618 AOG	122	31st overall, 5th in class
		P.Ozanne/P.Allison	850	617 AOG	120	Retired
June	Alpine Rally	T.Gold/M.Hughes	850	TMO 561	19	14th in category, 1st in class
		A.Pitts/A.Ambrose	850	TMO 560	1	4th in class
		K.James/R.Jones	850	TMO 559	5	Crashed
November	RAC Rally	D.Seigle-Morris/V.Elford	850	TMO 559	183	6th overall, 2nd in class
		M.Sutcliffe/D.Astle	850	TMO 561	170	8th overall, 4th in class
		T.Christie/N.Paterson	850	TMO 560	174	Retired
1961						
January	Monte Carlo Rally	P.Garnier/R.Jones	850	TMO 559	254	Retired
		T.Christie/N.Paterson	850	TMO 560	227	Retired
		D.Astle/S.Woolley	850	TMO 561	226	Retired
March	Lyons-Charbonnières	P.Moss/A.Wisdom	850	TMO 560	81	Retired
May	Tulip Rally	P.Riley/A.Ambrose	850	TMO 561	136	12th overall, 1st in class
		D.Seigle-Morris/V.Elford	850	TMO 559	135	23rd overall, 3rd in class

Month	Rally	Crew	cc	Reg.	No.	Result
May	Acropolis Rally	M.Sutcliffe/D.Astle	850	619 AOG	115	Retired
		D.Seigle-Morris/V.Elford	850	TMO 560	125	Retired
		D.Morley/A.Wisdom	850	363 DOC	117	Crashed
1962						
January	Monte Carlo Rally	P.Moss/A.Wisdom	997	737 ABL	304	26th overall, 7th in class, Ladies
		R.Jones/P.Morgan	850	363 DOC	97	77th overall, 3rd in class
		R.Aaltonen/G.Mabbs	997	11 NYB	100	Crashed
May	Tulip Rally	P.Moss/A.Wisdom	997	737 ABL	104	1st overall, 1st in class, Ladies
		D.Seigle-Morris/A.Ambrose	850	363 DOC		Retired
June	Alpine Rally	R.Aaltonen/G.Palm	997	407 ARX	63	Retired
August	1,000 Lakes Rally	R.Aaltonen/A.Ambrose	997	407 ARX		Retired
September	Baden-Baden Rally	P.Moss/P.Mayman	997	737 ABL		1st overall, 1st in class, Ladies
October	Geneva Rally	P.Moss/P.Mayman	997	737 ABL	135	3rd overall, 1st in class
November	RAC Rally	R.Aaltonen/A.Ambrose	997	977 ARX	6	5th overall, 1st in class
		T.Makinen/J.Steadman	997	407 ARX	38	7th overall, 1st in class
		L.Morrison/R.Finlay	997	477 BBL	32	13th overall, 3rd in class

1963

Month	Event	Crew	cc	Reg	No.	Result
January	Monte Carlo Rally	R.Aaltonen/A.Ambrose	997	977 ARX	288	3rd overall, 1st in class
		P.Hopkirk/J.Scott	997	407 ARX	66	6th overall, 2nd in class
		P.Mayman/V.Domleo	997	737 ABL	58	28th overall, 4th in class
		L.Morrison/B.Culcheth	997	477 BBL	155	44th overall, 1st in class
April	Tulip Rally	P.Hopkirk/H.Liddon	997	17 CRX	130	2nd overall, 1st in class
		P.Mayman/V.Domleo	997	737 ABL	129	21st overall, 4th in class
May	Trifels Rally	P.Mayman/V.Domleo	997	737 ABL		1st in class, Ladies
June	Scottish Rally	L.Morrison/D.Brown	997	477 BBL		Crashed
June	Alpine Rally	R.Aaltonen/A.Ambrose	1,071	277 EBL	63	1st in category, 1st in class, Coupe
		P.Mayman/V.Domleo	997	18 CRX	73	6th in category, 1st in class, Ladies, Coupe
		J.Sprinzel/W.Cave	997	977 ARX	24	Crashed
		D.McCluggage/R.Seers	997	17 CRX	64	Retired
September	Tour de France	P.Hopkirk/H.Liddon	1,071	33 EJB	38	3rd overall, 1st in class
		R.Aaltonen/A.Ambrose	997	477 BBL	24	44th overall
		T.Makinen/L.Morrison	997	407 ARX	27	Retired
		P.Mayman/E.Jones	997	277 EBL	39	Retired
November	RAC Rally	P.Hopkirk/H.Liddon	1,071	8 EMO	21	4th overall, 2nd in category
		L.Morrison/R.Finlay	990	407 ARX	36	19th overall, 1st in class
		P.Mayman/V.Domleo	1,071	277 EBL	38	30th overall

1964

Month	Event	Crew	cc	Reg.	No.	Result
January	Monte Carlo Rally	P.Hopkirk/H.Liddon	1,071	33 EJB	37	1st overall, 1st in class
		T.Makinen/P.Vanson	1,071	570 FMO	182	4th overall, 2nd in class
		R.Aaltonen/A.Ambrose	1,071	569 FMO	105	7th overall, 3rd in class
		R.Baxter/E.McMillan	997	477 BBL	39	43rd overall, 2nd in class
		P.Mayman/V.Domleo	1,071	277 EBL	189	Crashed
		J.Thompson/F.Heys	970	18 CRX	187	Crashed
		Manufacturers' Team Prize				
April	Tulip Rally	T.Makinen/A.Ambrose	1,275	AJB 66B	119	1st overall, 1st in class
		Manufacturers' Team Prize with P.Riley, J.Vernaeve				
May	Acropolis Rally	P.Hopkirk/H.Liddon	1,275	AJB 55B	67	Retired
		R.Aaltonen/A.Ambrose	1,275	AJB 33B		Retired
June	Alpine Rally	R.Aaltonen/A.Ambrose	1,275	AJB 55B	70	4th in category, 1st in class, Coupe
		P.Mayman/V.Domleo	970	AJB 66B	8	6th in category, 1st in class, Ladies
		P.Hopkirk/H.Liddon	1,275	AJB 44B	18	Retired
		T.Makinen/P.Vanson	1,275	BJB 77B	19	Retired
		Manufacturers' Team Prize				
August	1,000 Lakes Rally	T.Makinen/P.Keskitalo	1,275	AJB 33B	50	4th overall, 1st in class
August	Spa-Sofia-Liège	J.Wadsworth/M.Wood	1,275	570 FMO	68	20th overall
September	Tour de France	P.Mayman/V.Domleo	970	AJB 66B	20	1st in class
		P.Hopkirk/H.Liddon	970	AJB 44B	19	Retired
		R.Aaltonen/A.Ambrose	1,275	AJB 55B	30	Retired
		T.Makinen/P.Easter	970	BJB 77B	18	Crashed

Month	Event	Crew	cc	Reg	No.	Result
November	RAC Rally	P.Hopkirk/H.Liddon	1,275	CRX 90B	1	Retired
		R.Aaltonen/A.Ambrose	1,275	CRX 89B	2	Retired
		C.Orrenius/R.Dahlgren	1,275	AJB 44B	37	Retired
		H.Kallstrom/R.Haakansson	1,275	AGU 780B	42	Retired
1965						
January	Monte Carlo Rally	T.Makinen/P.Easter	1,275	AJB 44B	52	1st overall, 1st in class
		P.Hopkirk/H.Liddon	1,275	CRX 91B	56	26th overall, 1st in class
		D.Morley/E.Morley	1,275	CRX 90B	72	27th overall, 2nd in class
		R.Aaltonen/A.Ambrose	1,275	CRX 88B	273	Retired
		H.Kallstrom/R.Haakansson	1,275	AGU 780B	176	Retired
		R.Baxter/J.Scott	1,275	8 EMO	91	Retired
February	Swedish Rally	P.Hopkirk/H.Liddon	1,275	AJB 33B	25	Retired
		R.Aaltonen/A.Ambrose	1,275	DJB 93B	22	Retired
		T.Makinen/P.Easter	1,275	DJB 92B	31	Retired
		H.Kallstrom/R.Haakansson	1,275	AGU 780B		Retired
March	Circuit of Ireland	P.Hopkirk/T.Harryman	1,275	CRX 89B	2	1st overall, 1st in class
April	Tulip Rally	T.Makinen/P.Easter	1,275	AJB 33B	124	3rd in category, 1st in class
May	Acropolis Rally	T.Makinen/P.Easter	1,275	DJB 93B	60	Retired
June	Scottish Rally	P.Hopkirk/H.Liddon	1,275	CRX 89B	3	Retired
June	Geneva Rally	R.Aaltonen/A.Ambrose	1,275	EBL 55C	64	1st overall, 1st in class
July	Czech Rally	R.Aaltonen/A.Ambrose	1,275	EJB 55C	102	1st overall, 1st in class
		T.Makinen/P.Easter	1,275	AJB 66B	100	Retired
July	Nordrhein–Westfalen Rally	P.Hopkirk/H.Liddon	1,275	DJB 92B	58	6th overall, 1st in class

Month	Rally	Drivers		Reg.	No.	Result
July	Alpine Rally	T.Makinen/P.Easter	1,275	AJB 33B	70	2nd in category, 1st in class, Coupe
		P.Hopkirk/H.Liddon	1,275	EBL 56C	60	4th in category, 2nd in class, Coupe
		P.Mayman/V.Domleo	1,275	DJB 93B	66	13th in category, Ladies
		R.Aaltonen/A.Ambrose	1,275	EBL 55C	56	14th in category
		Manufacturers' Team Prize				
July	Polish Rally	R.Aaltonen/A.Ambrose	1,275	CRX 89B	55	1st overall, 1st in class
August	1,000 Lakes Rally	T.Makinen/P.Keskitalo	1,275	AJB 33B	28	1st overall, 1st in class
		R.Aaltonen/A.Jaervi	1,275	EBL 55C	26	2nd overall, 2nd in class
		P.Hopkirk/K.Ruutsalo	1,275	EBL 56C	22	6th overall
		Manufacturers' Team Prize				
October	Munich–Vienna–Budapest Rally	R.Aaltonen/A.Ambrose	1,275	CRX 89B	72	1st overall, 1st in class
		A.Fall/R.Crellin	1,275	AJB 66B	65	2nd in class
		G.Halliwell/M.Wood	1,275	CRX 90B	71	Crashed
		Manufacturers' Team Prize				
November	RAC Rally	R.Aaltonen/A.Ambrose	1,275	DJB 93B	5	1st overall, 1st in class
		J.Lusenius/M.Wood	1,275	DJB 92B	44	6th overall, 1st in class
		P.Hopkirk/H.Liddon	1,275	EBL 56C	8	13th overall, 2nd in class
		A.Fall/R.Crellin	1,275	CRX 89B	36	15th overall, 3rd in class
		H.Kallstrom/N.Bjork	1,275	EJB 55C	37	Retired

1966

Month	Event	Drivers		Reg.	No.	Result
January	Monte Carlo Rally	T.Makinen/P.Easter	1,275	GRX 555D	2	Disqualified (1st overall)
		R.Aaltonen/A.Ambrose	1,275	GRX 55D	242	Disqualified (2nd overall)
		P.Hopkirk/H.Liddon	1,275	GRX 5D	230	Disqualified (3rd overall)
		R.Baxter/J.Scott	1,275	GRX 195D	87	Disqualified
February	Swedish Rally	R.Aaltonen/H.Liddon	1,275	GRX 310D		Retired
		T.Makinen/P.Easter	1,275	DJB 92B	35	Retired
February	Flowers Rally	P.Hopkirk/R.Crellin	1,275	GRX 309D	50	15th overall, 6th in category
		A.Fall/H.Liddon	1,275	GRX 5D	15	Disqualified
April	Circuit of Ireland	A.Fall/H.Liddon	1,275	DJB 92B	4	1st overall, 1st in class
		P.Hopkirk/T.Harryman	1,275	GRX 55D	1	Crashed
April	Tulip Rally	R.Aaltonen/H.Liddon	1,275	GRX 310D	89	1st overall, 1st in class
		T.Makinen/P.Easter	1,275	GRX 5D	100	9th overall, 1st in class
		Manufacturers' Team Prize with R.Freeborough				
May	Austrian Alpine Rally	P.Hopkirk/R.Crellin	1,275	DJB 93B	58	1st overall, 1st in class
		A.Fall/M.Wood	1,275	GRX 310D	97	Retired
May	Acropolis Rally	P.Hopkirk/R.Crellin	1,275	GRX 311D	67	3rd overall, 1st in class
		T.Makinen/P.Easter	1,275	HJB 656D	82	10th overall, 2nd in class
		R.Aaltonen/H.Liddon	1,275	JBL 172D	77	Retired
June	Scottish Rally	A.Fall/M.Wood	1,275	DJB 93B	2	1st overall, 1st in class
June	Geneva Rally	A.Fall/M.Wood	1,275	EBL 56C	75	2nd overall, 2nd in class
		P.Hopkirk/T.Harryman	1,275	JBL 495D	50	Retired
		Manufacturers' Team Prize with G.Theiler and D.Friswell				

Month	Rally	Drivers	Capacity	Registration	No.	Result
June	London Rally	P.Hopkirk/R.Crellin	1,275	JBL 495D	6	Retired
		A.Fall/M.Wood	1,275	DJB 93B	4	Retired
July	Czech Rally	R.Aaltonen/H.Liddon	1,275	JBL 494D	75	1st overall, 1st in class
		T.Makinen/P.Easter	1,275	JBL 493D	77	3rd overall, 2nd in class
		S.Zasada/Z.Leszczvk	1,275	EBL 56C	16	4th overall, 1st in class
		Manufacturers' Team Prize				
July	German Rally	P.Hopkirk/A.Nash	1,275	GRX 311D	42	Retired
		A.Fall/H.Liddon	1,275	JBL 172D	49	Retired
August	Polish Rally	A.Fall/A.Krauklis	970	GRX 309D	56	1st overall, 1st in class
		T.Makinen/P.Easter	1,275	GRX 555D	37	2nd overall, 1st in class
		R.Aaltonen/H.Liddon	1,275	HJB 656D	29	Retired
August	Welsh Rally	A.Fall/M.Wood	1,275	GRX 309D		Retired
August	1,000 Lakes Rally	T.Makinen/P.Keskitalo	1,275	JBL 493D	45	1st overall, 1st in class
		R.Aaltonen/V.Numimba	1,275	GRX 310D	49	3rd overall, 2nd in class
		J.Lusenius/K.Lehto	1,275	JBL 494D	27	6th overall, 3rd in class
September	Alpine Rally	R.Aaltonen/H.Liddon	1,275	JBL 495D	62	3rd overall, 2nd in class
		P.Hopkirk/R.Crellin	1,275	GRX 311D	67	Retired
		T.Makinen/P.Easter	1,275	JMO 969D	68	Retired
		A.Fall/M.Wood	1,275	GRX 195D	66	Retired
October	Munich–Budapest Rally	T.Makinen/P.Easter	1,275	HJB 656D	57	1st overall, 1st in class
	Vienna–	A.Fall/H.Liddon	1,275	JBL 494D		Retired

Month	Event	Drivers				Result
November	RAC Rally	H.Kallstrom/R.Haakansson	1,275	JBL 494D	66	2nd overall, 1st in class
		R.Aaltonen/H.Liddon	1,275	GRX 310D	18	4th overall, 2nd in class
		A.Fall/M.Wood	1,275	GRX 195D	21	5th overall, 3rd in class
		M.Aaltonen/C.Tyler	1,275	EBL 56C	117	37th overall
		P.Hopkirk/R.Crellin	1,275	JMO 969D	10	Retired
		T.Makinen/P.Easter	1,275	GRX 5D	12	Retired
		S.Lampinen/A.Ambrose	1,275	JBL 495D	29	Crashed
		G.Hill/M.Boyd	1,275	GRX 309D	5	Retired
1967						
January	Monte Carlo Rally	R.Aaltonen/H.Liddon	1,275	LBL 6D	177	1st overall, 1st in class
		P.Hopkirk/R.Crellin	1,275	LBL 666D	205	6th overall, 5th in class
		A.Fall/R.Joss	1,275	LBL 606D	32	10th overall
		S.Lampinen/M.Wood	1,275	HJB 656D	178	15th overall
		T.Makinen/P.Easter	1,275	LBL 66D	144	41st overall
February	Swedish Rally	R.Aaltonen/H.Liddon	1,275	JBL 495D	26	3rd overall, 1st in class
		T.Makinen/P.Easter	1,275	JMO 969D	22	Retired
February	Flowers Rally	P.Hopkirk/R.Crellin	1,275	LBL 590E	67	2nd overall, 2nd in class
		A.Fall/M.Wood	1,275	GRX 195D	82	4th overall, 4th in class
March	East African Safari	R.Aaltonen/H.Liddon	1,275	HJB 656D	8	Retired
March	Circuit of Ireland	P.Hopkirk/T.Harryman	1,275	GRX 5D	1	1st overall, 1st in class
March	Sebring 3 Hour Race	P.Hopkirk/J.Rhodes	1,275	GRX 309D	48	1st in class
April	Tulip Rally	T.Makinen/P.Easter	1,275	LRX 827E	64	2nd overall, 1st in category
		R.Aaltonen/H.Liddon	1,275	LRX 829E	65	3rd overall, 2nd in category
		D.Benzimra/T.Harryman	1,275	GRX 5D	73	Retired
		Manufacturers' Team Prize with J.Vernaeve				

Month	Rally	Drivers	cc	Registration	No.	Result
May	Acropolis Rally	P.Hopkirk/R.Crellin	1,275	LRX 830E	89	1st overall, 1st in class
		R.Aaltonen/H.Liddon	1,275	LRX 828E	92	Retired
		T.Makinen/P.Easter	1,275	GRX 195D	99	Retired
June	Scottish Rally	L.Ytterbring/L.Persson	1,275	GRX 311D	1	2nd overall
		A.Fall/M.Wood	1,275	GRX 5D		Retired
June	Geneva Rally	A.Fall/M.Wood	1,275	LRX 827E	79	1st overall, 1st in class
		J.Vernaeve/H.Liddon	1,275	LRX 829E	80	2nd overall, 2nd in class
July	London Rally	A.Fall/M.Wood	1,275	GRX 5D	8	Retired
July	Danube Rally	R.Aaltonen/H.Liddon	1,275	LRX 828E	34	Disqualified
August	1,000 Lakes Rally	T.Makinen/P.Keskitalo	1,275	GRX 195D	29	1st overall, 1st in class
August	84 Hour Marathon	A.Fall/J.Vernaeve/A.Hedges	970	GRX 5D	39	2nd overall, 1st in class
		A.Poole/R.Enever/C.Baker	970	LRX 830E	40	Retired
September	Alpine Rally	P.Hopkirk/R.Crellin	1,275	LRX 827E	107	1st overall, 1st in class
		R.Aaltonen/H.Liddon	1,275	JBL 172D	106	Retired
		T.Makinen/P.Easter	1,275	GRX 311D	103	Retired
		A.Fall/M.Wood	1,275	GRX 310D	40	Retired
November	Tour de Corse	P.Hopkirk/R.Crellin	1,275	GRX 5D	79	Retired
		R.Aaltonen/H.Liddon	1,275	JBL 172D	73	Retired
1968 January	Monte Carlo Rally	R.Aaltonen/H.Liddon	1,275	ORX 7F	18	3rd overall, 1st in category
		A.Fall/M.Wood	1,275	ORX 707F	185	4th overall, 2nd in category
		P.Hopkirk/R.Crellin	1,275	ORX 777F	87	5th overall, 3rd in category
		T.Makinen/P.Easter	1,275	ORX 77F	7	55th overall
		Manufacturers' Team Prize				

Month	Event	Drivers	cc	Reg.	No.	Result
February	Flowers Rally	R.Aaltonen/H.Liddon	1,275	ORX 77F	40	Retired
		A.Fall/M.Wood	1,275	ORX 777F	44	Retired
April	Tulip Rally	J.Vernaeve/M.Wood	1,275	ORX 707F	74	3rd overall, 1st in category
		T.Makinen/P.Easter	1,275	LBL 66D	73	41st overall
April	Circuit of Ireland	P.Hopkirk/T.Harryman	1,275	JMO 969D	1	Retired
		L.Ytterbring/L.Persson	1,275	OBL 46F	3	Retired
April	Canada Shell 4000	P.Hopkirk/M.Kerry	1,275	GRX 5D	119	Disqualified
May	Acropolis Rally	R.Aaltonen/H.Liddon	1,275	RBL 450F	46	5th overall, 1st in class
		T.Makinen/P.Easter	1,275	GRX 310D	49	Retired
June	Scottish Rally	L.Ytterbring/L.Persson	1,275	JMO 969D	3	2nd overall, 1st in class
August	1,000 Lakes Rally	T.Makinen/P.Keskitalo	1,275	ORX 77F	47	Retired
		L.Ytterbring/L.Persson	1,275	ORX 777F	41	Retired
October	Portuguese Rally	P.Hopkirk/A.Nash	1,275	LBL 606D	71	2nd overall, 1st in class
1969						
March	Brands Hatch	J.Rhodes	1,275	OBL 45F	125	Crashed
		J.Handley	1,275	OBL 46F	126	Crashed
March	Silverstone Daily Express	J.Handley	1,275	LRX 827E	15	10th overall, 4th in class
		J.Rhodes	1,275	GRX 310D	14	11th overall, 5th in class
April	Snetterton Guards Trophy	J.Rhodes	1,275	GRX 310D		12th overall, 4th in class

Month	Event	Drivers	cc	Reg.	No.	Result
April	Thruxton	J.Handley J.Rhodes	1,275 1,275	LRX 827E GRX 310D	24 23	9th overall, 4th in class 22nd overall
April	Circuit of Ireland	P.Hopkirk/A.Nash	1,275	GRX 311D	2	2nd overall, 1st in class
May	Silverstone Martini Trophy	J.Rhodes J.Handley	1,275 1,275	LBL 666D LRX 827E	17 16	6th overall, 2nd in class 7th overall, 3rd in class
May	Crystal Palace Annerley Trophy	J.Handley J.Rhodes	1,275 1,275	LRX 827E LBL 666D	135 134	3rd overall, 3rd in class 4th overall, 4th in class
June	Hockenheim	J.Rhodes J.Handley	1,275 1,275	URX 560G URX 550G	1 2	6th overall, 3rd in class 5th in class
June	Brands Hatch Six Hours	J.Handley/R.Enever J.Rhodes/P.Hopkirk	1,275 1,275	RBL 450F GRX 310D	74 75	4th overall, 2nd in class 7th overall, 3rd in class
June	Mallory Park Guards Trophy	J.Rhodes J.Handley	1,275 1,275	LBL 666D LRX 827E	118 117	8th overall, 4th in class Retired
July	Nurbürgring Six Hours	J.Handley/R.Enever J.Rhodes/G.Mabbs	1,275 1,275	RBL 450F GRX 310D	74 73	Retired Retired
July	Silverstone Grand Prix	J.Rhodes J.Handley	1,275 1,275	LBL 666D LRX 827E	16 15	8th overall, 4th in class 10th overall, 6th in class
July	Spa 24 Hours	J.Handley/R.Enever J.Rhodes/G.Mabbs	1,275 1,275	RBL 450F RJB 327F	78 79	Retired Retired
August	Oulton Park	J.Rhodes J.Handley	1,275 1,275	LBL 666D RJB 327F	75	12th overall, 4th in class 15th overall

	Event	Drivers		Reg.	No.	Result
September	Tour de France	P.Hopkirk/A.Nash	1,275	OBL 45F	57	14th overall, 1st in class
		B.Culcheth/J.Syer	1,275	URX 550G	12	5th in category, 2nd in class
		J.Handley/P.Easter	1,275	URX 560G	56	Crashed
September	Brands Hatch Guards Trophy	J.Rhodes	1,275	LBL 666D	244	10th overall, 4th in class
		J.Handley	1,275	LRX 827E	245	Retired
October	Salzbürgring	J.Rhodes	1,275	LBL 666D	30	1st overall, 1st in class
		J.Handley	1,275	LRX 827E	31	2nd overall, 2nd in class
1970 April	World Cup Rally	J.Handley/P.Easter	1,275	XJB 308H	59	Retired
June	Scottish Rally	P.Hopkirk/A.Nash	1,275	XJB 308H	14	2nd overall, 1st in class
July	Nurbürgring	J.Handley/A.Poole	1,275	LBL 606D		Retired
September	84 Hour Marathon	J.Handley/A.Poole/J.Vernaeve	1,275	SOH 878H	20	Retired
October	Southern Cross Rally	A.Cowan/R.Forsyth	1,275	YMO 881H		Retired
		B.Culcheth/R.Bonhomme	1,275	RJB 327F	12	Retired
November	Rally of the Hills	B.Culcheth/R.Bonhomme	1,275	RJB 327F		4th overall

Works Mini Race Championships

The following are the achievements of the works-supported Mini racing teams in the British and European Saloon Car Championships.

Year	Title	Result	Driver	Team
1962	British Championship	1st overall, 1st 1,000 cc class	John Love	Cooper
1963	European Championship	1st 1,300 cc class	Rob Slotemaker	Downton
1964	British Championship	1st 1,300 cc class	John Fitzpatrick	Cooper
1964	European Championship	1st overall, 1st 1,000 cc class	Warwick Banks	Tyrrell
1965	British Championship	1st 1,000 cc class	Warwick Banks	Cooper
1965	British Championship	1st 1,300 cc class	John Rhodes	Cooper
1966	British Championship	1st 1,300 cc class	John Rhodes	Cooper
1967	British Championship	1st 1,300 cc class	John Rhodes	Cooper
1968	British Championship	1st 1,000 cc class	Gordon Spice	Arden
1968	British Championship	1st 1,300 cc class	John Rhodes	Cooper
1968	European Championship	1st overall, 1st 1,000 cc class	John Handley	British Vita
1968	European Championship	1st 1,300 cc class	John Rhodes	Cooper
1969	British Championship	1st overall, 1st 1,000 cc class	Alec Poole	Arden

The Works Mini Rally and Race Cars

The following is a list of all the Abingdon-built works Minis with the events in which they competed, their drivers, and the results. Throughout the book I have refrained from recording whether cars were Austin or Morris Minis or Mini-Coopers. This was mainly because I did not think that anyone would be interested and, furthermore, Abingdon regularly changed the badges from one to the other for various reasons. Timo Makinen, for example, had a close relationship with his local BMC Dealer in Finland who was strictly a Morris man. There was always a last minute panic to ensure, therefore, that Timo's cars were Morris and not Austin. In many countries either Austin or Morris was the favoured marque and thus on some events all of the team cars had to run as one marque or the other. This did lead to one or two amusing incidents and I recall a somewhat awkward scrutineering session on the Tulip Rally when the scrutineers were not at all happy to find that the badge on the bonnet said Austin and the badge on the boot said Morris. To make matters worse the car's log book would have shown that the registered owner was the MG Car Company!

Reg No	Model	Registered	Events	Driver	Result
YOP 663	850	August 1959	1959 Viking Rally	M.Chambers	51st overall
TJB 199	850	August 1959	1959 Portuguese Rally	N.Mitchell	54th overall
			1960 Tulip Rally	J.Sprinzel	43rd overall, 2nd in class
TMO 559	850	October 1959	1959 RAC Rally	P.Ozanne	Retired
			1960 Monte Carlo Rally	P.Ozanne	Retired
			1960 Circuit of Ireland	D.Hiam	Retired
			1960 Alpine Rally	K.James	Crashed
			1960 RAC Rally	D.Seigle-Morris	6th overall, 2nd in class
			1961 Monte Carlo Rally	P.Garnier	Retired
			1961 Tulip Rally	D.Seigle-Morris	23rd overall, 3rd in class

Car	Engine	Date	Event	Driver	Result
TMO 560	850	October 1959	1959 RAC Rally	A.Pitts	Retired
			1960 Monte Carlo Rally	A.Pitts	73rd overall
			1960 Tulip Rally	T.Christie	36th overall, 1st in class
			1960 Alpine Rally	A.Pitts	4th in class
			1960 RAC Rally	T.Christie	Retired
			1961 Monte Carlo Rally	T.Christie	Retired
			1961 Lyons–Charbonnières	P.Moss	Retired
			1961 Acropolis Rally	D.Seigle-Morris	Retired
TMO 561	850	October 1959	1959 RAC Rally	K.James	Retired
			1960 Monte Carlo Rally	D.Morley	33rd overall
			1960 Tulip Rally	P.Ozanne	72nd overall, 6th in class
			1960 Alpine Rally	T.Gold	14th in category, 1st in class
			1960 RAC Rally	M.Sutcliffe	8th overall, 4th in class
			1961 Monte Carlo Rally	D.Astle	Retired
			1961 Tulip Rally	P.Riley	12th overall, 1st in class
617 AOG	850	November 1959	1960 Monte Carlo Rally	N.Mitchell	Retired
			1960 Geneva Rally	P.Ozanne	27th overall, 2nd in class
			1960 Acropolis Rally	P.Ozanne	Retired
618 AOG	850	November 1959	1959 Portuguese Rally	P.Riley	64th overall
			1960 Monte Carlo Rally	P.Riley	23rd overall
			1960 Geneva Rally	D.Morley	14th overall
			1960 Acropolis Rally	M.Sutcliffe	31st overall, 5th in class
619 AOG	850	November 1959	1960 Monte Carlo Rally	T.Wisdom	55th overall
			1960 Geneva Rally	A.Pitts	Crashed
			1960 Acropolis Rally	J.Milne	16th overall, 4th in class
			1961 Acropolis Rally	M.Sutcliffe	Retired
363 DOC	850	March 1961	1961 Acropolis Rally	D.Morley	Crashed
			1962 Monte Carlo Rally	R.Jones	77th overall, 3rd in class
			1962 Tulip Rally	D.Seigle-Morris	Retired

Reg.	Model	Date	Rally	Driver	Result
11 NYB	997		1962 Monte Carlo Rally	R.Aaltonen	Crashed
737 ABL	997	November 1961	1962 Monte Carlo Rally	P.Moss	26th overall, 7th in class
			1962 Tulip Rally	P.Moss	1st overall, 1st in class
			1962 Baden-Baden Rally	P.Moss	1st overall, 1st in class
			1962 Geneva Rally	P.Moss	3rd overall, 1st in class
			1963 Monte Carlo Rally	P.Mayman	28th overall, 4th in class
			1963 Tulip Rally	P.Mayman	21st overall, 4th in class
			1963 Trifels Rally	P.Mayman	1st in class
407 ARX	997	March 1962	1962 Alpine Rally	R.Aaltonen	Retired
			1962 1,000 Lakes Rally	R.Aaltonen	Retired
			1962 RAC Rally	T.Makinen	7th overall, 1st in class
			1963 Monte Carlo Rally	P.Hopkirk	6th overall, 2nd in class
			1963 Tour de France	T.Makinen	Retired
			1963 RAC Rally	L.Morrison	19th overall, 1st in class
977 ARX	997	March 1962	1962 RAC Rally	R.Aaltonen	5th overall, 1st in class
			1963 Monte Carlo Rally	R.Aaltonen	3rd overall, 1st in class
			1963 Alpine Rally	J.Sprinzel	Crashed
477 BBL	997	April 1962	1962 RAC Rally	L.Morrison	13th overall, 3rd in class
			1963 Monte Carlo Rally	L.Morrison	44th overall, 1st in class
			1963 Tour de France	R.Aaltonen	44th overall
			1963 Scottish Rally	L.Morrison	Crashed
			1964 Monte Carlo Rally	R.Baxter	43rd overall, 2nd in class
17 CRX	997	December 1962	1963 Tulip Rally	P.Hopkirk	2nd overall, 1st in class
			1963 Alpine Rally	D.McCluggage	Retired
18 CRX	997	December 1962	1963 Alpine Rally	P.Mayman	6th in category, 1st in class
			1964 Monte Carlo Rally	J.Thompson	Retired
8 EMO	1071	May 1963	1963 Monte Carlo Rally	P.Hopkirk	4th overall, 2nd in category
			1965 Monte Carlo Rally	R.Baxter	Retired

Car	Engine	Introduced	Event	Driver	Result
277 EBL	997	May 1963	1963 Alpine Rally	R.Aaltonen	1st in category, 1st in class
			1963 Tour de France	P.Mayman	Retired
			1963 RAC Rally	P.Mayman	30th overall
			1964 Monte Carlo Rally	P.Mayman	Crashed
33 EJB	997	May 1963	1963 Tour de France	P.Hopkirk	3rd overall, 1st in class
			1964 Monte Carlo Rally	P.Hopkirk	1st overall, 1st in class
569 FMO	997	November 1963	1964 Monte Carlo Rally	R.Aaltonen	7th overall, 3rd in class
570 FMO	997	November 1963	1964 Monte Carlo Rally	T.Makinen	4th overall, 2nd in class
			1964 Spa–Sofia–Liège	J.Wadsworth	20th overall
AJB 33B	1275	February 1964	1964 Acropolis Rally	R.Aaltonen	Retired
			1964 1,000 Lakes Rally	T.Makinen	4th overall, 1st in class
			1965 Swedish Rally	P.Hopkirk	Retired
			1965 Tulip Rally	T.Makinen	3rd overall, 1st in class
			1965 Alpine Rally	T.Makinen	2nd in category, 1st in class
			1965 1,000 Lakes Rally	T.Makinen	1st overall, 1st in class
AJB 44B	1275	February 1964	1964 Alpine Rally	P.Hopkirk	Retired
			1964 Tour de France	P.Hopkirk	Retired
			1964 RAC Rally	C.Orrenius	Retired
			1965 Monte Carlo Rally	T.Makinen	1st overall, 1st in class
AJB 55B	1275	February 1964	1964 Acropolis Rally	P.Hopkirk	Retired
			1964 Alpine Rally	R.Aaltonen	4th in category, 1st in class
			1964 Tour de France	R.Aaltonen	Retired
AJB 66B	1275	February 1964	1964 Tulip Rally	T.Makinen	1st overall, 1st in class
			1964 Alpine Rally	P.Mayman	6th in category, 1st in class
			1964 Tour de France	P.Mayman	1st in class
			1965 Czech Rally	T.Makinen	Retired
			1965 Three Cities Rally	A.Fall	2nd in class

Reg.	Engine	Date	Event	Driver	Result
BJB 77B	1275	June 1964	1964 Alpine Rally	T.Makinen	Retired
			1964 Tour de France	T.Makinen	Crashed
CRX 88B	1275	October 1964	1965 Monte Carlo Rally	R.Aaltonen	Retired
CRX 89B	1275	October 1964	1964 RAC Rally	R.Aaltonen	Retired
			1965 Circuit of Ireland	P.Hopkirk	1st overall, 1st in class
			1965 Scottish Rally	P.Hopkirk	Retired
			1965 Polish Rally	R.Aaltonen	1st overall, 1st in class
			1965 Three Cities Rally	R.Aaltonen	1st overall, 1st in class
			1965 RAC Rally	A.Fall	15th overall, 3rd in class
CRX 90B	1275	October 1964	1964 RAC Rally	P.Hopkirk	Retired
			1965 Monte Carlo Rally	D.Morley	27th overall, 2nd in class
			1965 Three Cities Rally	G.Halliwell	Crashed
CRX 91B	1275	October 1964	1965 Monte Carlo Rally	P.Hopkirk	26th overall, 1st in class
AGU 780B	1275	November 1964	1964 RAC Rally	H.Kallstrom	Retired
			1965 Monte Carlo Rally	H.Kallstrom	Retired
			1965 Swedish Rally	H.Kallstrom	Retired
DJB 92B	1275	December 1964	1965 Swedish Rally	T.Makinen	Retired
			1965 German Rally	P.Hopkirk	6th overall, 1st in class
			1965 RAC Rally	J.Lusenius	6th overall, 1st in class
			1966 Swedish Rally	T.Makinen	Retired
			1966 Circuit of Ireland	A.Fall	1st overall, 1st in class
DJB 93B	1275	December 1964	1965 Swedish Rally	R.Aaltonen	Retired
			1965 Acropolis Rally	T.Makinen	Retired
			1965 Alpine Rally	P.Mayman	13th in category
			1965 RAC Rally	R.Aaltonen	1st overall, 1st in class
			1966 Austrian Alpine Rally	P.Hopkirk	1st overall, 1st in class
			1966 Scottish Rally	A.Fall	1st overall, 1st in class
			1966 London Rally	A.Fall	Retired

Reg	Engine	Date	Event	Driver	Result
EJB 55C	1275	March 1965	1965 Czech Rally	R.Aaltonen	1st overall, 1st in class
			1965 RAC Rally	H.Kallstrom	Retired
EBL 55C	1275	March 1965	1965 Geneva Rally	R.Aaltonen	1st overall, 1st in class
			1965 1,000 Lakes Rally	R.Aaltonen	2nd overall, 2nd in class
			1965 Alpine Rally	R.Aaltonen	14th in category
EBL 56C	1275	March 1965	1965 Alpine Rally	P.Hopkirk	4th in category, 2nd in class
			1965 1,000 Lakes Rally	P.Hopkirk	6th overall
			1965 RAC Rally	P.Hopkirk	13th overall, 2nd in class
			1966 Geneva Rally	A.Fall	2nd overall, 2nd in class
			1966 Czech Rally	S.Zasada	4th overall, 1st in class
			1966 RAC Rally	R.Aaltonen	37th overall
GRX 5D	1275	January 1966	1966 Monte Carlo Rally	P.Hopkirk	Disqualified
			1966 Flowers Rally	A.Fall	Disqualified
			1966 Tulip Rally	T.Makinen	9th overall, 1st in class
			1966 RAC Rally	T.Makinen	Retired
			1967 Circuit of Ireland	P.Hopkirk	1st overall, 1st in class
			1967 Tulip Rally	D.Benzimra	Retired
			1967 Scottish Rally	A.Fall	Retired
			1967 London Rally	A.Fall	Retired
			1967 84 Hour Marathon	A.Fall/A.Hedges/J.Vernaeve	2nd overall, 1st in class
			1967 Tour de Corse	P.Hopkirk	Retired
			1968 Canada Shell 4000	P.Hopkirk	Disqualified
GRX 55D	1275	January 1966	1966 Monte Carlo Rally	R.Aaltonen	Disqualified
			1966 Circuit of Ireland	P.Hopkirk	Crashed

GRX 195D — 1275 — January 1966

Event	Driver	Result
1966 Monte Carlo Rally	R.Baxter	Disqualified
1966 Alpine Rally	A.Fall	Retired
1966 RAC Rally	A.Fall	5th overall, 3rd in class
1967 Flowers Rally	A.Fall	4th overall, 4th in class
1967 Acropolis Rally	T.Makinen	Retired
1967 1,000 Lakes Rally	T.Makinen	1st overall, 1st in class

GRX 309D — 1275 — January 1966

Event	Driver	Result
1966 Flowers Rally	P.Hopkirk	15th overall, 6th in category
1966 Polish Rally	A.Fall	1st overall, 1st in class
1966 Welsh Rally	A.Fall	Retired
1966 RAC Rally	G.Hill	Retired
1966 Sebring 3 Hours	P.Hopkirk/J.Rhodes	1st in class

GRX 310D — 1275 — January 1966

Event	Driver	Result
1966 Swedish Rally	R.Aaltonen	Retired
1966 Tulip Rally	R.Aaltonen	1st overall, 1st in class
1966 Austrian Alpine	A.Fall	Retired
1966 1,000 Lakes Rally	R.Aaltonen	3rd overall, 2nd in class
1966 RAC Rally	R.Aaltonen	4th overall, 2nd in class
1967 Alpine Rally	A.Fall	Retired
1968 Acropolis Rally	T.Makinen	Retired
1969 Silverstone	J.Rhodes	11th overall, 5th in class
1969 Snetterton	J.Rhodes	12th overall, 4th in class
1969 Thruxton	J.Rhodes	22nd overall
1969 Brands Hatch	J.Rhodes/P.Hopkirk	7th overall, 3rd in class
1969 Nurbürgring	J.Rhodes/G.Mabbs	Retired

GRX 555D — 1275 — January 1966

Event	Driver	Result
1966 Monte Carlo Rally	T.Makinen	Disqualified
1966 Polish Rally	T.Makinen	2nd overall, 1st in class

GRX 311D — 1275 — February 1966

Event	Driver	Result
1966 Acropolis Rally	P.Hopkirk	3rd overall, 1st in class
1966 German Rally	P.Hopkirk	Retired
1966 Alpine Rally	P.Hopkirk	Retired
1967 Scottish Rally	L.Ytterbring	2nd overall
1967 Alpine Rally	T.Makinen	Retired
1969 Circuit of Ireland	P.Hopkirk	2nd overall, 1st in class

Registration	Engine	Date	Event	Driver	Result
HJB 656D	1275	April 1966	1966 Acropolis Rally	T.Makinen	10th overall
			1966 Polish Rally	R.Aaltonen	Retired
			1966 Three Cities Rally	T.Makinen	1st overall, 1st in class
			1967 Monte Carlo Rally	S.Lampinen	15th overall
			1967 East African Safari	R.Aaltonen	Retired
JBL 172D	1275	April 1966	1966 Acropolis Rally	T.Makinen	Retired
			1966 German Rally	A.Fall	Retired
			1967 Alpine Rally	R.Aaltonen	Retired
			1967 Tour de Corse	R.Aaltonen	Retired
JBL 494D	1275	May 1966	1966 Czech Rally	R.Aaltonen	1st overall, 1st in class
			1966 1,000 Lakes Rally	J.Lusenius	6th overall, 3rd in class
			1966 Three Cities Rally	A.Fall	Retired
			1966 RAC Rally	H.Kallstrom	2nd overall, 1st in class
JBL 495D	1275	May 1966	1966 Geneva Rally	P.Hopkirk	Retired
			1966 London Rally	P.Hopkirk	Retired
			1966 Alpine Rally	R.Aaltonen	3rd overall, 2nd in class
			1966 RAC Rally	S.Lampinen	Crashed
			1967 Swedish Rally	R.Aaltonen	3rd overall, 1st in class
JBL 493D	1275	June 1966	1966 Czech Rally	T.Makinen	3rd overall, 2nd in class
			1966 1,000 Lakes Rally	T.Makinen	1st overall, 1st in class
JMO 969D	1275	July 1966	1966 Alpine Rally	T.Makinen	Retired
			1966 RAC Rally	P.Hopkirk	Retired
			1967 Swedish Rally	T.Makinen	Retired
			1968 Circuit of Ireland	P.Hopkirk	Retired
			1968 Scottish Rally	L.Ytterbring	2nd overall, 1st in class

Reg	Engine	Date	Event	Driver	Result
LBL 666D	1275	December 1966	1967 Monte Carlo Rally	P.Hopkirk	6th overall, 5th in class
			1969 Silverstone	J.Rhodes	6th overall, 2nd in class
			1969 Crystal Palace	J.Rhodes	4th overall, 4th in class
			1969 Mallory Park	J.Rhodes	8th overall, 4th in class
			1969 Silverstone	J.Rhodes	8th overall, 4th in class
			1969 Oulton Park	J.Rhodes	12th overall, 4th in class
			1969 Brands Hatch	J.Rhodes	10th overall, 4th in class
			1969 Salzbürgring	J.Rhodes	1st overall, 1st in class
LBL 6D	1275	December 1966	1967 Monte Carlo Rally	R.Aaltonen	1st overall, 1st in class
LBL 606D	1275	December 1966	1967 Monte Carlo Rally	A.Fall	10th overall
			1968 Portuguese Rally	P.Hopkirk	2nd overall, 1st in class
			1969 Nurbürgring	J.Handley/A.Poole	Retired
LBL 66D	1275	December 1966	1967 Monte Carlo Rally	T.Makinen	41st overall
			1968 Tulip Rally	T.Makinen	41st overall
LBL 590E	1275	January 1967	1967 Flowers Rally	P.Hopkirk	2nd overall, 2nd in class
LRX 827E	1275	March 1967	1967 Tulip Rally	T.Makinen	2nd overall, 1st in category
			1967 Geneva Rally	A.Fall	1st overall, 1st in class
			1967 Alpine Rally	P.Hopkirk	1st overall, 1st in class
			1969 Silverstone	J.Handley	10th overall, 4th in class
			1969 Thruxton	J.Handley	9th overall, 4th in class
			1969 Silverstone	J.Handley	7th overall, 3rd in class
			1969 Crystal Palace	J.Handley	3rd overall, 3rd in class
			1969 Mallory Park	J.Handley	Retired
			1969 Silverstone	J.Handley	10th overall, 6th in class
			1969 Brands Hatch	J.Handley	Retired
			1969 Salzbürgring	J.Handley	2nd overall, 2nd in class
LRX 828E	1275	March 1967	1967 Acropolis Rally	R.Aaltonen	Retired
			1967 Danube Rally	R.Aaltonen	Disqualified

Registration	Engine	Date	Event	Driver(s)	Result
LRX 829E	1275	March 1967	1967 Tulip Rally 1967 Geneva Rally	R.Aaltonen J.Vernaeve	3rd overall, 2nd in category 2nd overall, 2nd in class
LRX 830E	1275	March 1967	1967 Acropolis Rally 1967 84 Hour Marathon	P.Hopkirk A.Poole/R.Enever/C.Baker	1st overall, 1st in class Retired
ORX 7F	1275	January 1968	1968 Monte Carlo Rally	R.Aaltonen	3rd overall, 1st in category
ORX 77F	1275	January 1968	1968 Monte Carlo Rally 1968 Flowers Rally 1968 1,000 Lakes Rally	T.Makinen R.Aaltonen T.Makinen	55th overall Retired Retired
ORX 777F	1275	January 1968	1968 Monte Carlo Rally 1968 Flowers Rally 1968 1,000 Lakes Rally	P.Hopkirk A.Fall L.Ytterbring	5th overall, 3rd in category Retired Retired
ORX 707F	1275	January 1968	1968 Monte Carlo Rally 1968 Tulip Rally	A.Fall J.Vernaeve	4th overall, 2nd in category 3rd overall, 1st in category
OBL 45F	1275	January 1968	1969 Tour de France 1969 Brands Hatch	P.Hopkirk J.Rhodes	14th overall, 1st in class Crashed
OBL 46F	1275	January 1968	1968 Circuit of Ireland 1969 Brands Hatch	L.Ytterbring J.Handley	Retired Crashed
RBL 450F	1275	January 1968	1968 Acropolis Rally 1969 Brands Hatch 6 Hours 1969 Nurburgring 6 Hours 1969 Spa 24 Hours	R.Aaltonen J.Handley/R.Enever J.Handley/R.Enever J.Handley/R.Enever	5th overall, 1st in class 4th overall, 2nd in class Retired Retired
RJB 327F	1275	January 1968	1969 Oulton Park 1969 Spa 24 Hours 1970 Southern Cross Rally 1970 Rally of the Hills	J.Handley J.Rhodes/G.Mabbs B.Culcheth B.Culcheth	15th overall, 4th in class Retired Retired 4th overall

Reg.	Engine	Date	Event	Drivers	Result
URX 550G	1275	May 1969	1969 Tour de France 1969 Hockenheim	B.Culcheth J.Handley	5th in category, 2nd in class 5th in class
URX 560G	1275	May 1969	1969 Tour de France 1969 Hockenheim	J.Handley J.Rhodes	Crashed 6th overall, 3rd in class
XJB 308H	1275	January 1970	1970 World Cup Rally 1970 Scottish Rally	J.Handley P.Hopkirk	Retired 2nd overall, 1st in class
YMO 881H	1275	January 1970	1970 Southern Cross Rally	A.Cowan	Retired
SOH 878H	1275	January 1970	1970 84 Hour Marathon	J.Handley/A.Poole/ J.Vernaeve	Retired

Works Mini Milestones

The first to drive a works Mini in an international event was the first competitions manager, Marcus Chambers, who took an 850 on the 1959 Viking Rally.

The first international class win for the works Minis was by Don Morley on the 1960 Geneva Rally in an 850.

The first international outright win for the works Mini was by Pat Moss on the 1962 Tulip Rally in a 997 Mini-Cooper.

The most successful works Mini was 737 ABL, driven in seven events by Pat Moss and Pauline Mayman, finishing every event and claiming two outright wins and four class awards.

The most successful works Mini driver was Rauno Aaltonen, who in 41 drives scored eight outright wins, two category wins, 14 class victories, and the European Rally Championship title in 1965.

Pat Moss was the most successful of the ladies who drove the works Minis, claiming two outright wins and four class awards.

The most successful of the works Mini co-drivers was Tony Ambrose, who partnered Peter Riley in 850 days and later Rauno Aaltonen to claim six outright victories, two category wins, and 11 class awards.

The works Mini which registered the most events was GRX 310D, which between 1966 and 1969 was driven on 12 events, seven European Rally Championship rounds and five races.

Paddy Hopkirk's success in the 1964 Monte Carlo Rally was the most significant victory for the works Minis and unquestionably the most publicized British rally victory of all time.

Timo Makinen's victory in the 1965 Monte Carlo Rally is generally recognized as being one of the greatest rally drives of all time.

The most successful event for the works Minis was the Monte Carlo Rally, bringing outright victories in 1964, 1965 and 1967 and class awards every year from 1963 to 1968 (except for the disqualification year of 1966).

The most successful works Mini race driver was John Rhodes, who won the 1,300 cc class in the British Saloon Car Championship every year from 1965 to 1968.

Works-supported Minis won the British Saloon Car Championship twice, John Love

(Cooper Car Company in 1962) and Alec Poole (Equipe Arden in 1969) on both occasions driving a 1-litre car.

The works Minis won every major European Rally Championship event during the 1960s except the Swedish Rally, the East African Safari, the Italian Flowers Rally and the Liège Marathon.

A total of 71 works Minis were built at Abingdon between 1959 and 1970, made up as follows: 850 (9), 997 (11), 1,071 (1) and 1,275 (50).

The most 'reliable' works Mini was LBL 66D, which contested eight events and finished every one.

The least successful works Mini was JBL 172D which failed to finish all four events for which it was entered.

The most successful year for the works Minis was 1965, when Timo Makinen won the Monte Carlo Rally, the Touring Category of the Alpine Rally, and the 1,000 Lakes Rally; Paddy Hopkirk won the Circuit of Ireland; and Rauno Aaltonen won five events (the Geneva Rally, Czech Rally, Polish Rally, Three Cities Rally, and RAC Rally) and took the European Rally Championship.

One of the fastest ever recorded stage times for a works Mini was on the 1965 Munich–Vienna–Budapest Rally, when Rauno Aaltonen was reputed to have averaged 75 mph!

The shortest rally sortie for the works Minis was on the 1967 Scottish Rally, when Tony Fall stopped 10.1 miles from the start at Blythswood Square in the centre of Glasgow with incurable fuel problems.

John Rhodes scored the works Mini's only outright race win at the Salzbürgring in 1969.

The works Minis contested a total of 116 events representing 263 individual entries, and the crews collected a total of 109 major awards.

The records show that the works Minis were crashed on 15 occasions during their 263 entries. It is a testimony to the car's strength that, apart from brief local hospitalization in one or two cases, none of the crews involved received any serious injuries.

Almost exactly one third of the 263 works Mini entries in events retired with mechanical problems – the most common being drive shaft failures, transmission problems, and overheating.

The last to drive a works Mini was Brian Culcheth, who contested the 1970 Rally of the Hills in Australia.

Of the 71 works Minis built at Abingdon, 58 have either been restored, are awaiting a rebuild, or their whereabouts are known.

Index